ADVANCED

TRIAGE

COUNSELING

COUNSELING THAT HEALS TEENAGERS & PARENTS

ADVANCED
TRIAGE
COUNSELING

COUNSELING THAT HEALS TEENAGERS & PARENTS

SARA TROLLINGER D.D.
Founder & President, House of Hope

HigherLife Press

Hear what is being said about House of Hope...

I travel around the country making people laugh. That's what I do. After all, I'm a comedian. Almost every night I talk with parents thanking me for the opportunity to laugh even though at the same time they are crying on the inside about family problems. Many of them are desperate to find a solution for their teenagers in trouble.

It is my honor to be spokesperson for National House of Hope. It soothes my heart to direct these folks to a place that has an incredible track record of healing and restoring teenagers and families.

House of Hope has outstanding professionals who view each case, each heart-ache and each trouble as an opportunity to see the glory of God in their lives. I wholeheartedly recommend House of Hope as the answer for this generation of hurting teens and families. Advanced Triage Counseling provides the techniques they use for wholeness.

—Chonda Pierce
Recording Artist
Comedian and Author
National HOH Spokesperson

Sara Trollinger's love for teens is evident to anyone who knows her. This book shares Sara's insights into healing the damaged emotions teens often experience. It is a must-read for anyone who cares about rescuing teens from destruction. Having had the pleasure of knowing Sara for many years and the joy of seeing hurting teens transformed by the power of Christ through the ministry of House of Hope, I am thrilled to see how this book will help others to help teens.

There is a war going on for the hearts and souls of young people. The early years of life are the most important years. When emotions are damaged during formative years, that damage is often manifested in self-destructive behavior, and self-destructive behavior eventually hurts others.

Sara is right when she observes that secular programs are not effective. Only the love and transforming power of Jesus Christ can completely heal and restore hurting teens. Our teens need emergency triage, and this book is a life-saving manual that should be in everyone's library.

—Mathew D. Staver, Esq.
Founder and Chairman, Liberty Counsel
Dean and Professor of Law, Liberty University School of Law

I have personally known Sara and witnessed her ministry at House of Hope since the first month I was in Orlando, and I can without hesitation say that this is not a hypothetical or theoretical book about ministry; this is a practical and applicable book born out of forty years of loving teenagers. It is simply about what she already does to make a difference in our world one teen at a time. If you care about teenagers, you must read this book!

—Dr. David Uth
Senior Pastor, First Baptist Church of Orlando

I was introduced to House of Hope in the year of 1987 and began my journey as a House staff. I am currently the voice of House of Hope when hurting families call concerning their children. I personally have been blessed by being a small part of the healing process in families and look forward to each day on campus.

—Brenda Gaines, Receptionist

After volunteering for twenty two years and looking back over my personal experience with House of Hope, I credit the counseling I have received in making me the best parent I could possibly be. Now my daughter is a counselor and my son an engineer. I am now working at House of Hope and am extremely blessed.

—Margaret Stokes, Board Member

I have counseled for twenty two years and been at House of Hope for six years. I am so grateful that God has placed me in a ministry where I am able to practice my faith in practical ways that work. I am able to minister a process that is essential to healing. I have not only counseled teens and parents but also grown spiritually and relationally myself. This is the most fulfilling, interesting and challenging work I have ever done!

—Elaine Coleman, Counselor

Since I have been working here for six years, I have become a better husband, better father and all around better person. because of the counseling skills I've learned.

—Tim Jones, Vice Principal

One of my greatest blessings was receiving counseling myself at House of Hope when I first arrived. I had no idea how much pain I had in my soul until He allowed the bandages to be pulled back. Over one and a half years, God disinfected my wounds through the five-step process and the ministry of the counselors at House of Hope. House of Hope helped me to become all that I am today, and I am very grateful.

—Deanne Torell, Dean

Sara and House of Hope were here for me and my family when our daughter rebelled at the age of fourteen. We were Pastors and should have known what to do, but when my daughter came in we were treated with respect and love and no condemnation. My daughter was taught things about the Lord and given a healing through the five-step process—all things that she would never have received from us. I so appreciate the spirit in which House of Hope operates. Now I am a counselor at House of Hope and am able to lead other teens and parents through this same process.

—Linda McCullom, Counselor
Former Missionary to Africa

I am continually blessed by the parents and teens especially as I do the initial interviews to come into the program. They come into my office despondent and broken. I get to see hope in their eyes, possibly for the first time, as and they realize that there is an answer to their pain.
—Sandy Carpenter, Vice President

Within a short period of time here I have obtained a better relationship with God and have found true unconditional love. I no longer have the desire to cut myself.

—current girl resident

Being at House of Hope has helped me come back to the Lord when I thought it was impossible. My hurting heart is being healed.
—current girl resident

Being in House of Hope has introduced me to the Lord. It has made my family life so much better, and I am free from the bondage of sex and pornography.
—current boy resident

Being in House of Hope has given me a fresh, new start in life. It has brought me and my family closer together, and I am set free of my generational curses.

—current boy resident

Since I have been at House of Hope my family and I have forgiven each other and I no longer crave drugs.

—current boy resident

More products and training resources from Sara Trollinger and House of Hope are available by calling: 407-843-8686 or online at houseofhopesara@aol.com or www. nationalhouseofhope.org

Advanced Triage Counseling: Answers that Unlock and Heal Teens and Parents

By Sara Trollinger

Published by
HigherLife Press
2342 Westminster Terrace
Oviedo, Florida 32765

For reasons of privacy, the names of the teens and parents quoted in this book are fictitious.

Cover design by Dennis Claypoole and The Think Agency
Interior design by Cathleen Kwas

Dedication

This book is lovingly dedicated to all the affiliate Houses of Hope under the National House of Hope umbrella. Thank you for being on the frontlines helping win this raging battle to save this generation of teens and parents. May your strength in Jesus Christ be renewed daily, knowing that one day in His courts is worth a thousand in warfare!

Acknowledgments

Thanks to the following people for their assistance on this book:

Maureen Haner and Jessica Gilstrap, who share the vision and lent their incredible talent to assist me in writing this book,

Mike Yorkey and Karen Buck for critiquing the manuscript and providing insight and valuable input to make a cleaner and more effective work,

Deanne Torrell for editing the first draft. Her incredible talents, efficiency and passionate heart for healing this generation made this manuscript a better work,

Amy Schipper and Laura Montgomery for their tireless effort when inputting the manuscript into the computer in its many drafts and revisions...and keeping it all straight...and never giving up!

My deepest gratitude to Jane Chambers, Sandy Carpenter, Sarah Nelson, Linda McCollum, Jillian Yeates and Shay Crump for their prayers and proofreading and care for the details.

To the parents and teens from HOH for allowing us to use their personal stories to help other who are in similiar situations.

Contents

Step V Set Up Counseling

Conclusion

Foreword by Dr. Tim Clinton

I once heard somebody say that a child smiles forty-five times an hour — and has a good belly laugh every seven minutes. That's how life should be when you grow up. Safe. Fun. Free. Loved. And wide open.

When I think about the teen years, my mind wonders back to: Hometown football games. School parties. Good friends. Being crazy. Searching for identity. Zits— especially the one that popped out on what seemed the tip of your nose that you thought kids could see from a mile away. Dating. And yes, we all struggled with raging hormones, peer pressure and the quest for life in a "sex, drugs, and rock 'n' roll" culture.

A life full of opportunity? Yes. Uncertainty. Lots of it.

Especially for today's kids.

Life has changed. And so has growing up. And for that matter, so has parenting. It's tough. Really tough.

Today's teens face challenges and issues that didn't even register on most of our radars "back in the day." Fatherlessness is off the charts. There is rampant sexual and physical abuse. Huge numbers of kids see Mom and Dad fight a lot, and nearly half will watch Mom and Dad split up, changing their lives forever.

Not long ago, kids settled their frustration and anger with each other by heading to the playground or bathroom to shove and take a swing at each other. Now they pull out guns and "go off" on each other. Bullying has always been around, but it has gone to another level. Over the last decade, the violence has soared. Columbine, Jonesboro and Virginia Tech are schools that have become household words that remind of tragedy.

Working and alcoholic parents. Loss. Substance abuse. Need I say more?

Our teens are living in a whirlwind of conflicting beliefs, values and lifestyles ripping at their hearts.

Before long, they can start spinning out of control and making some really poor choices.

Anger, loneliness and isolation, disillusionment and confusion usually surge. It precipitates a search, a deeper pattern of escapism to help cope with all the chaos and pain. Drugs. Sex. Music with filthy lyrics. Video games. Eating disorders. Cutting. Promiscuity. Running away. You get the idea.

Such chaos leads to lives that quickly fill with more poor choices and more pain. Hell loves to rejoice in it all. Evil loves to get parents to believe that the child has no potential, to get kids to believe that they have no future, no hope. Even suicide, for far too many, seems like a way to cope or get away from it all.

I read a quote by Fran Stott that said, "Every kid needs someone who is crazy about them." They need someone who can see them and see *into* them. They need advocates fighting for and reaffirming their potential and the endless possibilities that await them. They need hope.

Solomon understood this when he wrote, "You who are young, make the most of your youth. Relish your youthful vigor." (Ecclesiastes 11:9, The Message)

Now I am sure that if you're reading this book you're probably reading it for a reason. You already know the painful world we live in. You're a youth leader with troubled teens coming to your youth group or a teacher with hurting students walking in and out of your classroom every day. Or maybe you're a parent worried about your own adolescents at home.

Let me give you some good news. If you feel completely out of control, all is not lost. Most of the hurt and the pain that pours out of them is a cry for relief, an ache for new life. Tough to see and understand? Sure. Frustrating? Yep. But is it a real cry for hope and a better life? Absolutely.

The National House of Hope (HOH) offers just that—hope and a better life. It is a safe place of refuge for teens and parents. Don't get me wrong. It isn't a place to drop off your teen and hope things will get better. No, it is a place that firmly believes in and cares for today's teens by offering the love of Christ with professional care, and by connecting the hearts of parents and their teens together again through hard work.

HOH strongly advocates for the involvement of the family and the teen in the solution to life's biggest challenges and problems. They are aware of the myriad of influences that bring on pain and frustration and are not afraid to tackle the tough issues during life's darkest hours. Most important, they stand firm in their faith and anchor their plan of hope for a new and better life in Him.

HOH provides a consistent, safe harbor to foster deep, transformational change. At the heart of the ministry are Sara Trollinger and her team. A woman who absolutely loves kids, Sara's journey is marked by twenty-five years of teaching elementary school and, later, emotionally handicapped children. After retiring from teaching, Sara went to work in the juvenile justice system but became discouraged at the number of juveniles who kept coming back. As she realized the absence of the Lord in the juvenile justice system, she vowed to see transformation. And so began the dream and vision for House of Hope.

No matter the obstacle or challenge, Sara never shies away from doing what God has called her to do. Saved at a Billy Graham crusade at the University of North Carolina during her freshman year, Sara is a woman who truly believes in the power of the Holy Spirit to transform lives. She is a pioneer, a dreamer and an encourager. She loves people, she loves teens, but—most important—she loves God.

This work reflects her uncompromising belief that if you can reach into the soul of a teen and offer the transforming power of Christ, then there is always hope. Not one teen has to be lost. Families can be restored. And they are.

Preface

MY FAVORITE SAYING IS, "GOD WILL BE AS BIG IN OUR LIVES AS we allow Him to be." In this book you will discover new ways that we can allow God to be *big* in changing the lives of our hurting teenagers and parents by using proven counseling techniques that are incorporated in National Houses of Hope. Later I'll share some ideas of how faith can change their worlds of chaos.

As counselors, we are looking for new ways to accomplish two goals: 1) to help teens navigate through the turbulent period when they rock the family boat and threaten to capsize everything and 2) to help parents keep calm waters. The good news is that these goals can be achieved with a lot of love and attention, firm and consistent discipline, and tons of relationship building based on faith. Parents and teens can be victorious in their chaotic storms and build a solid faith foundation that will smooth the waves and stabilize their futures.

This book addresses the glaring problems that hurting teens and families face every day, such as divorce, anger, alcohol, drugs, porn, sex abuse, the occult and body mutilations. All these symptoms are signs of a deeper deficit. The missing factor is often a stable faith foundation.

Ron Luce, founder of Teen Mania, has been an evangelist to teenagers for twenty years and sees an alarming slide away from faith among teens. He estimates that only 4 percent of today's youth will be "Bible-believing" Christians when they grow up.[1]

The big question is: how do we bring stability to hurting teens and parents by imparting salvation and faith in our counseling sessions? You will find the answers in this book. I will share the insights, methods and processes that we use at House of Hope Orlando to absolutely build faith in God and to stabilize teens and parents in a world of chaos. These are tried, true and practical tools that have revolutionized our counseling practices.

The Spiritual Side of the Problem

Before I get too serious, I want to tell you about a teenage girl who brought her new boyfriend home to meet her parents. They were shocked by his appearance—black leather jacket, baggy pants, nose ring, pierced ears, dyed hair and tattoos. The parents pulled their daughter aside and expressed their concern and horror. The daughter quickly replied, "Oh, please, Mom and Dad. If he weren't nice he wouldn't be doing five hundred hours of community service!"

When it comes to working with teenagers, you'll need a sense of humor!

I've been counseling teenagers for nearly forty years, and I'm still amazed at some of the deep things that they say. A couple of weeks ago, I met with one of our boys, a sixteen-year-old named Jacob. Jacob had been progressing well, and he was a joy to have in the program. He told me that before he came to our program, four or five clinical counselors treated him but nothing compared to the counseling he received at House of Hope.

I asked him, "What do you mean?"

"The other counselors never dealt with the spiritual side to my problems. They just skimmed the surface," he answered.

"Really?" I said and urged him to tell me more.

"Here's the difference between regular counseling and Christian counseling," Jacob offered. He proceeded to paint an interesting word picture. "Counseling is like cleaning a swimming pool. When you just skim the surface, you never get the deep areas cleaned. The leaves floating on the top may seem like the main issue, but what about the algae or silt at the bottom of the pool? If those problems aren't dealt with, then the whole pool remains dirty. You have to clean the entire pool, not just skim the leaves off the surface."

I found Jacob's words very profound, especially coming from a sixteen-year-old. But he wasn't finished. "There's one more thing I've learned after being in counseling for a lot of years," he said. "Once the pool gets cleaned up, leaves will fall on the surface unless you have a covering on the pool, and that covering is the protection of the Holy Spirit. Over time, there will also be other things or issues that float to the top from the deep water, so the healing process is never a one-time shot."

Weren't those insightful observations? To carry the swimming pool metaphor a step further, I would describe counselors as on-duty lifeguards—responsible for rescuing families in distress. With the way our culture is headed today, way too many kids are thrashing around in the water, nearly drowning from emotional and physical abuse, often at the hands of those who are supposed to love them unconditionally (their mothers and fathers.)

It's up to us to save these families or to throw the lifejacket to these parents before it's too late.

No One to Rescue Her: Jenny's story

I remember a girl named Jenny who came to House of Hope. She was a teenage dropout with self-image problems that began when she was just seven years old. She was walking home from elementary school one afternoon when a man in a car pulled up beside her.

The man jumped out of the car and asked the second-grader, "Will you help me find my puppy?"

"What did you say, mister?" Jenny asked.

She never received an answer. The man grabbed her and threw her in the car. He held her down in the front seat while he drove to a secluded area and proceeded to brutalize her for the next two hours. He raped her at least twice, and then he inserted a hairbrush into her. Jenny screamed for her mother, but no one came to save her.

For the next few years, Jenny would wake up in the middle of the night crying because of an intense pain between her legs. Her mother didn't understand, but she began asking questions, and that's when Jenny told her about the creepy man who kidnapped her and raped her. Jenny's mother believed her, but she had her own problems to deal with—like a husband who was destroying himself with drugs, alcohol and other problems.

One night when Jenny was in middle school, her father got drunk and exposed his genitals to her, and then he urinated on her. The event traumatized the young girl even more. She had never received healing from the horrible rape—and now this. She felt ugly and worthless—like she had been tossed on the scrap heap of life.

Young people like Jenny have emotional wounds just as deep as the wounds they would have received if they had been in a terrible car crash. Counselors will encounter dozens, if not hundreds, of hurting teens just like Jenny. How do we help a young girl or a young boy who has been battered, abused, and neglected? What is the best approach? How can we do more than just offer soothing words?

We at House of Hope have asked those same questions, and we're convinced more than ever that God must be the foundation in our counseling sessions. But as we all know, that is easier said than done because many hurting teens believe He doesn't love them, couldn't love them, or has forgotten about them.

Wrong Image of God

Two little brothers were extremely disruptive in their Sunday school class, and the teacher took them to the pastor's office. The pastor called the six-year-old into his office and left his four-year-old brother outside. The pastor looked at the six-year-old and asked him, "Where is God?"

The little boy didn't blink.

The pastor said again, "Son, where is God?"

Again, the boy didn't open his mouth.

The third time the pastor asked the question, the little boy ran outside grabbed his little brother's arm and said, "Let's get out of here! God's missing and they're blaming us!"

If you don't explain God clearly to kids, they will get a mixed up and blurry picture of Him. It is up to us to make the proper introduction to the Lord.

Even with the best of counseling situations, this isn't an easy task because many hurting teens and parents are mad at God. They ask, "If God loved me, why would He allow this to happen or allow me to hurt so badly?" I liken our situation in the counseling office to when the EMT (Emergency Medical Team) is called to a horrific car crash. By the time we arrive on the accident scene, the teens and parents are pretty banged up. They need immediate help for their physical hurts and emotional wounds.

We try to meet those needs as best we can, with the Lord's help. At House of Hope, we've developed a five-step treatment plan that has given us a high success rate in healing and restoring teens and their families. Our program is one of the few across the nation that strictly requires parents' involvement.

We are aware there are no "pat answers," but there are theraputic and spiritual techniques that we have found to be successful instruments in healing the whole person. I want to make it clear that we're not to throw away all the knowledge and counseling skills we've learned in textbooks. While we apply those things that we have learned previously, we lay the foundation of our counseling program on Scripture.

The Holy Spirit is our Counselor. His fees have already been paid. He is available 24/7—day or night. There is no waiting. He keeps no record of wrongs. We invite the Holy Spirit to guide us into biblical wisdom, knowledge, discerning of spirits, salvation, inner healing, freedom from bondage and breaking generational patterns. Through prayer we open the door for the Holy Spirit to run the session according to His agenda.

Bringing Parents Back into the Picture

Most parents do not know what their teens are doing! Ignorance is not bliss! They watch their children grow up and see them physically become larger, but in their minds, they remain that beautiful little girl or handsome little boy—prior to the problems. The adults tend to wear these designer glasses they purchased at the Naïve Store and usually they have rose-colored lens. Most parents we deal with can't relate to their teen because they don't spend enough time with them to understand and love them in the ways the teens need to feel loved.

We must make quality time and learn to actively listen and to be intimate with each other. Love is spelled *t-i-m-e*. Here are some ways we can change these negative statistics. As Dr. Tim Clinton, president of the America Association of Christian Counselors, has often said, "Every teenager deserves one person who is crazy about them." Love is desperately lacking in almost every teenager we see.

We set the example and teach the parents ways to help fill their teens empty love tanks. We say to them, "As gas prices go up, we pay the price to fill our tanks. What price are you willing to pay to fill your teens' love tanks?" It will cost parents time, but it will have an eternal impact.

I recently read a survey that asked teens, "If you had one wish, what would you wish for in order to create a better life for you and your family?" Most teens didn't wish for a bigger house, fancier cars, more money or material things. What they desperately wanted was more time with their families. Seventy-one percent of the youth said they would prefer a home-cooked meal over any other type of meal and over pizza or McDonalds. Young people *want*—they *yearn*—to be connected to their families and caring adults who will help them navigate their way and find solutions for their problems so they can be well-adjusted and healed.

Parents hold the vital keys to a healthy teen!

Parents carry far more weight for good or bad than they believe. How a teen thinks and acts is molded by his home life. Parents must take their responsible places with their teens. Parents have more than six times more influence than TV.

In a survey, 78 percent of teens said their parents mold and shape their attitudes. Parents have *three times* more influence over teens than anyone else. Parents have not only the greatest influence, but also the greatest opportunity to impart values and faith to their teens. At House of Hope, we teach parents it's their responsibility to model a lifestyle of faith, by putting God in the center of their home. It is virtually impossible to see successful or long lasting changes without getting the family and teen on the same level playing field.

I want to give you a small glimpse of why our House of Hope programs are successful and how we're fulfilling Malachi 4:6. ("And he will turn the hearts of the fathers to the children, and the hearts of the children to their fathers, lest I come and strike the earth with a curse.") When a teen and parent come to House of Hope, most of them do not have a relationship with Jesus Christ. At House of Hope, we teach both teens and parents how to develop their faith. We constantly emphasize and teach the three faith-builders: what they think, what they say and what they hear.

1. Before they come in, it is clear to them what is expected of them—what is out of bounds and what is in bounds. Before they enter our program they are handed a booklet that explains our program.

2. In the course of twelve to eighteen months, we help them develop positive identity based on the Bible. We make sure they receive a strong sense of their purpose and worth, and that they understand the promises made to them by God. This helps them know who they are in Christ and develop positive esteem.

3. We teach them to know God's Word and use those principles to guide their choices. Key principles are integrity (conviction; standing up; honesty; telling truth when it's not easy) and restraint (refraining from sex, drugs, etc.)

Book Overview

My intention for writing this book is to share a balanced blueprint model that is based on biblical principles. It is my prayer that you as a counselor will investigate and incorporate our House of Hope model into your counseling. In the first chapter of this book I will give you a general overview of the five-step intervention and counseling plan we use. In the sections that follow, I will give specific details about how to implement each step.

Advanced Triage Counseling Steps

I have divided *Advanced Triage Counseling* into five categories, just as EMT triage categorizes for medical assistance at the scene of an accident. Each area is tagged with a color denoting the seriousness of the person's condition.

STEP 1: CHECK THE HEARTBEAT

Step 1 is the action you take when your patient has a life-threatening injury, which means not having spiritual life through a personal relationship with Jesus Christ. The two most important therapies in Step 1 are salvation and forgiveness.

STEP 2: TREAT THE WOUNDS

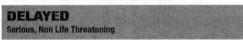

When you have reached Step 2, the patient is stable for the moment but still has wounds that require treatment. This is when you provide therapy for inner healing.

STEP 3: ASSESS FAMILY HISTORY

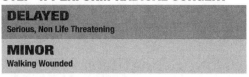

During or after Step 2, you will want to determine the cause and depth of the woundedness. This is done by assessing the client's family history. At this point the client is stable but needs to be monitored.

STEP 4: PERFORM RADICAL SURGERY

By Step 4, the healing process has begun, but you have determined that the client needs supernatural deliverance. The need for therapy may be urgent or delayed, depending on the individual circumstances.

STEP 5: SET UP THERAPY

MINOR
Walking Wounded

MINOR
After Care

The client has made excellent progress and is now ready to return home. You will teach the client about the therapy they will need to continue in order to live off campus successfully. Additional counseling should always be available for future scrapes or bruises. After-care counseling ensures their survival.

Every story told here is true. We have changed the names of the people involved to protect their privacy, but the things that have happened are real events involving real people. These parents and teens—many of them alumni—have gone through trials and temptations, but through House of Hope counseling methods they have found healing. They desire to share their stories of life-threatening problems to give you hope and proof that the five-step counseling process at House of Hope works.

—Sara Trollinger, D.D.
Founder/President of House of Hope

CHAPTER 1

Overview of a Triage Approach to Counseling: The Five-Step Process

Step 1: Check the Heartbeat (Salvation, Forgiveness)

Whenever paramedics race up to an accident scene, the first thing they do is check victims for a heartbeat. They treat the most seriously injured first. These are usually given a red tag. Those in life-or-death situations must be stabilized.

In the same way, when a counselor meets with a new client, the first few counseling sessions are to gauge the counselee's emotional, mental and spiritual health.

When a hurting teen is brought to House of Hope, our initial step is to check for a spiritual heartbeat. Is there a pulse? Is there any sense of spiritual life beating underneath the surface?

The overwhelming majority of the time, our teens appears spiritually DOA (dead on arrival). The EMTs would give them a black tag, but at House of Hope we never give up on anyone, even if they appear half-dead. A typical example would be Charlie, who arrived at House of Hope wearing white pancake makeup and black eyeliner. He was dressed in a black shirt and black stovepipe pants with knee-high, front-lace Doc Martens black boots.

Charlie wore something else—a chip on his shoulder heavier than the knee-high leather boots he had on his feet. It was very apparent that he was into Goth—not God—but his eyes told me he had been mocked and rejected by his peers for years. His sullen attitude was probably why he didn't have many friends at school. Charlie was an outcast.

Even spiritually dead teens like Charlie can be revived. The first thing we do is tell the hurting teen that he or she is special—special in God's eyes. I remember saying to Charlie, "Charlie, we're pleased that you're here. You'll find that House of Hope is a place where love abounds. You are not here by accident. We believe you were handpicked and specially selected to come here, and I do understand that you're unhappy with the way your life has been going."

"You got that right," Charlie mumbled as he looked out the window.

I waited until I could lock eyes with Charlie. Then I said to him, "We believe God has called us to share His love with you—a love that is patient and kind, a love that will heal your deepest hurts. Your days with us will be full, and you will grow and learn as never before."

God works in the midst of pain and brokenness. Those who are hurting are incredibly open to receiving and knowing the Lord. No one has ever told them that God loves them unconditionally. Often we have the opportunity to be the first person to do that. Many troubled teens are driven by self-hate and shame, believing they are so bad that *nobody* could love them. But we know God does, and sometimes we are totally surprised at how open teens become when we quietly introduce them to a new kind of love—God's love.

The Vital Sign of Salvation

There are two vital issues concerning the heart. The first is the vital sign of salvation. The second issue is in the area of forgiveness.

What hurting families and teens need most is salvation. As counselors, we have to share our hope in God with them. During my talk with Charlie, once I felt I had gained some trust as a loving adult, I said to him, "You know, Charlie, you're going to be involved in individual counseling, Bible studies, school, work duties, music, arts and sports here at House of Hope. We're going to put you in classes that will help you catch up academically, but you will also have a lot of fun. There's another thing you should know about us: House of Hope is a faith ministry. We have the freedom to offer you the opportunity to discover a meaningful, exciting, and lasting relationship with Jesus Christ. We *will not* force Christianity down your throat because that is not the way God wants us to come to Him. Our purpose is to help you develop into the person God created you to be. That's our sincere prayer for you, Charlie."

I must tell you, with that simple beginning, I've seen hundreds of teens who had appeared half-dead and hardened just melt over the years. It didn't happen overnight with Charlie, but it happened. Like most teens that come to House of Hope, no one had ever made him feel that he was special or loved. No one had ever shared Scripture with him or even prayed with him. At House of Hope, we are not shy in telling teens what it means to be born again and what salvation means. We use John 3:3: "Jesus declared, 'I tell you the truth, no one can see the kingdom of God unless he is born again'" (NIV). And then we explain what "born again" means.

> When President Reagan visited House of Hope in 1990, he said, "House of Hope is unabashedly a Christian organization. Secular programs do not work."

The young people we see are looking for a fresh start. Most of them have tried everything else. They are receptive to learning about salvation. We tell them that the word *salvation* comes from the Greek word *sozo*, which means "saved," "to heal," "keep safe," "rescue from danger," and "deliver." They want to be saved because they are tired of feeling the pain. They understand that salvation is the foundation for their healing. They want to the benefits of salvation—to be rescued from danger; they want to feel safe and secure.

Not all the teens immediately fall to their knees and ask Jesus Christ into their hearts. Sometimes, the pain, anger, and frustration are too great; they aren't ready yet. But I agree with Isaiah 55:11, where God says, "My Word... shall not return unto Me void, but it shall accomplish what I please" (NKJV).We minister God's love and gentleness and are always looking for the right way and the right time to introduce hurting teens and parents to the Great Physician. Research has proven that those who truly find Christ in the midst of their pain are most often the ones who continue to thrive for the rest of their lives. Few fall away after experiencing the unconditional love of Jesus Christ.

Salvation is an ongoing process. We are changed from glory to glory, not reaching perfection until we meet Jesus face to face. We have only to walk and appropriate the truth of His Word by living in the Spirit. There are five revolutionary keys that we use in healing the whole person that we have found to be effective. I will be unpacking these tools later.

The Vital Sign of Forgiveness

Let's look at the second issue of the heart, which is forgiveness. Forgiveness opens the door of all ministry areas and paves the way to freedom. It is required by God for all those who choose to be healed.

More times than not the teens and/or parents come into a session in the midst of crisis. They may be angry, hurt, bitter, etc. and may not feel like forgiving those who hurt them. We teach them that forgiveness is not an emotion but an act of our will and we show what God's word says about forgiveness.

Mark 11:25–26 says, "And when you stand praying, if you hold anything against anyone, forgive him, so that your Father in heaven may forgive you your sins" (NIV). When the teenager and parents reach a place in their healing where they can forgive, the counselor leads them in prayer.

There are three main prayers of forgiveness that we pray with our parents and teens. The first is the prayers of forgiveness for their sins. The second is prayers to forgive others, and the third is a prayer to forgive them.

A Family Testimony of Forgiveness

During one of our Tuesday night parenting classes, the subject was forgiveness. After the guest speaker had finished his presentation, families were invited to come to the front for special prayers. This was the first night Amy's entire family had attended the classes together. One of the counselors approached them, seeing the biological father had tears in his eyes. He stood there with his arms around his daughter. For the first time since his divorce, he turned to Amy's mother and asked for forgiveness for all of the hurts he caused by leaving Amy and divorcing her. At that moment, the entire family broke into tears. With their arms around each other, they each repented and asked each other for forgiveness.

Even though Amy and her mother Jodi had been in counseling for months, it was at this moment when the real breakthrough came and the family began to heal. This took place six years ago, and today that same mother is now facilitating a forgiveness group for other parents (who are having the same problem) at House of Hope Orlando.

Forgiveness opens the door of hearts and lives to some other needed ministry areas that I share in the book, areas such as generational curses, sins of the fathers, vows and judgments, soul ties and ungodly beliefs. The end result is healing.

In bringing wholeness to the family, forgiveness is the spiritual ointment God uses to sooth our emotional wounds. Forgiveness removes the sting from the wound and in many instances restores relationships that have been broken.

Today Jody and her daughter Amy travel to other Houses of Hope across America sharing on the healing power of forgiveness.

The Next Step

After the patients are stabilized and the heart issues of salvation and forgiveness are addressed, the visible wounds are treated.

Step 2: Treat the Wounds (Healing for the Broken Heart)

Let's put our EMT hat back on. The first thing we do is check their heartbeat (salvation and forgiveness). The next step is treating the wounds.

Cutting to Stop the Pain: Rachel's Story

Rachel was fourteen when she spent the night with one of her classmates. After her friend's parents had gone to bed, the two girls were laughing and carrying on when Rachel mentioned that her friend's brother was cute. His was seventeen, and his bedroom was across the hall.

"Why don't you go and say hello to him?" her friend asked.

Rachel protested, but her friend gently pushed her out of her bedroom—then locked the door. Rachel pounded on the door until she heard a voice say from across the hall, "Can I help you?"

"Your sister won't let me back in her room," Rachel said.

Her friend's brother answered, "Why don't you come watch some TV with me?"

It turned out that the boy wanted to do a lot more than watch TV. He shut the door and locked it, and before Rachel could figure out what was happening, he forced himself on her. He raped her and stole her virginity in a matter of moments. Up until then, she had never even kissed a boy. And now she had been raped.

Rachel's heart was broken as she left the room and returned to her friend's bedroom. She pretended everything was fine. She didn't tell her friend what her brother had done, but Rachel was left feeling guilty, thinking it must be her fault. She felt so dirty after the horrible experience that for the next six months, she took six showers a day in a vain attempt to rid herself of how dirty she felt, trying to cleanse herself.

When she arrived at House of Hope, Rachel bore deep emotional scars—as well as physical scars. She was a "cutter," someone who wore sweatshirts even in Orlando's blazing summer heat because she wanted to cover up the cuts and jabs on her arms from sharp objects. She said the pain on the inside was so great that she couldn't feel the outside cuts. She said releasing the blood made her feel better, giving her a feeling she was in control.

When a teenager comes to House of Hope, we are always on the alert to look for the physical as well as emotional wounds. Once that assessment has been made, we can help them face their hurts and feelings, their bitterness and sorrow. First, the wounds must be thoroughly cleansed and cleansing starts with forgiveness. We have already discussed that unforgiveness is huge among parents and teens.

Our job is to ask them to recall those who wounded them and to allow us to lead them through an emotional minefield. After the perpetrator(s) are identified, we lead the counselees in a prayer to forgive those who have hurt them. This is where "healing the wounded heart" or "broken heart" or "inner healing" begins. Remember how sixteen-year-old Jacob talked about the dirt and grime at the bottom of the pool? Forgiveness is the cleansing agent. Each day our offices are filled with wounded souls who have never dealt with the issues that caused their pain.

I believe that the Song of Solomon is an allegory concerning Jesus and the body of Christ. Song of Solomon 2:9 paints a picture of God standing behind our wall, looking through the window of our heart. During our prayer sessions, I encourage the teen or parent to ask the Lord to show them the wall in their hearts. Most of the time, teens realize that the walls exist, but they don't know the reason why they built them. Some of the stones in the wall are fear, control, manipulation, addiction, abandonment and rejection. Anger seems to always be the plaster that holds their walls in place.

Most of us have walls because when we were hurt, we didn't have time to process the pain, nor anyone to talk to, and as a result we stuffed the hurt into our hearts. Sometimes we stuff so much that our hearts are wounded and broken. We don't know how to process the hurts, so we build walls and try to forget, but the pain is still there. Isaiah 61:1 tells us," He has sent Me to heal the brokenhearted, to proclaim liberty to the captives, and the opening of the prison to *those who are* bound" (NKJV). The Holy Spirit is our real Healer. It's all about our relationship with the Holy Spirit and inviting His power to operate in our lives.

At House of Hope during the prayer session, we encourage parents and teens to find a quiet place and focus on the Lord. We instruct them to ask God to reveal the source of their walls and ask Him to take away and heal whatever has built up over the years. The results are astounding! Afterward there are usually tears, laughter, joy, peace and as one teen said, "I feel a weight lifted from my back."

To make sure all potential areas of deep hurts are addressed, we use a Counseling Checklist for each client. We also a Behavior Checklist at regular intervals to ensure progress is being made in their actions. Both forms are in Appendix A.

The next thing we do is to examine their family history so that inner healing can begin. Emotional wounds come from past hurts and broken relationships. I can't remember the last teen at House of Hope who *wasn't* suffering from several deep, emotional wounds. Somewhere along the way, a parent, sibling, friend, acquaintance, or stranger shattered their trust, injured and wounded them badly.

Step 3: Assess Family History (Generational Patterns)

Now let's get back to our five-step triage analogy for treating emotionally wounded teens and their families. First, check their heart-beats (salvation and forgiveness). Second, take care of the wounds (inner healing), and third, check out their family histories.

When you visit a doctor for the first time, he or she will ask you questions about your health and request records from previous doctors. This is known as taking a patient's medical history. Each person has an emotional and spiritual history as well. The Bible tells us that our history goes back three or four generations; therefore, we counselors need to ask probing questions about history because we need to learn about the past so we can counsel for the future. (We have developed a Client Evaluation Questionnaire that is a good tool for gathering this information. You can see it in Appendix A.)

When we interview teens who come to House of Hope, we hear about family situations like this:

"Dad was in jail because he was busted for dealing drugs. When he was home he was angry, fighting and full of rage."

- ⅄ "My mom is an alcoholic."
- ⅄ "Dad cheated on my mom."
- ⅄ "Mom's second husband sexually abused me before he disappeared."

The Bible tells us that the effect of sin is passed on from generation to generation. I am convinced generational patterns are real. It breaks my heart to think that half of the teens in America wake up every morning with no biological father in the home. It breaks my heart that teens have parents who are alcoholic and full of rage. It breaks my heart when children are sexually abused or come home to an empty home after school every day. At the same time, I make a point to tell parents we understand that it's not all their fault. Their parents probably didn't parent them the proper way either.

This parental influence cuts both ways because mothers and fathers who aren't good role models can really do a number on their children. Teens who grow up in homes bursting with drugs, pornography, adultery, sexual sin, alcoholism, divorce and violence are much more apt to carry those behaviors into their own lives, and this is why sin is passed on to the next generation. Exodus 20:5-6 says, "You shall not bow down to them or worship them; for I, the LORD your God, am a jealous God, punishing the children for the sin of the fathers to the third and fourth generation of those who hate me, but showing love to a thousand {generations} of those who love me and keep my commandments" (NIV).

I don't know how far back you can go in your family tree. Personally, I have no direct knowledge of went on in my relatives' lives three or four generations ago, but I can see things that were passed down to my immediate family and I've had to deal with them.

A classic example of the power of generational patterns comes from the research of Richard L. Dugdale, who was hired in 1874 to interview inmates in six different prisons. He discovered that their relatives were mostly criminals or paupers. For the next three years, he traced the lives of 540 descendants and five generations of one man—a fellow named Max Juke.

Here are some of the statistics he reported:

> Max Juke was born in 1720.
>
> Dugdale was able to directly study 540 of his descendants plus 169 people who married into the family (a total of 709).
>
> Dugdale estimated that Juke's had 1200 descendants by the end of the eighteen century.
>
> Out of the 1200 estimated descendants, 280 were paupers and 140 became criminals. Seven were convicted of murder.
>
> Out of the 540 descendants who were studied directly, 52.4 percent were described as "harlots." In Dugdale's day, "harlot" did not mean prostitute. Instead it meant women who were sexually active, or "impudent," but not paid.
>
> However, Dugdale also said that 128 out of the 709 descendants and in-laws were "common prostitutes" for some period of time. That is about 25 percent.
>
> All in all, Dugdale estimated that Juke's twelve hundred descendants cost the U.S. government more than $1.25 million in nineteenth-century dollars. Most of this was the cost of venereal disease passed down through prostitution.[1]

That's not much of a legacy to leave. In contrast, in 1900 a man named A.E. Winshop studied the descendants of Jonathan Edwards, who was born in the early 1700s like Max Jukes. Jonathan Edwards was a Congregational preacher, a theologian, and a missionary to the Native Americans. His electrifying preaching touched off the Great Awakening that swept through the colonies in 1740.

He and his wife had 1,394 descendants by the late nineteenth century. Listen to this roll call of accomplishment:

- ⅄ thirteen college presidents
- ⅄ hundreds of college professors
- ⅄ sixty physicians
- ⅄ one hundred clergymen, missionaries, and theological professors
- ⅄ sixty authors, with one hundred and thirty-five books of merit
- ⅄ seventy-five army or navy officers
- ⅄ three mayors
- ⅄ three state governors
- ⅄ several members of Congress
- ⅄ three U.S. senators
- ⅄ one vice president of the United States, Aaron Burr[1]

Many teens that we counsel come from dysfunctional families like Max Jukes', inheriting the legacy of messed-up parents, grandparents and great-grandparents who were trying to hack their way through life. The incredible grip of generational sin can only be broken through the healing power of Jesus Christ.

Step 4: Perform Essential Surgery (Being Set Free from Oppression)

After we've learned about a client's family history, we as counselors may recognize that a fourth step is needed to save the patient—essential surgery. Some teens and parents have such messed-up lives that they need surgery to help them stop the generational cycle of sinful patterns. Teens have participated in hook-up sex, smoked a lot of weed, used heavy drugs, participated in witchcraft and the occult, and acted defiantly before authorities—just to name a few. By opening the door so wide to sinful behavior, they have invited ungodly spiritual activity to oppress them.

Time after time we've seen the effects of this kind of oppression at House of Hope. I'm talking about violence, involvement in the occult, witchcraft, torment, depression, alcohol, drugs, and perversion. In most cases, their parents need to experience freedom as well.

Ungodly Spiritual Forces

We counselors can be a ray of light in dark lives. We are on the front lines and are involved in warfare against the enemy. I believe God wants us to use our authority to help teens overcome the demonic forces in their lives. Luke 10:19 says, "Behold, I give you the authority to trample on serpents and scorpions, and over all the power of the enemy, and nothing shall by any means hurt you." We must call upon the name of Jesus to bring these influences under His authority.

Surgery—major surgery—involves seeing someone come to a place of freedom. Before a session like this, we need to prepare ourselves spiritually because this is not something done on the spur of moment and it is not something that should be done alone because we believe we are clearly involved in a spiritual battle. We need a prayer partner as we approach the date we've set the session. E-mail is a great tool to rally a prayer support team behind us. We must be sure to saturate our minds with the Word of God. Finally, we pray for the blood of Jesus to cover each one in the session for protection, peace and victory. Before some sessions, I've fasted.

During a session of this nature with the teen or parent, we begin by praying in the name of Jesus. We plead the blood of Jesus Christ over the teen, inviting Jesus, the power of His Holy Spirit and His presence to fill the room. We ask the person to confess and renounce the specific areas of sin, and then ask in the name of Jesus that each stronghold be broken in the person who has been oppressed. We then ask Jesus to heal any emotional, spiritual or physical wounds from the past that may be serving as footholds for the current oppression.

As counselors, we have no reason to be intimidated by demonic activity as long as we are avoiding sin and trusting in Jesus Christ as our Lord and Savior. God has given us the authority and the spiritual surgical tools to confront the evil and restore wholeness to the teens and parents who are seeking freedom from oppression and sin.

Now we are ready for our fifth treatment step, which is physical therapy.

Step 5: Set Up Counseling

Our fifth step is counseling. Football players who are injured and undergo knee surgery often begin physical therapy within twenty-four hours of the surgery. The same should happen to those who have received in-depth counseling, healing for a wounded heart or freedom from strongholds: they need to start counseling right away.

The counseling process for teens and parents has three parts: 1) building their relationship with God and making Him a fundamental part of their lives and 2) restoring broken relationships between parents and teens and others and 3) establishing relationships with people who know God.

Building Relationship with God

To build their relationship with God, teens and parents learn spiritual principals by reading God's Word, listening to the Lord, fellowshipping with believers, and having intimate times with God through prayer and praise.

Restoring Relationships with Others

Teens don't wake up one morning and say, "Wow, I think I'm going to make everyone's life a living hell today." No, they had to learn it from somewhere, and most likely it was Mom, Dad, grandparents, aunts and uncles who were the teachers. Sure, the media plays a huge role as well, but 78 percent of teens said in a recent poll that it was their parents who molded and shaped their attitudes. Parents have *three* times more influence over their lives than anyone else.[2]

Our job, as counselors, is to teach hurting teens and parents how to set reasonable boundaries as described in detail in the book *Boundaries* by Dr. Henry Cloud and Dr. John Townsend. They wrote about how you should begin by describing what physical boundaries are appropriate. For instance, who may touch them? Under what circumstances? They explain how mental boundaries will give them the freedom to have their own thoughts and opinions. Emotional boundaries will help them deal with their own emotions and recognize harmful, manipulative emotions from others. Spiritual boundaries help them distinguish God's will from their own.

Starting New Relationships with People Who Know God

To establish positive relationships with those who know God, we teach teens especially how to discern between "safe" and "unsafe" friends. In the teen world, it's all about who you hang out with. We encourage them to make friends with other Christians.

Going into Detail

You now have a good overview of the five key steps of triage counseling for teens and their parents.

1. Check the heartbeat (salvation and forgiveness).

2. Treat the wounds (healing for the wounded heart).

3. Assess family history (generational patterns, soul ties, etc.).

4. Perform essential surgery.

5. Set up counseling (relationship with God and family). Show them how to have a deep and abiding relationship with each other and with Jesus Christ, their Savior and Healer (John 15:5).

This introduction shows you the tip of the iceberg. In the following chapters you will learn step by step how the counselors at House of Hope integrate and implement these five methods.

Most important, I want you to know that these steps are not just a philosophy or an untested theory. We have been practicing them and refining at House of Hope for the past twenty-two years. Before you read how to implement each step in your own counseling, I believe it will help you to see how they are put into practice at the House of Hope every day. The next chapter shows what makes House of Hope work, starting with its beginning in 1985.

CHAPTER 2

What Makes House of Hope Work

IN THIS CHAPTER, I WILL DO MORE THAN JUST SHARE WITH YOU THE series of miracles that God used to establish House of Hope in Orlando. I will show you that God can work in any situation when we ask Him to help us. He takes teens who have been abused, misused and rejected and gives back their self-esteem and passion for life. He takes whatever resources we have to offer and turns them into a faith debt-free home for teens and parents. It is our privilege to partner with Him in this work.

A Vision, But No Money

During one of my early morning prayer times, God spoke to me in His still, small voice and said, "Sara, your ministry is going to branch out into a new direction." One year later, that new direction became House of Hope, a Christian home for hurting teenagers.

After the Lord spoke with me about starting a treatment center for teens, I shared this vision with the Fellowship of Faith Ministry, Inc. Their hearts were touched and they wanted to join with me in this opportunity to help change the lives of hurting young people and their parents permanently!

We had no money, no house, no facility, but I had a vision and knew God was directing me. One day as I was praying and asking God about a location, the name of a lady who owned a Bible bookstore came strongly to my mind and I felt impressed to call her. I asked if she might know a location for a home we could use for teenagers. She said she had a friend who was getting ready to sell two houses, a garage, and three lots. After seeing the site and talking with the lady, we immediately knew this was to be the first House of Hope. The first price quoted was $117,000. That seemed like a million dollars to us because we had not money — except for $200. Since the owners were Christians, we asked if they would pray about a final price.

In the meantime, someone suggested we write a grant request to the Edyth Bush Foundation. The person went on to say, "But they never give to Christian groups—only the arts, sciences, and theater." I had no experience with grant writing, but several of us once again asked God for guidance and, after much prayer, submitted a grant request for $95,000. At this point I had no idea why God told us to ask for $95,000.

The property owners called a few days later (not knowing about the amount of our grant request) and said, "We've decided to let you have the property for $95,000." Now we knew and rejoiced, believing we would get the grant. By faith I said, "Fine, we'll take it." They prepared for the closing, but we still had no money. Two weeks before the closing date, I received a letter from the Edyth Bush Foundation saying, "We are happy to announce that you will receive your request of $95,000!" God is so good. He is never late! We left the closing with the same $200 we had when we started praying about our facility. It was the down payment to start House of Hope.

As we began the task of preparing the property, I was a guest on a television program that followed an interview with Charley Reese, a nationally syndicated columnist for the *Orlando Sentinel*. During my interview, he heard me describe how House of Hope was a faith ministry, totally dependent upon the local businesses, corporations, church support, and caring people who have a heart for helping hurting teenagers. He was so impressed that we refused government funds that he asked if he might write an article about House of Hope. The article was scheduled to appear in the *Sentinel* on May 29, 1985, the same day that President Reagan would visit EPCOT Center in Orlando at its dedication. He was only scheduled to be in Orlando for three hours, but we prayed that somehow, in spite of his busy schedule, the president would read the article.

Once again, God answered our prayer. The president read the article, wrote a letter of congratulation and encouraged the community to get involved. He included a $1,000 check from his personal account. Another God incident!

The community began to become aware of what we were doing and the great need for this unique home. Carpenters donated materials and labor, and plumbers, electricians, painters and repairmen, etc., rallied to God's calling. One house had a large hole in the roof. Early one morning when I arrived at the property, I was surprised to see five men on top of the house building a new roof! These men were unknown to us but known to God.

Our doors to House of Hope opened August 22, 1985. Exactly what we needed— beds, furniture, appliances, dishes, linens, pots and pans, clothing—came from individuals, organizations and churches.

God Meets Our Needs

Shortly after we moved in, we found that the carpet in one house was full of fleas! An exterminator came and told us that the rug was infested with fleas and eggs, which would be impossible to take care of in one trip, and each visit would cost us forty dollars. We had no funds for this. When volunteers and children walked into the house, their legs were peppered with fleas—and the best three girls were coming the next day. In desperation I felt impressed to use my authority as a Christian.

Luke 10:19 says, "Behold, I give you the authority to trample on serpents and scorpions, and over all the power of the enemy, and nothing shall by any means hurt you." I believed that included fleas and went through each room, asking God to remove every flea. Since that day there has never been another flea at House of Hope! Praise the Lord!

When I told this story at a men's club one day, a man on the front row was a veterinarian and he said enthusiastically, "Lady, come on down to my place!"

I laughed and said, "We'll never put the exterminators out of business, but God answered our prayer that day!"

Another time we had a need for some office furniture and chairs. As I looked in the yellow pages, one name seemed to stand out. The next day while looking at newspaper ads, the same name seemed to leap from the page. I called that number and introduced myself. The lady practically shouted with excitement—she had been trying to get in touch with me for two days. She went on to say if it had not been for our twenty-four-hour prayer hotline, she would not be alive today. If one of our prayer counselors had not prayed with her she would have committed suicide. Now she had hope through Jesus Christ. This grateful lady happened to own a furniture store and told me, "Come down right now and pick out what you need." God had provided again.

A lady came to House of Hope and volunteered to clean and wax the floors. However, she needed a buffer. At that time we had very few phone calls, so we were surprised when the phone rang at that moment. When we answered the line, a voice on the other end asked us if we needed a buffer! What a confirmation! This precious volunteer waxed the floors and went on to become a valuable member of the staff.

One night the girls prayed for a color television. The very next day a stranger delivered a beautiful color television.

The Lord's blessings continued to flow! The girls loved grilled cheese sandwiches for lunch and for a while we had no cheese. The girls decided they had better pray! Two days later a fifty-pound hoop of cheese arrived at the door! Only the Lord knew who delivered it.

On October 28, 1985, our part-time bookkeeper let me know that it was time to pay the bills. We owed $6,000 in bills and we only had $5,700. We agreed together in prayer (Matthew 18:19) that God would touch someone's heart to give. Two days later a letter arrived from someone in New York State. You guessed it! Enclosed was a check for $300! From finances and fleas to cheese, God cares about the hurting teenagers at House of Hope!

Addressing a Staggering Need

The number of teenagers who desperately need this facility staggers the imagination. We maintain a maximum capacity of twenty-four girls and sixteen boys in our program because we want each teen to get the individual attention and home atmosphere they so desperately need and may have never received before. However, there are thousands of other teens across America needing help too.

Our vision is to see Houses of Hope spring up across the nation and around the world. We hold national training seminars to teach others how to start a facility in their area. Today House of Hope Orlando is the model for a national network of Houses of Hope. I'm proud to say we now have seventy-four facilities in process across America, and the number is growing steadily.

Our program is based on Malachi 4:6, and our mission is to turn the hearts of fathers and mothers to the children, and to turn the hearts of children back to their fathers and mothers.

Reconciling the family is a vital key to the success of House of Hope. Our goal is to return each teen to a healthy and loving home. We therefore require all parents and other family members to participate in once-a-week individual counseling and a weekly parenting class.

For teens and their families who are not in the residential program, we also offer non-resident counseling.

House of Hope is a holistic ministry to body, soul, and spirit. We have a full-size, fully equipped gymnasium with exercise equipment, aerobic classes and intramural games. Our A.C.E. (Accelerated Christian Education) School offers an accredited high school diploma. Extracurricular classes include etiquette, health, social graces, beauty, dance, drama and art.

Our goal at House of Hope is to prevent hundreds of hurting young people from being destroyed on the streets in our community. We want to protect them from our drug-altered, child-abusing, sex-for-sale society where children are being exploited, facing horrors and experiencing defeat. Social agencies and institutions try to help teenagers, but young people continue to desperately yearn for love and a sense of being wanted.

Designed to be an anchor to hurting teenagers drifting in troubled waters, House of Hope proves an atmosphere of love—Christian love—through Christian counseling and intervention techniques to reconcile and restore the family. Our Christian staff is well-qualified to provide assistance in meeting each teenager's need. This ministry has a ripple effect, for not only are the girls' and boys' lives touched but also their families, friends and everyone with whom they come in contact.

Sir Edmund Burke, noted British statesman, said something to the effect of, "A sure way for evil to triumph is for good men to do nothing." House of Hope is doing something. We are changing lives—the lives of our young people, our most precious natural resource and America's future—and causing evil not to triumph.

House of Hope is a unique experience for everyone. From the first phone call that a tired, frustrated and worn-out parent makes to the graduation ceremony, the one constant lesson that is taught involves *h-o-p-e.*

Of course what makes this facility unique is the required involvement of the parents. We spend innumerable hours working with the teen to turn their lives around by giving up those old negative habits. But it does not stop there! We work with the parents in counseling, parenting classes and spiritual encouragement, and we require them to spend time with their children. It would be worthless to fix the teens and get them all spruced up, looking good and ready to face the world, but then return them to a chaotic and dysfunctional environment at home. That doesn't work!

Through many years of trial and error, we are now perfecting a model that is successful. The journey is not a temporary, quick-fix for teens. The transformation reaches into the entire family and can change every aspect of living. Below are two good examples of the kind of transformation that we see.

On the Road to Destruction: Laura, age 14

My name is Laura, and I am fourteen years old. I have been at House of Hope for eight months. I grew up with an alcoholic mother and basically had to take care of myself—and took care of her, too. She was never there for me.

I had a stepfather who criticized everything I did and brought me down for my faults. I could never live up to his standards. He called me names like "slut" and "whore." He caused me to have no respect for my authority figures.

As I grew older, my stepfather started to hit and curse me out. I was molested by one of his friends when I was only seven. For five years my mother denied that it ever happened because my stepfather denied it to my mom.

I started to defile my body, smoke cigarettes, have sex and use cocaine and other drugs. I began to fail, not only in school, but in every area of my life. I began to fight with my mom over everything. I took advantage of her when she was drunk, and would not listen or do anything that she told me to do. I was a mess, and she was a mess. I was confused and full of shame. I hated myself and the mistakes I had made.

I did not know about Jesus until I came to House of Hope. Since I have been here, I have come to know Him as my personal friend and Savior. Through counseling, I have a better relationship with my mom. I have also learned to have more respect for myself and for authority figures. People say my whole countenance has changed.

Before House of Hope I was on a fast road to destruction. House of Hope saved my life. My mom and I are getting the help and tools we need to survive in this world.

My favorite verse is Psalm 9:9: "The Lord is the refuge for the oppressed, A refuge in times of trouble." Now I run to Jesus when I am down or in trouble.

And by the way, to all you mothers and grandmothers I say, "Please spend time with your children. Be a mother to them. Don't get on the same level as a friend. Be a mom. Be there for them and listen to them."

Rejected by Mom and Step Dad: David, age 17

My name is David. I am seventeen. I was born in Orlando. My mom cheated on my dad with a guy from church. When I was five years old, my parents were divorced. My mom met a guy at a bar and they went out a couple of times. Then he moved in with us. He got my mom pregnant, and I had a sister on the way. All the attention was lost from me and went toward my sister.

I spent a lot of time either being punished or just being locked in my room. One time I was so frustrated that I kicked out the bottom of the door and bent it forward so I could crawl out. Another time I just threw my shoe and, not meaning to, I broke through the window. I always wondered why I was stuck in my room every day and every weekend while my parents were out playing with my sister, watching movies and having fun.

When I was nine years old, I was miserable. I had thought about suicide and thought about running away. My mom and step dad would not let me see my dad. Because of anger and rejection, I got into a lot of trouble.

My life continued to be horrible, and my mom and step dad continued to refuse to let me see my dad. My mom was looking at a whole bunch of juvenile facilities to send me to because she wanted to wash her hands of me.

My dad said he did not want me to go. He wanted me to come live with him. My mom refused. My dad hired a private investigator and got enough information on her to use in court. He then told her that he would fight her in court for custody of me. She said, "No, you can have him." So on my twelfth birthday, my dad got custody of me.

Everything was perfect for three years, but then during those last two years, I started rebelling against my dad and getting into trouble at school.

I was failing all my classes. I was arrested for getting in a fight with my dad. I locked myself in my room until the cops showed up a few minutes later and arrested me. My dad found out about House of Hope.

House of Hope is a safe place. I knew about Jesus but did not have a strong relationship with Him.

I have always thought that tall, handsome, strong guys were the most popular and most important. Then I learned the story of how Samuel picked David, who was young and watching sheep and not as handsome and strong as his brothers, to be king because he had a pure heart after God. I love God and I want to serve Him even though the popular people may not accept me. I want God to look at my heart. Man looks on the outside, but God looks at the heart.

My dad and I have a very good relationship now. When I graduate, I want to be a counselor to help other teenagers who, like me, are having problems.

At House of Hope We Never Give Up Hope!

I want to leave you with a final story that I love sharing about House of Hope because it captures what we're trying to do here. We make our teens feel special by loving them as much as we can. One of the ways we love them is by tucking them in every night.

Now, I know what you're thinking: "You cannot be serious, Sara. Did you say tucking in teenage boys and girls? Aren't they a little old for that?"

No, they aren't too old. Our house parents tuck in every teen every night, not with a kiss as most parents do, but with a warm hug. Yes, our street-hardened boys— some standing six feet, four inches tall and weighing 250 pounds—are tucked in at bedtime. Initially, they are not used to this display of love, but after a month or two they can't go to sleep without the touch of a warm hug and someone praying for them. At House of Hope we say: "The streets and institutions don't tuck them in at night, but we do at House of Hope."

If you're counseling teens in a group home situation, think about tucking them in with a hug before they fall asleep. Then stand back and watch their hearts melt. You'll be amazed what love can do. What a privilege that God counts us worthy to love, serve and help hurting teenagers and parents.

The Cycle of Hope

I still remember the long drive on that Saturday morning. I had just been released from a psychiatric hospital where I had been committed following a drug overdose. I had intended to end my life and stop the pain and torment that had been a part of my life for years. My head was swimming with conflicted thoughts. I felt hopeless and alone.

As we pulled into the drive I lifted my head just long enough to read the sign: "House of Hope." I remember thinking, "Yea, hope, whatever." I had no other place to go. I had been told that the people here would agree to let me stay if I agreed with their rules. As if I had a choice. It was here or another psychiatric facility.

Sara came out to greet me with a hug. I wanted to pull away, but I let my guard down long enough to allow her. She spoke to me with a genuineness that I could not quite comprehend. How could a woman I had only just met possibly be this concerned about my situation? I did not understand the emotions that were being brought to the surface, but I now understand that it was the Holy Spirit beginning an incredible work in and through me. God used House of Hope to save me—to save me from myself, from my torment, and from an eternal life in hell.

When I looked in the mirror I saw a grotesque monster. I had become convinced that I was evil and undeserving of anything good. I had been sexually abused by a family member since the age of four. I had been taught to believe that I was responsible for the abuse. I believed I was dirty, and I deserved it.

I would not allow myself to think into the future. I could not see myself grown. I was not worthy of an education, the love of a husband or the gift of children.

I was determined to die and put an end to my pain. I was obsessed with suicide. I felt I had no other choice, and I could not control my thoughts. Drugs and alcohol no longer numbed the suffering I was experiencing.

The counselors began to minister to me immediately. They showed Christ to me daily in real, very practical ways. The staff sat with me when I woke up screaming in the night. They gave me opportunities to express my fears and gave me Scripture to use to fight the spiritual warfare that I encountered.

I accepted Christ, and over time I began to see myself differently. The counselors prayed for me to be delivered from my fears and to be healed from hurts I had not dealt with inside from all the sexual abuse. They taught me about my true identity in Jesus Christ. I no longer saw the monster I had become so familiar with. I began to understand that I was a creation of my heavenly Father, and that to choose suicide would hurt Him terribly.

When I was ready to graduate from the program I was unable to return to my hometown. House of Hope placed me in a Christian foster home where I continued to receive the support and counseling that promoted my healing. I lived there until I left for the University of Florida.

It has been twenty-one years since I graduated from House of Hope. I am now a high school English teacher and a leader in the Fellowship of Christian Athletes. God has continued to richly bless me. I am not sure I would even recognize the young girl I once was.

Even after accepting Christ, I found it difficult to dream about marrying and having children. I still felt incapable of, and perhaps unworthy of, the love someone might share with me. I was especially frightened that I would fail as a parent and inadvertently repeat the evil cycle of perversion or abuse.

God was and is bigger than any of my fears! The Holy Spirit led a godly man to me. He accepted me as I was and enabled me to see beyond my long-held reservations involving parenthood. We have been married nearly sixteen years and have two young daughters.

They don't understand what a gift they are to me. They sing the "House of Hope" song with me but are too young to understand the significance of the words to mommy.

Without House of Hope, I am not sure that I would be alive. I can never repay the gift of life and the prayer that gave me eternal life. I have had several opportunities to pray with other young girls to accept Christ. With each opportunity I must acknowledge that without House of Hope I would not have been there for those prayers. God continues to use House of Hope in my life. The cycle of hope continues...

The Need for Counselors

There is a ripe harvest of teenagers who need to experience the Lord's touch through people who are called and equipped to welcome them into His love and walk with them through their darkness. These people are counselors like you who have a burden for the hurting and the capacity to nurture them into spiritual and emotional health. You are desperately needed.

Our mission is "to turn the hearts of the fathers and mothers to the children, and to turn the children back to the fathers and mothers, lest there be a curse on this land." Please notice which comes first—the hearts of the fathers and mothers. As children recognize those with unwavering values and a firm faith foundation, they will begin to find security in the Lord we speak of and in their ability to pursue Him for themselves. Together, we will break this curse.

The Lord has given a special, sacred trust to those He has called to work with youth. So much has been deposited in our youth, and we have the privilege of helping them discover this reality. We also have the privilege of ensuring that our Lord has a good return on His investments in these young lives. Youth need to be told that they are destined for greatness and that no power can stop them unless they allow it. It is important to remind them of the great call on their lives and to assist them as they walk through their darkness until they can come to the place where they believe and are able to lay aside meaningless pursuits and strive for the excellence of their call.

As counselors, we are agents of the Lord. Just as the Holy Spirit is called the "Counselor," we are able to join with Him to see radical change and bear witness to the Lord's marvelous works. There is no greater miracle than the power of a transformed life. Please join us as we endeavor to move the mountains of despair and clear the clouds of impending doom from this generation. Daniel 12:3 (NIV) says, "Those who are wise will shine like the brightness of the heavens, and those who lead many to righteousness, shine like the stars for ever and ever."

You are the wise teachers, and those who shine like stars. This task becomes lighter as we synergize. I look forward to reaping this precious harvest with your help. The parents and teens are waiting....

Preparing for Ministry

Now I want to share with you the five-steps of the Triage Approach to Counseling that House of Hope uses to bring God's healing touch into hopeless situations. In Emergency Triage Counseling, we often meet the patients at the scene of the accident, when there has been a serious crisis in their lives. At this point, we take Step 1: Checking the Heartbeat. The next section will teach you how to do this.

CHAPTER 3

Salvation

AT THE SCENE OF AN ACCIDENT, AN EMT WOULD assess the victimsand put a red tag on those in life-and-death situations and need to be stabilized to be kept alive.

In the same way, as counselors we need to focus on the life-and-death issues for our clients. The first thing we do is assess the client's spiritual heartbeat. Is he or she spiritually alive? Does he or she have salvation?

Healing the Whole Person

Unless you and I impart a Bible-based foundation and demonstrate God's healing power (which builds their faith), our efforts become no different than the secular world.

America is facing a crisis with the youth of this nation. In 2005 President George W. Bush invited me along with three hundred people across America to attend the first White House conference called "Helping America's Teens." House of

Hope is different because we have not received any government funds in the past twenty-three years of our operation.

President Ronald Reagan and his wife Nancy visited House of Hope Orlando in 1990. He commented, "There needs to be a House of Hope within driving distance of every major city across America."

That's our mission at House of Hope, to help wounded people find Jesus Christ and teach them principles based on God's Word. That is the only thing that will bring long-lasting healing! **Secular programs can only address part of the problem!** In this chapter I'll share with you the types of healing that bring change and a renewed sense of freedom to our young people and parents.

At House of Hope, the staff and I have a great advantage for caring for teenagers and families God's way. We have forty boys and girls on campus in our residential facility and many in our non-residential counseling program in Orlando, Florida, which is our national model. In agreement with President Reagan, my goal is to have a House of Hope within driving distance of every major city across America and in other countries. Presently there are seventy-one centers open or in process under our national umbrella. We are the only residential program (that I know) that requires intensive parental involvement through individual Christian clinical counseling along with specialized groups. Parents must attend a church that teaches the Trinity, attend weekly parenting classes, *and* visit their teens on Sunday afternoons for two hours. In most cases, the teens love their parents' attention.

Our program is based on Christian principles of healing the whole person—body, mind and spirit. We have an outstanding success rate of healing and returning teens to their families, fulfilling our mission in Malachi 4:6: "And he shall turn the heart of the children to their fathers."

We receive an abundance of calls weekly from youth workers, pastors and counselors who are crying out for Christian residential facilities that require parents to be involved. We all know we cannot send a teen home to a dysfunctional family and expect them to succeed. Therefore it is crucial and required that parents actively participate in our programs. Research consistently shows that teens that have positive connections to their families are far less likely to engage in risky behavior than those who do not.

Supernatural Awakening:
Jonathan, fifteen years old

Hi, my name is Jonathan and I am 15 years old. I've been in House of Hope for several months. Before I came to House of Hope, I barely knew of God. Honestly, the only thing I knew was using His name the wrong way. It only took a few months in House of Hope before I actually had a salvation experience in my life. I had broken my foot and was in a brace on crutches.

What I am about to share is the experience that caused me to have a relationship with Jesus Christ. It was my first prayer night in House of Hope, and at the end of the meeting they prayed for my foot. I was shocked to find that the pain was gone. I took off my brace and stomped my foot. There was no pain!

At once I fell to my face; thanking God for showing me He is real. The other boys on campus noticed that I was no longer on crutches, and it caused them all to come together and worship. I'll never again doubt my salvation experience. Because of what Jesus did in my life, some of the other boys asked Jesus into their hearts. Jesus Christ is real!

Becoming a born-again Christian is *the* most significant experience in a person's life, like in Jonathan's. Great healing can follow the salvation experience. However, becoming saved does not usually bring immediate healing to our whole being. Years of unmet needs and pain are not going to be immediately understood. It is the Lord's desire to bring every person through the many facets of the healing process to free them from their past pains, including false beliefs and lies.

We have become so adept at avoiding pain that we tend to flee when the Lord begins to work. We are driven by our needs. Until we can truly experience a deep sense of intimacy with God, we won't necessarily go to Him to get our needs met. After Jonathan's experience, he was ready to allow his counselor to begin the healing process of his years of pain, which began by forgiving those people who had caused his pain.

What about the parents' responsibility? We share with the parents the importance of walking the walk, not just talking the talk. Most parents like to tell the kids, "Do what I say do, not what I do." The teen's response is, "Your actions speak so loud I can't hear what you're saying." Parents must model and demonstrate their love and devotion toward God in front of their children. Paul said in Ephesians 5:1–2, "Therefore, be imitators of God, as beloved children, walk in love, just as Christ also loved you."

Kids with Passion

This generation does not lack passion. The challenge is to open their eyes so they can discover something *worth* their passion. As parents, teachers, counselors and youth workers, we need to communicate our faith to our teens. Deep down our teens want to know that God is real. They have tried everything else that didn't work.

Out of Control: Missy, age 14

Growing up, all I can remember is that my mother and father argued a lot and that my older sister, Martha, and I didn't get along. Perhaps that's because Martha and I came from completely different planets. I'm the sporty, tomboy sort who likes to break a sweat, while Martha was the girly-girl type who is into music and art.

My argumentative parents finally threw in the towel and separated when I was eight years old, and for the next few years, all I can remember is Mom going in and out of relationships with different boyfriends.

Dad? He was always gone for business. They somehow managed to share joint custody: We lived with my mother during the week and then spent the weekend with Dad after he got home from yet another business trip. Even after they broke up, Mom and Dad still argued, and their number one topic of contention was custody issues.

One weekend while at Dad's house, Martha and my father got into—you guessed it—an argument. Dad lost his temper and slapped Martha across the face. Martha was shocked, and she continually rubbed where she had been whacked. The rubbing caused the wound to look much worse, and when Martha and I returned home, Mom naturally wondered what happened.

"He beat me," Martha said, and before you could say the words "restraining order," Mom traveled to an emergency courtroom, where a judge granted her sole custody and ordered my father not to see us for three weeks. Afterward, a representative from the police department had to be present during all visits.

A couple of weeks passed, and I called Dad to see how he was doing. He sounded angry, but then he calmed down.

"I love you," he said.

"I love you too, Dad, but don't do anything stupid because of your anger issues."

Then I gave the phone to my sister and ran to the next room and picked up another phone so I could listen in.

Dad began yelling at Martha, saying that he hated her and my mom and that he could never forgive them.

That's when I heard the phone drop and a bunch of static.

"Dad! Dad!" my sister cried out.

Then we heard a loud bang [through the telephone] that sounded like a gunshot! All I can remember is running to the next room, screaming for Mom, before I passed out in shock.

When I came to, Mom was out in the middle of the street, talking with the police. I walked outside to talk to her, and when she saw me, she collapsed in a heap. While she was tended to, a social worker escorted me back to the house, where she told me that my dad had committed suicide.

*Following Dad's death, I became very rebellious. I was
nine years old, and Mom had to take me out of a private
Catholic school and put me into a public school, where I got
introduced to a whole lot of things. For the next couple of
years, I started hanging out at teen clubs, where I got into
smoking and drinking.*

*I never wanted to come home. I preferred hanging out
with my new friends, Mary Ann and her brother Brad. They
were into things like stealing cars and dealing drugs, and
that seemed exciting to me. Since Brad sold marijuana and
ecstasy, he didn't charge us anything.*

*As I got older, I started going to more teen bars, especially
the ones where the bouncers didn't do anything about the
kids doing drugs inside the club. Mary Ann and I also got
into guys, and I became sexually active when I was thirteen.
We would stay out at clubs until four or five o'clock in the
morning, not caring what anyone thought or said to us.*

*Mom, meanwhile, was flipping out. I was gone all the time,
totally out of control, while my older sister was getting really
rebellious. Mom found out about House of Hope, and she
made us go to Tuesday night family counseling, but I didn't
like it when the counselors would pinpoint things I didn't like
about myself—like no self respect or respect for others. Those
counseling sessions made me so mad that I would race out to
the car and sulk.*

*My sister started acting better, which put all the attention
on me. Finally, Mom had enough: after I stayed up all night
at some club and slept until four o'clock in the afternoon,
Mom announced that she had had enough and that I was
making a move—to House of Hope.*

*I hated Mom so much for making me go there. I didn't
want to be at House of Hope, so I didn't show any emotion
and wanted to prove to everyone that they couldn't reach
me.*

*Then I saw God's love for me through the people at
House of Hope. As I was beginning to deal with my issues*

in counseling, I knew my heart was softening, but I still had rebellious thinking. After four months, I no longer had the desire to go out with my old friends. This was not how I wanted to live.

Although my attitude changed, I was still getting into trouble for breaking the rules. Three other girls and I decided to run away from the program. Once we were back on the streets, the old pressures started kicking in. Someone had some weed, and at first I said no, but when everyone was smoking, I thought, Why not?

One of the girls that ran away with me has an uncle who is a local sheriff, and he had all the cops looking for us. We were found and brought back, and when I returned, my heart was softened to God. I had a big heart change, and at chapel I gave my life to Christ. Two weeks later, Mom did the same thing! Since then, life has been so much better.

What I've learned through all this is that God has a plan for you. He did for me, even though I thought my future consisted of sitting around an apartment watching TV, selling drugs, driving around in stolen cars, and making dirty money. At one time, I really thought I was going to do that the rest of my life.

But God knew better, and I'm glad He did. He disciplines the ones He loves, and I sure got disciplined, but I also know He loves me and wants me to be His.

I was brokenhearted. Part of the problem with me was that I didn't want to be under authority. Eventually I learned that in life everybody is under an authority of some kind. I feel safer now because there is someone besides God who loves me and will not give me the wrong advice . . . my mom.

He heals the brokenhearted and binds up their wounds.—Psalm 147:3, NIV

Salvation is the first part of checking the heartbeat of a wounded person. However, salvation is not a cure-all for every spiritual, psychological or physical problem.

We counselors must determine the source of our teens and families' problems—whether it is spiritual, psychological, or physical. Often problems in one area will spill over into other areas. For example, most teens that come to House of Hope are heavily medicated, meaning they take a lot of prescription medications. We always check with their doctors so that we understand their physical diagnoses. However, we often find that spiritual and psychological problems are at the root of their need for the medication. After properly identifying and addressing these spiritual and psychological problems, we find that many of our residents can gradually come off their medication. (We *always* get their doctor's approval first and consult with the doctor regularly during the process.) It is our responsibility to identify the problems correctly so we can administer the right course of action.

After explaining salvation, the next thing you need to do for your clients in Step 1 is talk about forgiveness. In the next chapter you will learn how willingness to forgive opens the door to healing broken hearts and relationships.

Chapter 4

Forgiveness: The Key to Freedom

AT HOUSE OF HOPE WE BELIEVE FORGIVENESS IS REQUIRED BY GOD and is the principle key to unlock the door to freedom in all ministry areas.

Our Symbol

House of Hope logo is a symbol of total forgiveness. The circle around the house represents when a "house becomes a home." It is a symbol of healing for the entire family, both parents and children.

A Family Repents and Forgives: Amy and Her Family

During one of our Tuesday night parenting classes, the subject was forgiveness. After the guest speaker had finished his presentation, families were invited to come to the front for special prayers.

This was the first night Amy's entire family had attended the class together. One of the counselors approached them, seeing the biological father had tears in his eyes. The father stood there with his arm around his daughter Amy. For the first time since his divorce from Amy's mother, he turned to her and asked for forgiveness for all of the hurts he caused both by leaving Amy and divorcing her mother.

At that moment, the entire family broke into tears. With their arms around each other, they each repented and asked each others' forgiveness. Even though Amy and her mother had been in counseling for months, it was at this moment when the real breakthrough came, and their family actually began to heal.

This took place six years ago, and today that same mother is now facilitating a forgiveness group for other parents (who are having the same problems) at House of Hope Orlando. The mother and daughter travel to speak at other Houses of Hope across America on the importance of forgiveness.

Prayers of Forgiveness

Unforgiveness is an area where we address healing the whole person. Parents and teens come to us angry, hurt and bitter. They are full of resentment, rejection, self-pity and hatred, and they feel incapable of forgiving and loving those who hurt them. We teach that forgiveness is not an emotion, but an act of our will.

> And whenever you stand praying, if you have anything against anyone, forgive him, that your Father in heaven may also forgive you your trespasses. But if you do not forgive, neither will your Father in heaven forgive your trespasses. –Mark 11:25-26

When the teenager and parents reach a place in their healing where they can forgive, the counselor leads them in prayer. There are three main prayers of forgiveness that we pray with our parents and teens.

Prayer 1: Asking forgiveness for sins committed
Prayer 2: Forgiving those who hurt them
Prayer 3: Forgiving themselves

We believe forgiveness opens the doors of our hearts and lives to some other needed ministry areas that we will discuss in the following chapters, areas such as generational curses, sins of the fathers, vows and judgments, soul ties and ungodly beliefs. Forgiveness begins healing for all of these.

What Is Forgiveness?

Forgiveness means "to pardon or excuse an offense without attaching a penalty; to cancel a debt." To forgive is to release from judgment and give up the right to get even. Nobody could ever do anything to us that the blood of Jesus could not wash away. Forgiveness is consistently and freely offered to everyone by a merciful God.

Forgiveness should never start with feelings; it is primarily dependant upon our wills. If we wait until we feel like forgiving, we may never forgive. The decision to forgive is made with our wills, and we submit our feelings to God. He will change our feelings in due time.

> Forgiveness is the spiritual ointment God uses to remove the sting from our emotional wounds.

I acknowledged my sin to You, and my iniquity I have not hidden. I said, "I will confess my transgressions to the Lord," And You forgave the iniquity of my sin. —Psalm 32:5

For You, Lord, *are* good, and ready to forgive, and abundant in mercy to all those who call upon You. —Psalm 86:5

As far as the east is from the west, so far has He removed our transgressions from us. —Psalm 103:12

I, even I, am He who blots out your transgressions for My own sake; and I will not remember your sins. —Isaiah 43:25

...For I will forgive their iniquity, and their sin I will remember no more. —Jeremiah 31:34

But I tell you not to resist an evil person. But whoever slaps you on your right cheek, turn the other to his also. —Matthew 5:39

Then Jesus said, "Father, forgive them, for they do not know what they do. —Luke 23:34

If you forgive the sins of any, they are forgiven them; if you retain the sins of any, they are retained. —John 20:23

...Their sins and their lawless deeds I will remember no more. —Hebrews 10:17

Who Needs to Be Forgiven?

The Bible has many verses about who needs to be forgiven. Let's look at these different types of people.

1. The people we love the most are often the people we have to forgive the most.

We need to be sure that we have forgiven all the people that we are close to and we need to be sure that we are on the same playing field. And ready for the next step in counseling.

Brethren, I do not count myself to have apprehended; but one thing I *do*, forgetting those things which are behind and reaching forward to those things which are ahead. —Philippians 3:13

Finally, *all of you* be of one mind, having compassion for one another; love as brothers, *be* tenderhearted, *be* courteous; Do not repay evil with evil or insult with insult but with blessing, because to this you were called so that you may inherit a blessing. —1 Peter 3:8-9

2. We must forgive people who hurt us repeatedly.

Jesus said to him, "I do not say to you, up to seven times, but up to seventy times seven." —Matthew 18:22

3. We must forgive people who don't act like us—opposite in temperament and personality.

Finally, brethren, whatever things are true, whatever things *are* noble, whatever things *are* just, whatever things *are* pure, whatever things *are* lovely, whatever things *are* of good report, if *there is* any virtue and if *there is* anything praiseworthy—meditate on these things. —Philippians 4:8

4. We must forgive people in authority over us when they tell us to do what we don't want to do.

God will vindicate us (clear us of blame or accusation) if we give up trying to protect ourselves and let God protect us. In the end, He will balance it out.

If the spirit of the ruler rises against you, Do not leave your post;
For conciliation pacifies great offenses. —Ecclesiastes 10:4

5. Sometimes we need to forgive God.

This is a problem that we face frequently as we bring adolescents into the program because so many of them blame God for what has happened to them. It is easy to blame God because we can't see how He intervened in our troubles or because life isn't fair. We must never blame God, and I'm not saying that He has done anything sinful, but we must recognize these temptations as Satan's attack. We try to show our teens who their enemy really is.

Every good gift and every perfect gift is from above, and comes down from the Father of lights, with whom there is no variation or shadow of turning. —James 1:17

When Do We Forgive?

1. We must forgive every time there is unforgiveness in our hearts.

If we are depressed; plagued by unbelief, doubt or ingratitude; if we are constantly sick or impatient, full of self-pity or resentment, or if we feel rejected and withdraw, we could need to forgive somebody. Also, if we are bitter, unfeeling around certain people, jealous, have unrighteous anger, rigid, legalistic, manipulative, or if we have hatred, we need to forgive. The Scripture states:

> And do not grieve the Holy Spirit of God, by whom you were sealed for the day of redemption. Let all bitterness, wrath, anger, clamor, and evil speaking be put away from you, with all malice. And be kind to one another, tenderhearted, forgiving one another, even as God in Christ forgave you. —Ephesians 4:30–32

2. Forgiveness is an on-going process.

Sometimes we need to forgive for things as simple as daily irritations; other times we are affected by a deep hurt or sting. Unforgiveness must be recognized and acted upon as a sin. The Holy Spirit is very able to convict us of any and all sin. We must trust Him to convict us and then bring ourselves under His guidance and authority. Again, Scripture states:

> And do not be conformed to this world, but be transformed by the renewing of your mind, that you may prove what is that good and acceptable and perfect will of God. —Romans 12:2

Why Is It Important to Forgive?

1. Forgiveness is the principle key to open the door to freedom in all ministry areas.

Unforgiveness is a very important area that must be addressed in healing the whole person. We can receive nothing from God (we even forfeit the right to have our prayers answered) if we harbor unforgiveness in our hearts. Unforgiveness (toward God, toward others, toward ourselves) is a sin, and the Bible tells us that if we regard iniquity (sin) in our heart, the Lord cannot hear us (Ps. 66:18). If a person is living in sin, the only prayers God is committed to answer are the prayers for salvation and forgiveness.

2. Forgiveness is required by God and is non-negotiable.

Even if the need for forgiveness and love toward those who have wronged us is very real, even if we feel incapable of forgiving and loving, we must understand that forgiveness and love are not basic emotions. They are *acts of the will in obedience to Jesus*. We make a quality decision to love and to forgive. God will take care of our emotions in time; we may not feel them at first. Our part is to make the decision to love and to forgive and to refuse and reject any thought that would interfere with that decision. We must turn those thoughts over to Jesus and ask Him to fill us with thoughts of love and forgiveness for that person.

> But I say to you, love your enemies, bless those who curse you, do good to those who hate you, and pray for those who spitefully use you and persecute you. —Matthew 5:44

> Should you not also have had compassion on your fellow servant, just as I had pity on you?' And his master was angry, and delivered him to the torturers until he should pay all that was due to him. "So My heavenly Father also will do to you if each of you, from his heart, does not forgive his brother his trespasses." —Matthew 18:33–35

> "And whenever you stand praying, if you have anything against anyone, forgive him, that your Father in heaven may also forgive

you your trespasses. But if you do not forgive, neither will your Father in heaven forgive your trespasses." —Mark 11:25–26

"Be angry, and do not sin." Do not let the sun go down on your wrath. —Ephesians 4:26

3. Forgiveness breaks the negative spiritual bond between people, releasing both sides.

Our Lord commanded us to forgive. He commanded us to love, and He never expects us to do something unless He has made the way possible for us to do it. So we must *decide to* lay aside the resentment and the self-pity and the hurt, *decide to* obey our Lord's words to love and forgive. The decision is ours to make; God won't do it for us, but once we've done it, He will move heaven and earth to make it real within us!

> If it is possible, as much as depends on you, live peaceably with all men. Beloved, do not avenge yourselves, but *rather* give place to wrath; for it is written, *"Vengeance is Mine, I will repay," says the Lord.* —Romans 12:18–19

> Pursue peace with all people, and holiness, without which no one will see the Lord: looking carefully lest anyone fall short of the grace of God; lest any root of bitterness springing up cause trouble, and by this many become defiled. —Hebrews 12:14

4. Unforgiveness affects us emotionally, psychologically, and physically.

When we don't forgive, we are dying inside, and the pain is intense. Hurt has sown seeds of destruction. Some medical studies say that unforgiveness and bitterness can impair physical functions of the body. Unforgiveness can bring depression, which depletes the serotonin level in the brain, takes its toll on our immune systems, and opens up the body to cancer, viruses, arthritis, etc. As you can see, when we keep our joy and peace levels up, we can fight much more effectively.

And the peace of God, which surpasses all understanding, will guard your hearts and minds through Christ Jesus. —Philippians 4:7

How Do We Forgive?

1. We must allow ourselves to hurt.

We must be "willing to be willing." We have to get to a place where we hurt so badly that we are willing to do anything God requires to relieve our pain. Many are too hurt to even think about forgiving someone, so we must ask God to heal them enough so that they can forgive. We cannot deny the hurt, and the counselee may need time to grieve.

> The Lord is close to the brokenhearted and saves those who are crushed in spirit. —Psalm 34:18 (NIV)

2. We must assume our responsibility in the hurt.

When our hearts and minds are clouded by unforgiveness, our perception of truth is often blurred and distorted. All we can see is the other person's faults. When we forgive, it moves dark clouds away, and we can see our own responsibility and error in the situation. We must be honest with ourselves and with God.

We can't blame others when there is sin in our own lives. We must not ignore the truth when we have a part in it or when we allowed it to happen. We must pray that God will forgive us for any disobedience.

> And why do you look at the speck in your brother's eye, but do not consider the plank in your own eye? Or how can you say to your brother, 'Let me remove the speck from your eye'; and look, a plank *is* in your own eye? Hypocrite! First remove the plank from your own eye, and then you will see clearly to remove the speck from your brother's eye. —Matthew 7:3–5

3. Forgiveness is a decision, not just a feeling.

People will say, "After what he/she did to me, I cannot—I will not-forgive them." It will matter little what someone did to us after this short testing time here on earth when we stand before the Almighty God and tell Him by our unforgiveness that His Son Jesus' death on the cross wasn't enough for us, that we held the unforgiveness higher than His atoning death!

> "For if you forgive men their trespasses, your heavenly Father will also forgive you. But if you do not forgive men their trespasses, neither will your Father forgive your trespasses." —Matthew 6:14–15

> "So My heavenly Father also will do to you if each of you, from his heart, does not forgive his brother his trespasses." —Matthew 18:35

4. We must drop it, leave it, and let it go.

We try to hang on and remember offenses, but this makes us gossip and talk about the offense to others. We don't always have to forget, but God can take the sting out.

We walk in the flesh, but that does not mean that we have to do war in the flesh!

> For though we walk in the flesh, we do not war according to the flesh. For the weapons of our warfare *are* not carnal but mighty in God for pulling down strongholds, casting down arguments and every high thing that exalts itself against the knowledge of God, bringing every thought into captivity to the obedience of Christ. —2 Corinthians 10:3–5

We free ourselves from demonic influences by releasing those who have wounded us.

How Do We Help Others Forgive?

Clean hands and a clean heart are vital to be effective in counseling others.

It's helpful to go through a preparatory and purifying forgiveness prayer in order to be effective in counseling. We must examine our own hearts and be quick to repent and forgive before asking the Holy Spirit to be the Counselor on behalf of the counselee.

> And a servant of the Lord must not quarrel but be gentle to all, able to teach, patient, in humility correcting those who are in opposition, if God perhaps will grant them repentance, so that they may know the truth.—2 Timothy 224-25

Prayer 1: Asking Forgiveness for Sins Committed

In this prayer we ask the counselee to pray out loud and renounce any sin they remember and also pray that God brings to their mind all the sins for which they need to repent.

First, lead the counselee to ask for God's forgiveness.

> *Father, now I come to You through the shed blood of Your Son, Jesus, my Savior, and ask You to forgive me for _____, _____, _____, etc. (it is important that the counselee name the specific offenses). I acknowledge and take responsibility for each and every time I have sinned against You and violated Your commandments as well as for the sinful thoughts and plans that have been in my heart. Forgive and cleanse me, and restore me into fellowship with You. Holy Spirit, I thank You for working forgiveness in and through me, healing me and cleanse me from all unrighteousness. In Jesus' name, AMEN*

> If we confess our sins, He is faithful and just to forgive us our sins and to cleanse us from all unrighteousness. —I John 1:9

Prayer 2: Forgiving Those Who Hurt Them
Second, help the counselee to forgive others.

> *Lord Jesus, I choose to forgive _____ for _____. I desire*
> *the healing for me that forgiveness brings. I have chosen to*
> *forgive and to be forgiven. I release them from all debts, judg-*
> *ment and punishment that I wanted to put upon them. I now*
> *place them into Your hands. I choose to be obedient to You,*
> *Lord. I recognize that if I forgive man their trespasses, our*
> *heavenly Father will also forgive me; if I do not forgive others;*
> *neither will I receive forgiveness from God. In Jesus' name I*
> *pray, AMEN.*

And forgive us our debts, as we forgive our debtors. —Matthew
6:12

Prayer 3: Forgiving Themselves
Third, we must help the counselee to forgive himself/herself.

> *Father, because You have forgiven me, I choose to forgive*
> *myself for all the ways I have hurt others out of my own*
> *hurts and the ways I have hurt myself. I choose to forgive and*
> *release myself from all hatred, accusations, and judgments I*
> *have made against myself. I choose to accept and see myself*
> *as You see and accept me, as You will not leave me in this*
> *condition. You have something good in mind for me, and I am*
> *now on the right road, walking out the process. Thank You,*
> *Holy Spirit. I give You permission to work on me, embracing*
> *Your process of changing me into the image of Jesus Christ. In*
> *Jesus' name I pray, AMEN.*

Everyone who thirsts, come to the waters; and you who have no
money, come, buy and eat. — Isaiah 55:1

Total Forgiveness
We know that we have completed the step of forgiveness when:

1. We do not want anybody else to be hurt because of what was done to us.

2. We want the offender to know God and be healed.

3. We do not want the offender to feel condemned, angry at themselves, or afraid.

4. We make it easy for others to forgive themselves.

5. We keep on forgiving the offender—two months later, two years later. The forgiveness lasts.

After Forgiveness, What Is Next?

Forgiveness is a major key in all ministry areas and is always available to all who choose to walk in daily righteousness.

Forgiveness opens the doors of our hearts and lives to other needed ministry areas of which many born-again Christians are unaware. The Bible says, "My people perish for lack of knowledge" (Hosea 3:6). The Christian walk is a day-by-day process of restoration and transformation into His likeness.

As far as God is concerned, when forgiveness is given, it is finished—done! Sanctification, however, is an on going process. We are changed from "glory to glory" (2 Corinthians 3:18). We won't be perfect until we meet Jesus face-to-face. Our responsibility is to live in the Spirit and appropriate the truth of His Word as we go through life.

Dealing with a Crisis

After salvation and forgiveness, with the help of the Holy Spirit, we take step 2 in the Triage Approach to Counseling, which is treating the wounds. This will help calm the crisis and bring stabilization to the parent and teen.

CHAPTER 5

Healing the Broken Heart

AFTER AN EMT HAS STABILIZED A PATIENT, A yellow tag is given. The patient is then ready to have any wounds assessed and treated. As Christian counselors, we want to treat the hidden wounds of teens and parents, with the help of the Holy Spirit. A broken heart is the main area that is hidden at the bottom of the pool Jacob talked about earlier.

Every human being has a deep-rooted, basic need for love, acceptance and a sense of worth. God established the parents to be a model for the relationship He wants to have with humanity. When a child is born into this world, the parents are responsible to provide the child's needs. However, in reality, only God can truly meet the root needs of love, acceptance and self-worth. When God is absent in a family's life, deep wounds can occur.

Causes of the Broken Heart

If a child grows up in a stable, secure environment where parents consistently model the love and acceptance of God, the child develops a sense of value. It is quite natural for the child to develop a desire for God and to find a deeper sense of worth. Unfortunately, teens often get a false sense of worthlessness due to dysfunctions in their families passed down through the generations or due to the influence of the ways of the world.

In many families, the children have needs that are never met. For example, most children (and adults) have a need to be encouraged when they attempt a new skill. Some parents are unable to meet that need, and their lack of encouragement causes pain to a child. When a child is overwhelmed by this pain, he or she will develop a variety of insecurities and fears.

In trying to cope with these insecurities, the child, without a clear understanding of whom God is and what He can do, turns to various negative alternatives in the world trying to meet unmet needs. This often leads to a variety of destructive behavior patterns. The person becomes so far removed from the pain that he or she sees the destructive behavior as the only source of relief (regardless of how much more pain, shame, guilt, etc. it creates).

When a person experiences trauma, abandonment, abuse, etc., especially at a young age, they usually have an even deeper and more complex system of coping mechanisms. In many cases where the parental structure is broken down, we find the teen loses all sense of trust and security.

The truth is that only God can meet our needs. We were not created to be able to meet our own needs; otherwise, we would not have to be dependent upon God.

Rather than repress the pain, lead your client to resist evil. The word *"repress"* means to press, or push, the pain back where it began so a person doesn't have to look at it. However, the hurt doesn't cease to exist; it's simply driven into the subconscious. Jesus will heal so they don't have to repress memories. To resist evil is the biblical alternative. The Bible says:

> We demolish arguments and every pretension that sets itself up
> against the knowledge of God, and we take captive every thought
> to make it obedient to Christ. —2 Corinthians 10:5, NIV

Submit yourselves, then, to God. Resist the devil, and he will flee from you. —James 4:7, NIV

Symptoms of a Broken Heart

We must rely on the Holy Spirit to direct our approach in ministering healing to broken hearts and to show us specific areas where teens need inner healing.

Inner healing is not a rehashing of past sins or a fruitless excavation into the past. Rather it is allowing God to bring things to the surface as He directs. It is not teaching people to forget their past hurts or giving advice on how to solve problems. It is not a psychological gimmick or a substitute for the cross but an encounter with the crucified and now resurrected Lord Jesus.

When a person has not experienced healing for a broken heart, one or more of the following symptoms will typically be apparent.

1. Abandonment—rejected by birth parents and given up for adoption
2. Abuse—physical, sexual, mental, emotional or verbal
3. Addiction problems
4. Allows others to walk all over them
5. Anger
6. Confusion; difficulty making decisions
7. Depression
8. Excessive need for attention
9. Fears
10. Guilt feelings
11. Hating the physical body
12. Hurts others
13. Identity distorted
14. Illegitimacy (a lack of feeling worthy; inability to feel ownership)
15. Lack of forgiveness

16. Lack of identity (Is there a private self and a public self? Does the client wear a mask?)
17. Lack of motivation
18. Loneliness
19. Losses
20. Lost joy of Christian life
21. Low self-esteem
22. Marital problems
23. Nightmares
24. Ongoing vulnerability
25. Physical problem without an identifiable cause
26. Purpose distorted or unfilled
27. Rejection—being unloved, given up for adoption, nearly adopted as baby
28. Restricted emotional growth
29. Sexual identity confusion
30. Shame
31. Trouble having eye contact with others
32. Very critical of others and/or self
33. Very defensive
34. Wrongful soul or sexual ties to others

If we are honest with ourselves, every person reading this book has, or had, a wall in their lives that holds, or held, them in bondage.

Healing Memories

Wounds from the past can be as crippling to our souls and spirits as debilitating diseases are to our bodies. The hurts are carried and experienced within the person himself, and sometimes they can cause a person to completely shut down.

For example, a little child running towards a lake hears a terrified scream from her mother: "Don't go near the water!" The child panics and a fear-based response has now found an open door to enter. It is important to bring a measure of healing to the memory of that moment.

We help heal that memory by first explaining to the now grown woman (who has never been able to "go near the water" from that day) that Jesus is the "same yesterday, today, and tomorrow" and He is not limited, as we are, to the boundaries of time and space, so He can transcend our limits. Our yesterdays can be—and are—His now.

Jesus can meet that little girl in that grown woman right at the point of that fear coming in and heal the pain of the memory, thus removing the "landing strip" for an automatic response of fear to come into that situation.

During the counseling session for inner healing, we pray and ask Jesus to do just that. Perhaps the counselee will experience an immediate release in her spirit, or perhaps she will notice some time in the future that she no longer fears the water.

Purpose of Inner Healing

The purpose of inner healing is found in Jesus' mission, as declared in Isaiah:

> The Spirit of the Sovereign Lord is on me,
>   because the Lord has anointed me
>   to preach good news to the poor.
>   He has sent me to bind up the brokenhearted,
>   to proclaim freedom for the captives
>   and release from darkness for the prisoners,
>
> and provide for those who grieve in Zion—
>   to bestow on them a crown of beauty
>   instead of ashes,
>   the oil of gladness
>   instead of mourning,
>   and a garment of praise
>   instead of a spirit of despair.
>   They will be called oaks of righteousness,
>   a planting of the Lord
>   for the display of his splendor. —Isaiah 61:1-3, NIV.

(See also Luke 4:18, Matthew 22:36–40).

Teach your clients that inner healing will help them to have:

- ⅄ A closer relationship with God. (Some feel closer to the Father, rather than the Son—until healed).
- ⅄ Freedom to love and accept yourself. (We see ourselves as others saw us—especially parents.)
- ⅄ An ability to forgive, restore and deepen relationships with "your neighbors." (Neighbors are those closest to you as well as those who live on your street. Relationships without strings.)
- ⅄ Wholeness enough to be about your Father's business. (Luke 2:49) We're to carry on the ministry of Jesus—sharing good news, healing broken hearts, setting captives free from prison, opening blind eyes.
- ⅄ Persistence to reach your fullest potential. (3 John 2, Ephesians 3:17-21, Romans 8:32)
- ⅄ A desire to become a vessel of honor and channel of love (2 Timothy 2:21).
- ⅄ A sense of purpose and passion given by the Holy Spirit to prepare the Body of Christ for His coming (Psalm 23,24, 1 Corinthians 11:28,31 (We examine).

Basically, inner healing gives a person the ability to walk out God's greatest commandments. As Jesus said,

> Jesus said to him, "'*You shall love the Lord your God with all your heart, with all your soul, and with all your mind*.' This is the first and great commandment. And the second is like it: '*You shall love your neighbor as yourself*.'" —Matthew 22:37-39.

Spiritual Preparation for Counselors

As we have ministered inner healing over the years to many people, we have learned that counselors need to take the following steps in spiritual preparation.

⅄ Ask the Holy Spirit to direct which prayer approaches to use.

⅄ Make sure everyone is forgiven—even if only on the level of the will.

⅄ Invite the power of the Holy Spirit to be present.

⅄ Ask God to provide cleansing from all sins in thoughts, word or deeds (James 5:16b).

⅄ Ask for the protection of Jesus' blood.

⅄ Ask God to be filled and stay filled with the Holy Spirit—and praise Him for it.

⅄ Ask God to become a conduit so that His healing love and light will flow through us.

⅄ Put on the whole armor of God (Ephesians 6:10–18)

⅄ Ask God to direct each day and learn to practice listening to and obeying His directions.

⅄ Teach the families how to walk in God's protection.

Counselor Tools for the Inner Healing Session

During the inner healing session, counselors need to know and do the following:

⅄ Use all the helps available but realize the great importance in depending on the Holy Spirit. One word from God can cut through a lot of human reasoning.

⅄ Evaluate whether the stories or events shared by the teen or parent are scriptural. They should show the nature of Jesus. (For example, Jesus would not be condemning according to John 3:17.) Set the teen or parent at ease about this, so he can just share without being concerned whether what he's saying is acceptable.

⅄ If what the teen or parent says is unscriptural, stop him, but do it gently.

⅄ If praying about childhood, encourage the teen or parent to stay in the scene with a child's point of view. Do not analyze or come into the adult viewpoint until prayer is completed. Children think in pictures; adults in concepts and pictures.

⅄ Be sure that parents and teens participate verbally in the prayers involving the healing of memories. We've found that it's much more effective if the teen or parent sees, feels and speaks about the scenes than if the counselor does it for him. Counselors will do more talking after the prayer session than during it.

⅄ During prayer, we must keep directing the teen or parent to Jesus and away from ourselves.

The Inner Healing Session

These are the steps that we have used with success at House of Hope to start clients on the process of inner healing.

Step 1: Confess the Desire for Help

Tell your counselees about King David's prayer:

> Search me, O God, and know my heart; try me, and know my anxieties; and see if *there is any* wicked way in me, and lead me in the way everlasting. —Psalm 139:23–24

Explain that people need to go behind the walls they build in order to heal the pain in their lives. Isaiah 61:1–3 states that Jesus came to heal the broken-hearted and bind up their wounds. Jesus can take them to the place where the pain first began and help them to begin the healing process. The next question to ask is, "Are you willing for Jesus to come and remove these walls?" If your client is ready, go to the next step.

Step 2: Look for the Source of the Wounds

Explain to your client that events in the past may have caused them to stuff their pain in their hearts. They built walls around their hearts because they had no way to process the hurt or they had no one to talk to.

To understand what wounds need healing, pray and ask the Holy Spirit to reveal the truth about the person. You may ask the parent or teen some of the questions below. Keep a pad of paper handy and write down significant answers or comments the teen or parent makes.

- ⅄ Who was the first person who loved you? [If the answer is not one or both of the parents, there is a deficiency.]
- ⅄ Who is the first person you ever really felt loved you?
- ⅄ Describe what you know about your birth and any special or unique situations about it.
- ⅄ How did you feel when you were with your father? Your mother? Other family members or neighbors?
- ⅄ Were you and your parents compatible in religion or did your parents have different beliefs?
- ⅄ Were your parents very controlling? Did you feel that they loved you?
- ⅄ Were you neglected or not nurtured? [Watch for childhood sickness or substance abuse in the family.]
- ⅄ Were you happy as a child? If not, when did you become unhappy? Did you like yourself as a child? When have you been happy?
- ⅄ What is the first hurtful memory you have?
- ⅄ How did or do you respond to hurts? (depression, anger, crying, acting out sexually, working harder for approval, escaping through drugs or alcohol, isolation, illness, repression, not admitting anything's wrong, revenge, controlling through temper or organizing people lives, having to be ahead of everyone)
- ⅄ What hurtful emotions have been surfacing lately?
- ⅄ What would you like God to do for you?

Step 3: Pray for Healing of Memories

After you have talked about the sources of hurt, you can choose a time to lead the teens and/or parents in a prayer session to start the healing process. Sometimes a person has to experience a measure of freedom before inner healing and/or during inner healing. (Later chapters of this book describe this process in detail.) That is why we recommend a second person be present. It is important that our counselors are sensitive to the leading of the Holy Spirit and the response of the teen or parent. Psalm 32:8 reads: "I will instruct you and teach you in the way you should go; I will guide you with My eye."

1. Begin with prayer, inviting the Holy Spirit to be the Counselor and search the teen or parent's heart and life for any hurts to be revealed and healed. REMEMBER: "What God reveals, He heals."

2. Wait on the Lord and expect the teen or parent to hear God's voice as a hurt comes to mind. (This could take fifteen to twenty minutes.)

3. Have the teen or parent share what he/she hears or sees.

4. Lead them in healing of memories prayers, making sure *the client repeats the prayers after you.* As you pray, gently touch the teen or parent on the hand/shoulder if appropriate, allowing them to get in touch with their emotions and know that they are with a safe person.

Pray: *"I release and give this hurt, pain, anger, frustration, and fear to You, God." Tell your client to be honest about how he/she feels, acknowledge any emotions, and describe feelings at the time of the hurt. For example, if the emotion is anger, ask the Lord to pull out that anger and fill that place in your clients' heart with His love.*

Pray: *"I release and forgive others for inflicting this and causing me pain." Name the people who caused the pain.*

Pray: *"I ask You to forgive me, Lord, for hurting others out of my heart. I repent for my attitude and behavior toward others."*

Pray: *"I forgive myself for letting this hurt control me."*

5. As the negative emotions are released, ask the Spirit of God to remove the hurt.

Pray: *"I ask You, Jesus, to come and heal the hurt." Be still and allow the Holy Spirit time to minister His healing touch.*

Pray: *"I receive Your healing." Be careful not to make leading suggestions about what they are feeling or not feeling.*

6. After prayer, have the teen or parent share whatever he/ she has seen, heard, or sensed.

7. Repeat the process to allow the Holy Spirit opportunity to reveal any more hurts.

8. Finally, pray for the sealing of the healing and the continuing of the healing process in the days to come.

To make this process clear to counselors, House of Hope has prepared a video demonstrating this type of counseling. Please use the information at the back of this book to contact House of Hope if you are interested in getting a copy.

CHAPTER 6

Testimonies of Inner Healing

You will be greatly encouraged to read the stories of young men and women who have experienced inner healing from a variety of wounds. Following is a sample from our ministry, addressing wounds and symptoms such as:

- ⅄ Abuse
- ⅄ Rejection from parents
- ⅄ Addiction
- ⅄ Cutting, or self-mutilation
- ⅄ Suicide
- ⅄ Fear of grieving
- ⅄ Uncontrollable anger

Abuse

Abuse can take many forms—physical, sexual, emotional, verbal, spiritual, or neglect. Each and every form can affect anyone. While some forms of abuse are easier to define than others, nonetheless they are all abuse. Physical abuse would be the quickest and most obvious to define because it is external and visible, while sexual, emotional, spiritual and verbal abuse and neglect would be more difficult because they are internal.

How would you recognize abuse that is not external? Behavior would give some signs, and clues, but only through relationship and trust built with a counselor or parent would you be able to dig through the layers of pain to uncover the internal abuse.

Stuck in the Pain of Sexual Abuse: Michelle

A Poem

This is my story as a teenage girl,
Who let liquid chains rule my world.
At the end of the day,
With an empty bottle and with my heart full of pain,
I'd fall away
And lose another part.
Without a sound, without a drop,
I'd scream and cry and wait for my heart to stop.
Then one night my hurts and actions caught up;
There was no escaping;
This time I was stuck.

I was stuck in the pain of my sexual abuse which began when I was only eight years old. He was a family member. Then my entire family life began to unravel. My parents divorced. I became angry, began lying and looking for acceptance and fulfillment through alcohol, drugs and guys. After coming to House of Hope, through counseling, I received healing for my heart broken by rejection, abuse and drugs, and now I am a changed young lady. My goal in life is to help other girls who have gone through the same hurts I have.

Addiction

Addiction comes in many packages—substances, relationships, sex, religion, food, entertainment, etc. Addiction is often described as "a compulsive or physical dependency upon a substance or person or behavior that provides a temporary sense of well-being"—with the emphasis on *temporary*. Truly, an addiction *never* satisfies; it is a neurological game of fooling the mind into believing the person is satiated.

In our fallen world, we have certain biological and neurological malfunctions, such as diabetes, cancer, depression and even predispositions to substance abuse. However, we as Christian counselors believe that when there is faith, applications of wisdom, godly therapeutic interventions, and healthy family and community support, grace can abound and restoration will be the result.

Becoming healed and satisfied involves maturity. Maturity enables a person to know where he/she is, where he/she is headed and what it will take to get there. When the aforementioned elements are in place, the need to "trick the brain" is more than likely to disappear, and people can be in life-giving relationships that are mutually satisfying. We must understand: *Recovery does not occur in isolation.* It takes a faith community. Jesus desires that we experience abundant life, not an addicted life. He leads the way to having our needs met.

Using Drugs to Deaden the Pain: Blake's story

I was adopted at birth. I have six brothers and sisters. When I was about nine years old, my parents got divorced and everything started to go down hill. I started not to care about anything, and when I got into high school, I got into the wrong crowd.

I wanted to do what I wanted to do when I wanted to do it. I started using drugs, having sex and stealing with my friends. I was heavily addicted to prescription drugs. That made my life very hard. I was a loner.

My family knew I needed counseling at House of Hope. When I came into the program at House of Hope, everything started getting a lot better. After five months, I found God.

But I still made a bad decision. I went home on pass, took thirty-six prescription drugs and nearly died. At that point, I made a decision to fully accept Jesus into my life. My counselor helped me get healing for my broken heart and deliverance from my addiction. I now depend on God and not drugs. I feel a lot better, I can think clearly, and my mind is open to what the Lord has to tell me.

I have always liked music. I play the guitar, the piano and the violin. I like to worship God through the talent that He has given me.

I have learned that I won't always get to do or go where I want to go, but as long as I obey God, I know I can be strong like Samson in the Bible. I know God will give me incredible strength. I am learning to trust God and to say no to the things that are not good for me. I like Proverbs 3:5–6 because I'm learning to trust in the Lord with all my heart and not lean on my own understanding.

Now I want to serve the Lord all my life.

Rejection from Parents

When a child is put up for adoption or experiences a divorce, he can feel rejection from the most important people in his life—mom and dad. After perceiving rejection from parents, many children do not bond with their parents. Bonding is vital to their physical, psychological and emotional health. Many teens that come to House of Hope have been traumatized, ignored and rejected by their biological parents or adoptive family. Many have frequently moved and been placed in foster care. These teens have feelings of rejection, hurt and pain so deep that they later form walls around their hearts as a shield against any further pain. This protective wall around their hearts is a form of survival and protects them from being attached to anyone who may hurt them again. The wall becomes difficult to remove, and they turn from anyone that may try to help them. This disorder is known as reactive attachment disorder, or attachment disorder. Some of the symptoms are:

- ⅄ Lack of eye contact
- ⅄ Inability to give and receive affection
- ⅄ Control issues
- ⅄ Very demanding

We have found that when parents and counselors build a close relationship with the hurting teen, healing the wounded heart gives us great success in this area.

Craving Acceptance and Attention: Ashley, age 16

I'm Ashley, and I'm sixteen years old. My biological father was a drug addict, alcoholic and an extremely violent man. Before I was old enough to go to school he got drunk one night, and he was screaming and throwing things at my mom. My baby brother was crying, and my mom was desperate to make him quiet. Because of that night, my mom ended up in jail, charged with manslaughter, because she abused my brother, and he died of Shaken Baby Syndrome.

As a child, I was passed back and forth between my aunt and my grandmother until I was five years old. The courts ordered them to either adopt me or put me in an orphanage. My aunt Susan adopted me into her family. My life was beautiful until my mom came back into the picture. Her values were not good. My mom got me on marijuana and beer and introduced me to a man ten years older than me to date.

I had written all these bad experiences in my journal. One day my aunt found the diary under my mattress. The police ordered me not to see my biological mother again.

The devil had a strong grasp on me, which caused me to make bad decisions. My life was going down the drain. I was like the women at the well, involved in many sexual relationships. I was seeking things that did not satisfy. I needed desperately to be accepted, and I would do almost anything to get attention. I was shattered and empty inside, and I didn't want to live anymore. I even thought about suicide.

My aunt saw my desperate condition and took me to House of Hope. I accepted Jesus Christ into my heart a week after I arrived. Through extensive counseling, I have dealt with the adoption, abandonment and rejection issues. I am learning how to take back what the devil stole from me. When I am faced with temptations or problems, I spend more time reading the Bible and praying. That's where I get my comfort, and I now know who I am. I know my identity, and I want to fulfill my destiny.

My past was full of sadness and hurt, but I know God has a bright future for me. I want to help girls who are hurting like I was when I came to House of Hope.

Happy to Leave Home: Beth's Story

I was abandoned as a baby and given up for adoption. After bouncing through several foster homes, I was finally adopted at the age of three—the second of five children adopted by my parents.

We were all considered special needs children. I was an ADHD kid, even though they didn't have a name for it back then. I was just known as a hyperactive child, as someone hard to handle.

Soon after I was adopted [at age three], my father would come into my room late at night and touch me where he shouldn't have. It was never rape, but it was more of a fondling thing. Although I can't remember what happened, his actions made a serious impact on me. For many years, I could not relate well to men in terms of relationships, and this was something that I carried with me into my teenage and adult years.

My parents sent me to a boarding school for three years where I had to cope with the harsh environment. When I came home, I wasn't allowed to make phone calls or accept phone calls. I couldn't go to the movies. I couldn't do anything. About the only thing I could do was go to the backyard.

One day Mom was hitting my brother with a switch for some minor offense. I pleaded with her to stop, but she told me to leave the house—immediately! So I did. I walked down the street to the Sunoco gas station and slept on the concrete out back for a night. I had no money in my pocket; the only thing I ate was the hot dog the attendant gave me.

The police picked me up. They gave me a ride home, but then my parents informed me that I wouldn't be living there any longer. My new home would be House of Hope. I was glad. I can honestly say that I was one of the rare ones who wanted to go. I couldn't wait to leave home.

House of Hope was all girls back then. I loved the loving environment provided by Miss Sara and the house staff. I just grew as a person. You see, I already knew the Lord. I had accepted Christ when I was eleven years old on August 8, 1984. But when I arrived at House of Hope, I began soaking up God's love like a sponge. Just the difference between my home life and how House of Hope met my needs emotionally, physically and spiritually helped me so much. I got the counseling I needed, and that's where it all came out—the sexual abuse. I also received healing for all the hurts of my past.

I've been married ten years, and we have four children. I sing in the choir at our church, and my husband and I enjoy running together.

Yes, He lifted me out of the slimy pit, out of the mud and mire; he set my feet on a rock and gave me a firm place to stand (Psalm 40:2, NIV).

*I have already attended a House of Hope seminar and
am working with someone from my church to start a House
of Hope in the state where I now live. That's my goal for the
future.*

Cutting or Self-Mutilation (Rooted in Poor Self-Esteem)

We deal almost daily with a symptom of emotional wounds that
literally causes physical wounds—cutting, or carving. More and more
teens are arriving at House of Hope with scars on their legs, arms
and wrists. Using X-Acto knives, razor blades, sharp knives and even
pens and pins, teens slowly and deliberately slice and dig at their flesh,
saying it gives them a sense of power or a tremendous release of stress
in their lives. It's as if they try to cut out the pain or bring it to the
surface so it can heal.

Josh, one of our seventeen-year-olds, explained his urge to carve
this way:

> *Carving is like self-mutilation. Carving brought me pain
> that I felt I deserved. I found that the physical pain of taking
> a razor and digging into my skin overtook the emotional pain
> that I was experiencing. I couldn't take how bad I was feeling,
> so I had to express it somehow. I got really creative, too, when
> I discovered that you can mix salt and ice to create an acid
> burn. I have a scar on my left hand from the acid.*

Self-mutilation is a manifestation of something painful inside.
Mutilations, carvings, piercing and tattoos are definite warning signs of
poor self-esteem.

This poem was found in the notebook of one of our girls at House
of Hope who was cutting herself. This was written during one of her
most depressed moments:

> *Blood is what keeps life flowing.
> You lose too much of it and you die.
> You have nothing left.*

> *But if you lose just a bit,*
> *Just enough to hurt, to feel weak,*
> *You know you're still breathing;*
> *You know that at any time you can make yourself lose more,*
> *And then you're in control...*
> *Life pours out of you."*

Today this young lady has received healing from her deep hurts and now has no need to cut.

Here is another poem by a different young lady who was a cutter but received healing through inner healing prayers.

To the Cutting...

A piece of glass may trigger my past,
But I will allow my thoughts to remind me of the precious jewel I have become to Christ.
Blood will no longer flow from me caused by my own hands.
Good bye to you.

Inflicting Pain on Myself: Monica, age 14

I was adopted when I was one day old by parents who divorced when I was three. This is when the hurting began at first. I was Daddy's girl, and he was not there for me. My mom worked a lot and was never home.

When I was eight, I had to cook dinner and keep up the house. No matter how much I did, it was never good enough for my mom. I just couldn't please her. She emotionally abused me, calling me names and telling me that I was nothing and I would never amount to anything. That hurt a lot. I became very angry. I began cutting myself with razors to try to make the pain go away.

Because of my poor self concept, I smoked marijuana, took ecstasy and became sexually active. I finally ran away, was hospitalized for cutting myself, and then admitted to House of Hope. I hated it because I was an atheist and didn't believe in God. My beliefs changed quickly for me at House of Hope.

Now I tell my friends about the Jesus I have found. I try to be a light in the dark world. I want them to see the change in me so they will come to know the Jesus Christ that I've met.

Here's a poem I wrote:

> *I thought I wouldn't make it.*
> *I thought I would be dead.*
> *I thought the deadly, depressing thoughts*
> *Would never leave my head.*
> *I afflicted pain upon myself*
> *And thought razors were my stress reliever.*
> *I thought the pain would go away*
> *If I cut myself deeper.*
> *Left one night in my own puddle of blood.*
> *No one heard the terrible cries...not a sound.*
> *I woke up afraid in a hospital room.*
> *I thought it was a dream.*
> *That got me to House of Hope,*
> *Where I am learning how to cope.*
> *Now I'm making it through my problems,*
> *Even if they all aren't yet gone.*
> *I know I have a purpose.*
> *Jesus Christ is His name.*
> *I know He really loves me.*
> *Now my life will never be the same.*

My life has been healed because my counselor prayed with me and broke the negative judgments spoken against

*me. Also she prayed with me to heal my hurting heart. I
have repented and have been forgiven for having sex before
marriage. I am a born-again virgin. I am saving myself for
the Christian man I will one day marry.*

*Matthew 10:30 says, God knows me so well that He even
knows how many hairs are on my head! I can trust Him to
take care of me no matter what kinds of things I am facing in
the future because I have made the choice to follow Him.*

Suicide

Since the 1950s, the suicide rate among teenagers and young adults
in America has increased by over 60 percent, from a rate of 6.3 in
1955 to 10.4 in 2004.[1] In 2004 there were 4,316 suicide deaths between
the ages of 15 and 24.[2] This number amounts to 11.8 teenage suicides per
day!

According to the American Association of Suicidology, suicide is the
third leading cause of death among today's youth. [3] Of the total number
of U.S. suicides age fifteen to twenty-four in 2001, 86% were males and
14% were female.[4] In 2002, it was estimated that about 2,000 teens were
committing suicide yearly.[5]

The following stories are proof that healing the hurting heart is real. I
will begin with the story of Jack, who lost the desire to live at a young age
due to the circumstances of his life.

Wanting to Get Life Over With: Jack, age 14

*My name is Jack and I'm 14 years old from Puerto Rico.
My parents got divorced when I was two years old, which
led my mother, my older brother and I to start a new life in
Miami. We started off in homeless shelters, and when I was
four my mother met another man. He was abusive, so my
mother ended up leaving him after he hit her with his baby
in her stomach.*

I never liked school from the beginning because I was always different, never fit in, and was always picked on. I went through my life not having a dad. And those years without my dad made me feel abandoned—until one day he got our number and we went to see him in Puerto Rico. In the end he moved in with us, after finding out my mother was pregnant again with his child.

My dad told me if anyone tried to pick on me or boss me around at school that I was to fight back. So I decided to do just that. I fought every kid that tried me. With my dad having such a bad temper, my mom was afraid to leave me with him. The abuse became so bad that one day we just got up and left. We ended up in shelters again in Alabama. In my school I was not accepted.

During Christmas my mom made a bad decision to go back with my father. The abuse did not stop, so we went to Florida again, starting off in shelters until my moms' parents took us in.

I just wanted to kill myself and get life over with. I grew up knowing God and thought God was like my dad and was never there for me. I thought people deserved to die. I had no reason to live. All I wanted was a dad.

After I was arrested the court recommended sending me to a program. I began living at House of Hope, and I've been here seven and a half months. Now I want to let God change me into His image, but it is hard.

The Scripture I am learning a lot from Proverbs 3:5-6 and it is teaching me to trust in the LORD with all my heart, and lean not on my own understanding; in all my ways acknowledge Him, and He shall direct my paths. I am learning to give it all up to God. He knows what is best. Will you pray for me and all the other boys who don't have a dad to love them?

Generational Curse of Witchcraft: Becca, age 16

My name is Becca. I'm 16 years old. I grew up with my mom and dad fighting all the time. Both of my parents were pagans. They were involved in witchcraft. I was taken to séances and believed in different gods, thinking that was normal.

When I was five, my mom and dad got a divorce. My mom got remarried. I intensely despised my stepdad for taking my mom away from me. I began to have a lot of anxiety and depression. The pain on the inside was so bad; I couldn't feel it when I cut my arms. Later I tried to kill myself by overdosing on drugs. My mom rushed me to the E.R.

After that I started cutting again and burning myself with cigarettes. I developed an eating disorder. Many times I would pass out because I had not eaten for weeks. I dropped twenty-five pounds in three months. One day my mom found my journal, realized that I needed help, and took me to House of Hope.

Since I've been at House of Hope, I've become more comfortable with my weight. I love myself the way God made me, and I am finding out who I am in Christ. I have an unbelievable relationship with my mom and have just started to write letters to my dad. In counseling, we broke the generational curses over my life. I also received deliverance from witchcraft and occult practices. Now that I have Jesus in my heart, I realize He will never leave me, no matter what. He is making my life so much easier and helping me feel so much happier.

I am still a virgin, and I'm saving myself for the man God wants me to marry. After I graduate, I want to be a psychiatrist to help hurting people like I was.

Fear of Grieving

Society over the years has told our young teen boys and more recently our young teen girls that it is not okay to cry. Brave little boys and girls don't cry. They should not show hurt, emotion or pain. But that is a lie from Satan!

Learning How to Grieve: James, age 15

I'm James, and I'm 15 years old. When I was born, my mother was very young and my father was in and out. My mother gave my sister and me up for adoption. She abandoned us, leaving us alone at home for several days. We were found in the closet with no one to care for us. My sister found some chicken bouillon cubes that we ate. The neighbors called HRS. Then we were adopted together into another bad situation. My adopted father and I always fought and argued.

Now I was rejected from both fathers. He never accepted me. I was never tough enough. He told me I wasn't allowed to cry. Big boys don't cry. I was never able to get in touch with my feelings. My dad hit me very often in the back with his belt and punched me in the head.

I felt I couldn't do anything to please him. I started looking for love in all the wrong places. With girls, sex didn't fix anything. It only made it worse. And now I was rebellious too, wanting to do my own thing. My parents dropped me off at House of Hope.

At House of Hope, I found the love and acceptance I had always longed for. My counselor prayed for healing of the hurts and helped tear down the walls I had put up to protect my feelings. As she was praying I had a picture in my mind of Jesus taking a big bulldozer, pushing down all those walls that had held me captive. I felt such a release and was able to cry. That was the beginning of my healing. I thank God for House of Hope.

One of the most important things we all need to learn is how to grieve. Grieving is the ability to recognize and mourn the losses we have experienced. God has given us the ability to grieve. If any of us has lost a family member, an animal or friend though death, we should have the opportunity to grieve that loss.

Problems arise within us when we experience losses in our lives but aren't allowed time or space or don't know how to grieve those losses. Many teenagers do not know how to cope with a significant loss and therefore, instead of grieving, allow themselves to become hardened or "stuff" the hurts inside. As a result, the hardened teen will react to things in the wrong way. They become resentful and angry. They do not know how to deal with the hurt, pain and loss and completely shut the Lord off from being able to minister to them in those areas.

Overwhelmed by Deaths: Chelsea, age 13

My name is Chelsea. When I was five years old, my mother was diagnosed with cancer and when I was six she passed away. When I was eight, both of my grandparents died. At the age of eight I found out I was adopted. Finding out I was adopted scared me. When I was nine, my dad's girlfriend Joy moved in with us and she was alcoholic. Joy was in an accident...a few days later she died.

This is when I went into a real deep depression. I started hating God and asking why? Why would he put a child through this grief? Why did he take three mommies away from me, and I was only eleven.

By age twelve, I was on the streets while my dad thought I was at a friend's. At age thirteen, I was a wild child, smoking, popping pills and all just to feel comfortable in my own skin. I got into more drugs like cocaine and ecstasy and selling drugs; just doing crazy stuff. I was partying with people

*almost twice my age. I was finally taken to a drug rehabilita-
tion center where I was diagnosed with manic depression.*

*At this time my dad was diagnosed with cancer. For six
months he didn't tell me until his hair was falling out from
the chemotherapy. After at least six surgeries he finally told
me and said he needed a place to save me from everything he
couldn't do, so he found House of Hope.*

*I've learned a lot about love and feel part of the family
here at House of Hope. In counseling my counselor and I are
dealing with the deep hurts from all the losses in my life. For
the first time in our lives my dad and I are going through a
grieving process. Jesus has healed me from the hurts of being
abandoned and rejected, and He's healing my broken heart.
Because of House of Hope I now have a positive attitude and
am finding how much I am loved. For the first time, I am
excited about my future.*

Uncontrollable Anger

Lucy, an eighteen-year-old runaway, had an extremely bad temper.
This is the story related to me when Lucy came for counseling

*When my stepmother says cruel things, it is hard for me
to cope with my emotions. Sometimes my anger outbursts
are so intense that I actually want to kill her. In a fit of rage,
I did try one time to kill her with a knife. My temper seems
almost uncontrollable. "Flying off the handle" seems to be a
daily problem for me, and, to top it all off, I scarcely realize
what I have done after the rage is over.*

Because of her past, Lucy was an emotional basket case. She had
experienced many unfortunate experiences. However, they were not of
her choosing. As a child, deep hurts had caused her to develop many
wrong attitudes.

When I first met Lucy, she had just returned home after running away. After a serious encounter with her stepmother she had run away in a fit of anger. She went on to say,

> *I can't even tell you why I feel like I do. All I know is that it's beginning to happen all the time. I know I have felt this way ever since I was a little child, actually as far back as I can remember. How can I change the way I feel? No matter how hard I try, I can't control my temper.*

We taught Lucy that when she found anger flaring up, she should check it immediately to keep it from getting out of hand. One of the biggest helps was the Scripture; "A soft answer turns away wrath, but a harsh word stirs up anger" (Proverbs 15:1). Through counseling, she learned not to store up anger but to quickly resolve her hostility with whomever she felt angry.

She daily made every little irritation a matter of prayer. She would deal with little irritations before they would grow, mount up, and cause a temper outburst. Jesus healed all the hurts from Lucy's past where the anger had originated, as she allowed her counselor to help her remove all her repressed hostilities. Along with her counselor's assistance, Lucy allowed Jesus to go back in her life and heal the hurts in that little girl that caused the anger. He filled the void with His peace.

Conclusion

In the next several chapters we will look at some worldly influences that have been detrimental and compounded the teen's pain. The first one is the Internet.

CHAPTER 7

Disaster Lurking on the Internet

FIVE YEARS AGO, IT WASN'T NECESSARY TO WRITE THIS CHAPTER, BUT what you're about to read could save you and your teens from a lifetime of hurt and regret.

The invention of the World Wide Web and a family's easy access to the Internet via a modem and home computer have brought cataclysmic changes in the way pornography and inappropriate material are made available to teenagers. Everything from erotic images, including "kiddie porn" to hate speech, directions on how to make pipe bombs, and even bestiality materialize in seconds as colorized pixel bits.

As reported in TIME magazine, polls indicated, "In 1998 17 million kids ages 2 to 18 were online. That number is expected to grow in five years to more than 42 million."[1] I am *very* concerned about the Internet and the danger it poses to teenagers because it's rather easy for them to find themselves in some awful porn-related websites. It's child's play! Don't believe me? Pretend you are a high school student and you've been given a homework assignment to write a report on Louisa May Alcott's *Little Women*. You begin your research by typing *little women* in a search engine such as HotBot. The browser brings you access to 500,000 matches. Some of those matches link you to legitimate web sites referencing Miss Alcott's famous book. But others point you toward sites like "Little Women Forum," a web address dedicated to "small breasts, tiny tops, and itty, bitty titties." I kid you not.

Welcome to cyberspace, and it's a brave new world out there. In case you're not computer savvy, you had better know that your teens are. What do you think they're learning at school? After all, 89 percent of public schools are connected to the Internet, and students are taught how to navigate the World Wide Web. What makes this interesting and a matter of grave concern is that the Internet is built on the back of the porn industry. Did you know that 60 percent of all web site visits are sexual in nature? Did you know that sex is the No. 1 searched-for topic on the Internet?

The Dangers of Internet Porn

For all their popularity, virtual companies such as Amazon.com—the leader in e-commerce—aren't profitable yet. But tens of thousands of hard-core XXX-rated sites are raking in *mucho* bucks to the tune of $1 billion a year. The *Washington Post* has called the Internet the largest pornography store in the history of mankind.

There's a reason why so many deviant men and testosterone-laden teens frequent this cyberstore. In the old days, you had to get in a car or take a bus to the seedy part of town to watch a dirty movie or buy glossy magazines depicting naked bodies performing sexual acts. That's no longer the case. Every kind of pornography imaginable can be brought to your teen's computer screen in the privacy of his bedroom. Sometimes it's free; sometimes he must pay, and if it's the latter, all he needs is dad's credit card—or a friend's. Many sites, however, allow voyeurs to download pornographic pictures without paying a cent. They figure a long peek will entice viewers to lay down some serious money—usually $19.95—to see more. Their advisory, "You must be eighteen years old to enter this site," is a joke.

Then there are the teen boys who don't intentionally seek out Internet porn. They stumble across XXX-rated sites by misspelling a word during a search (boys, toys, etc), coming upon a "stealth site' (there's a *big* difference between whitehouse.com and whitehouse.gov), or innocently typing in a brand name that links them to pictures of naked women. Twenty-five percent of porn sites are estimated to misuse popular brand names in search engine magnets, metatags and links. The top ten are: Disney, Barbie, CNN, Honda, Mercedes, Levis, ESPN, NBA, Chevy and Nintendo. Three of the top ten brand names used specifically target children—Disney, Barbie and Nintendo. (Cyveillance Survey, 1999, accessed at http://www.protectkids.com/dangers/childaccess.htm)

According to a Yankelovitch Partner survey, 91 percent of children accessing objectionable Websites did so unintentionally. The same survey found that 62 percent of parents were unaware that their children had accessed objectionable sites.

These web sites destroy women's dignity and respect. Martha, a House of Hope counselor, summed it up perfectly:

> *It doesn't take long to notice that women are used and abused in pornography. There has never been a pornographic movie or web site that added dignity or grace to a woman or caused a man to feel that a woman is special and should be treated as such.*

Ensnared by Porn While Doing Homework: Chad, age 12

I was trying to do an innocent assignment, which led me into pornography. I was doing a school project in sixth grade. We were learning how to start searching on the Internet. I was doing research for a social studies paper on the executive branch of government. A boy said I should click on www. whitehouse.com, which came up as pornography instead of the government.

Before that, friends had talked about pornography, but it wasn't something I chose to look at. It made me curious. Because of pornography, I then had a desire to start dating and having sex. Pornography made me look at my close friends who were girls differently, more like sex objects.

It really messed up my mind. I would get in chat rooms to talk to friends or groups based on a decent subject like the Chicago Cubs, and I would start receiving lots of pop-ups and instant messages from girls that would lead to pornography. Sometimes I would receive too many, and my computer would freeze. I'd be curious and go check out what I'd missed.

I now have realized it was stupid. I have to admit it was an everyday struggle to get the pornography images out of my mind.

Pornography really gave me the wrong impression of what sex was meant for. At House of Hope, I was convicted by God. The counselors prayed for me and I have been forgiven. My life would not have been as difficult if I had not been exposed to and held in bondage to Internet pornography.

Porn Warps the Beauty of Sex

Why am I concerned about pornography? It warps young minds regarding the beauty of sex. Teens hooked on Internet porn sites develop sexual attitudes that are coarse and debased. They want to "act out" what they see on the computer monitor.

For instance, teen boys influenced by porn believe:

⅄ All women want "it" any time, day or night.
⅄ When a woman says no, she really means yes. (This so-called rape myth is perpetuated throughout all strata of porn.)
⅄ All women are incredibly built with large bosoms, tiny waists, full thighs and tight buns. (Is this the real world? No.)
⅄ Women enjoy deviant sexual acts. (Again, not true.)
⅄ Women's basic role in life is to give sexual pleasure to men.

As for adolescent girls, a vast majority think porn is icky, but some are fascinated with the images. That fascination turns to daydreaming and playing "what-ifs" in their minds. They begin thinking that what is abnormal is really normal.

Are these the attitudes you want your teens to grow up with? I hope not. You want to nip Internet porn in the bud because pornography is progressive and addictive. Believe it or not, pictures of man and woman having intercourse get old after a while. Guys need something more stimulating, such as pictures of women being tied up and raped or a dominatrix performing S&M.

Men need more and more stimulation, which is why they eventually seek images of women having sex with dogs, couples spreading feces on each other, or scenes of bloody mutilations. I cannot warn you enough about the sick, sick stuff out there.

Ted Bundy's Slide into Porn

I'll never forget when convicted mass murderer Ted Bundy was scheduled to be executed in Florida State Prison back in 1989. On the eve of his date with the electric chair, Bundy gave a jailhouse interview to Dr. James Dobson, president of Focus on the Family and a person long involved in the fight against pornography.

Bundy told Dobson that his journey to where he was at that moment—facing certain execution in a matter of hours—began as a young boy twelve or thirteen years old when he found soft-porn magazines in trash cans near his home. He was fascinated by this pornography, and he wanted more. Bundy graduated to harder, more explicit porn, including "detective novels" that featured violence against women.

The interview, captured on a video called *Fatal Addiction*, featured this exchange between Dr. Dobson and Ted Bundy:

> **Dr. Dobson:** Now I really want to understand this. You had gone as far as you could go in your own fantasy life with printed material. Then there was this urge to take that little step or big step over to a physical event.
>
> **Ted Bundy:** Right. And it happened in stages, gradually. It didn't necessarily, to me at least, happen overnight. My experience with pornography that dealt on a violent level

with sexuality is that once you become addicted to it—and I look at this as kind of an addiction—I would keep looking for more potent, more explicit, more graphic kinds of materials. Until you reach the point where the pornography only goes so far. You reach that jumping-off point where you begin to wonder if maybe actually doing it will give you that [satisfaction] which is beyond just reading about it or looking at it.[2]

Chilling, isn't it? Bundy admitted to killing more than twenty women in four states, snuffing out innocent lives of young women and teen girls and absolutely devastating the families they left behind.

I know that there are benefits that make it worthwhile to have the Internet in your home. The Internet can open up educational vistas that were never available before. You can take a virtual tour of Buckingham Palace or explore the art found in the Metropolitan Museum of Art. This extraordinary communication vehicle delivers millions of resources to your fingertips.

At House of Hope, we have found that access to the World Wide Web has provided exciting educational advantages for our teens. They use the Internet to do copious amounts of research that would have taken days in a city library. We monitor their use, however, and we use blocking software, about which I'll have more to say later.

My concerns about the Internet, however, stretch beyond casual access to inappropriate content. Daterape.org, which billed itself as a "one-stop shop for all your date rape needs," was finally shut down by its Web hosting company following a volume of complaints. The site offered a $49.99 kit that included a *How to Date Rape Properly* manual, "Shut-the-Hell-Up-Bitch" duct tape, and a medical prescription guide to check the side effects of certain drugs. How thoughtful.[3]

If web sites aren't pushing the envelope of human decency in the area of rape, then thousands of other web sites and chat rooms are promoting violence, spewing hate speech toward minorities, and outlining easy-to-follow directions for making pipe bombs.

Chat Rooms

Chat rooms can be especially dangerous, especially to young women. An MSNBC survey found that women favor chat rooms twice as much as men.[4] Sexual predators have easy and anonymous access to unsuspecting kids they "meet" in their chat rooms. They will strike up a conversation and then ask your son or daughter to go to instant messaging (a form of one-on-one online chat), where they begin developing a cyber relationship.

In a chat setting, there's no way to know *anything* about the person with whom they're "talking." Researchers call them "gender switchers," "gender hackers" or "posers." Men, it is believed, switch roles online more than women.

Imagine a "gender hacker" posing as a teenage girl makes arrangements with your daughter for a meeting. Don't think it can happen! The newspapers are filled with stories about a "dirty old man" getting caught in a hotel room with a fourteen-year-old girl that he met in a chat room.

That point was driven home to us when we received a frantic phone call from the mother of a teenage girl, asking us if we could take in her daughter Hailey right away. It seems that Hailey had a little secret: some friends she had met in a chat room. One asked her to rendezvous in a nearby motel room, so Hailey ran away for a clandestine meeting. Her mother, naturally concerned about the whereabouts of her daughter, noticed her daughter had left her pager behind. She asked police to trace the last number that Hailey received, which they traced to the motel.

A police officer knocked on the door of the hotel room, which was answered by two men and a woman. They tried to run for it because they were making preparations to prostitute Hailey. The young girl ran into her mother's arms and burst into tears.

Hailey was one of the lucky ones! So was Teresa Stickland, who cried as she testified before a U.S. Congressional subcommittee on children and families. She shared that a forty-three-year-old man found her teenage daughter through the Internet and convinced her and a friend to run off with him. The daughter and her friend escaped from the man, who was sent to prison for felonies involving child pornography and exploitation. FBI officials testified at the same hearing that they have arrested hundreds of suspected child molesters through undercover monitoring of Internet chat rooms. According to the National Center for Missing and Exploited Children, a web site (cybertipline.com) created in 1999 to take complaints about suspicious or illegal Internet activity, has received more than twenty five thousand complaints (as of June 18, 2007).[5]

"Cyber sex is the crack cocaine of sexual addiction," said Dr. Robert Weiss of Sexual Recovery Institute.[6] Cyber sex is addictive. If your teen son is spending an inordinate amount of hours in his room surfing the Internet, he could be among the twenty-five million Americans who visit cyber sex sites between one to ten hours per week. Teenagers usually do it at home after school, when working parents are not at home. A survey released in 2000 estimated that at least 200,000 Internet users are hooked on porn sites, X-rated rooms or other sexual materials online.[7] If you think this is just a "guy problem" because they are hardwired this way, then know this: while boys prefer visual erotica twice as much as women, girls favor chat rooms twice as much as boys. So the porn sites are there to hook the boys, and the chat rooms are there to entrap the girls.

How to Keep Kids Safe on the Internet

A good friend, Donna Rice Hughes, made me aware of the problems of the Internet. If you're thinking, "Where have I heard that name?" you have a good memory.

After straying from her spiritual roots, Donna recommitted herself to God and her faith. She married and settled down. In the mid-1990s, Donna met Dee Jepsen, president of Enough Is Enough, a nonprofit organization dedicated to addressing the sexual exploitation of children, women and men by illegal pornography. Dee told Donna that one of the harms of pornography is the perpetuation of the rape myth—that when a woman says no, she really means yes. At that moment, Donna realized for the first time that she had been victimized in this manner when she lost her virginity against her will at the age of twenty-two.

Donna asked how she could help. Enough Is Enough needed a spokesperson to increase public awareness on the insidiousness of pornography, and Donna fit that role. She joined the organization as vice president of public relations and quickly emerged as a nationally known advocate for protecting children on the Internet. We've become friends since I served on the national board of Enough Is Enough. Donna has given over 1,200 TV and magazine interviews in the last few years on this topic and authored the book *Kids Online: Protecting Your Children in Cyberspace* (Revell). She helped me come up with some advice on how to fight against Internet porn on your computers and keep your kids safe.

1. Keep the computer in a public area. It's hard to monitor Internet use behind closed doors. Place the family computer in the family room or some other area that is out in the open. That way you can "drop in" unexpectedly. I would be very reluctant to allow a teen unrestricted Internet access in a bedroom.

2. Install blocking software or subscribe to an Internet serve provider (ISP) that screens out pornographic sites. Blocking software such as Cyber Patrol, Bess, Bonus. com, Cybersitter, SurfWatch and Net Nanny use teams of information specialist, parents and teachers to assist in classifying content. Please know that filtering solutions are not 100 percent foolproof or perfect because hundreds of new porn sites come online each day. Clean internet service providers (ISPs) are harder to find, but an Internet search should yield a company or two worth checking out. Donna highly recommends familyclick. com, a filtered Internet service provider that has five access levels.

   It will be interesting to see what happens in Australia, where the government banned pornographic Websites in 2000. Australian ISPs are also required to offer their customers filtering software. Internet content believed to be sexually explicit, overly violent, or otherwise offensive receive an "RC" rating for "refused certification." These offensive sites are ordered to "take down" their offensive pages by the Australian Broadcasting Authority. Rather than comply, the porn sites relocate to a U.S.-based server and are back in business—usually within twenty-four hours.

3. Check your teens' Bookmarks or Favorite Places. Netscape and Internet Explorer allow users to bookmark their favorite web sites. Check their browsers for telltale signs of where they've been spending their time in cyber-space. You can also do a search for .jpg or .gif files to find downloaded pictures.

4. Check your credit card statement. Many parents barely glace at their monthly credit card statements. What about you? See any unexplained charges? Porn companies often call themselves by innocuous names to disguise their services.

5. Spend some time online with your teen. You need to get up to speed with the Internet and what this is all about. Ask him to show you around the World Wide Web.

6. Only allow your child to use instant messaging with people you know and approve. You should sit in and monitor your teen's instant messaging. Watch for inconsistencies in statements. After all, you have more experience in judging people than he/she. Make sure that he/she does not have an online profile or give out personal information. Remind him/her that individuals who ask what you look like are often seeking sex.

7. Don't let your child surf the Internet late at night. Just like city streets, weird things happen in the wee late hours.

8. Tell your child never to give someone your phone number or street address and never, ever to meet someone in person, unless you are with them. You never know when a modern-day Ted Bundy is out there, waiting for prey.

9. Clean up your act. You don't have much credibility raising the Internet porn issue with your teens if you have Playboy lying around the coffee table or frequent porn sites yourself. Isn't it time you left this degrading stuff behind? If you need help, consult a counselor or pastor.

10. Finally, don't let Internet use dominate their lives. Teens need to be much more than spending six hours a day on the Internet. Limit use and plan things you all can do together to promote fellowship, conversation and recreation.

Imitating Porn: Danielle, age 13

One morning before school I was in a chat room talking with a stranger. He sent me nude pictures of himself and gave me some websites to visit, which had people having sex, masturbating and girls showing all kinds of body parts. We then had an unedifying conversation. I thought it was normal and wanted to be like those girls I saw on the Internet. I started doing the things I had seen and began stripping at parties, started prostituting and watching more pornography. It was addictive. Several of us would watch porn, and I would then imitate what I saw in front of people. I still am dealing with thoughts of what I've seen. It's hard to get them out of my mind. I have to make a decision and pray to not think about what I've seen.

I have asked forgiveness for what I've done. Now I have to read the Bible when the temptation comes to watch pornography. My counselor helped me bring healing to the sexual areas in my life. I had to forgive and break some ties with the people I had sex with.

Today I know the trust of what God's word says about sin and I'm walking in that truth.

Conclusion

Is the Internet destroying a generation? You decide. Technology has played a tremendous part in the lives of teenagers. While it instantly connects people around the world, Donna Hughes shows in her book that the Internet has also tried to destroy this generation. The paradox is that Americans have lost the fine art of communication in this process. That personal aspect has been lost. How important is eye-to-eye contact, a hand on the shoulder, a smile? None of these can be passed through a voice mail, e-mail or text message.

Hughes book is an excellent resource about the Internet. Supported by statistics of various law enforcement divisions, Hughes discusses the dangers of the internet trolling. What needs of predators and teens are being met on the internet? She also discusses the value of supervised use of MySpace.com, video games, IPODS and various other technologies. When kids generally know more about these technologies than the parents, parents and counselors need to educate themselves!

CHAPTER 8

Mass Media Culture

PROBABLY THE BIGGEST CAUSE OF CHAOS FOR THIS GENERATION IS media hype. Media hype is really hard for teens to ignore. In a matter of seconds, most youth can mimic a jingle or give other examples of what they have learned from media. Sadly, these examples may include naming a popular brand of beer or striking a "sexy pose." Teens only have to put a movie into the DVD player, open a magazine, click on a web site or turn on the TV to experience all kinds of negative messages. It *really* is that easy. What is *not* easy is walking away from the media hype.

Mass Media Culture

Did you know that a thirty-second ad during the Super Bowl now costs $2.3 million and reaches eighty million people? The average young person views more than 3000 ads per day on television (TV), on the Internet, on billboards, and in magazines.[1] A recent FTC investigation found that violent movies, music and video games have been internationally marketed to children and adolescents. According to the Consumer's Union, more than 160 magazines are now targeted at children. Young people see 45 percent more beer ads and 27 percent more ads for hard liquor in teen magazines than adults do in their magazines. On the Internet, an increasing number of the web sites try to make direct sales to children and teenagers. Teenagers account for more than $1 billion in e-commerce dollars.[2]

Teens are seeking the supernatural in the wrong spiritual world. In the last ten years, the Harry Potter book series has made a huge negative impact through witches and warlocks and has been a fantasy escape that has led many teenagers into witchcraft and other occult practices with devastating results.

As counselors, teachers, parents and youth leaders, we find ourselves in a critical time for this generation. They are crying out for help! We don't want to be convicted for our lack of assertiveness to help them. We cannot afford to allow this generation to continue to be lured by the demonic forces in media that capitalize on their fears and anxieties and produce hopelessness, self destruction and violence.

Music to Their Ears

When we were teenagers, we thought we'd be different once we became parents, didn't we?

Twenty or thirty years ago, when our parents let us listen to the car radio blaring "Jumping Jack Flash" by the Rolling Stones or "Do You Think I'm Sexy?" by Rod Steward, we invariably heard them mutter, "That music is awful! You can't even understand the words!"

We vowed that when we had kids, we would be more liberal regarding music. We couldn't imagine not liking the music our children would like. Then rap was invented (just a joke). Seriously, we were weaned on rock 'n' roll, rhythm and blues, disco, country, metal, and other kinds of music, and our brain cells remained intact. That's why we decided we would allow our kids to listen to popular music because we understood their desire to follow their musical heroes, who assume larger-than-life personas.

But something changed over the years. Popular music didn't die, as Don McLean sang in "American Pie," but it sure drove the Chevy to the levee and proceeded to sink underneath its own weight. Music morphed into a frenetic, bass-driven sound accented by raunchy lyrics that are played so loudly and so often that no one blushes anymore.

Rap music is one of the worst offenders. Rappers, in their stylized monotone, jive talk about "bustin' bitches" and "hos," and employ street terms to describe oral sex, anal sex, cop killing and drug dealing. Kids are susceptible to these inappropriate messages because they are antiauthority, and during these turbulent years of hormone development and pursuit for pseudo-maturity, their judgment becomes clouded.

Some Perspective, Please

Before I go much further, some perspective is called for. Our generation had a style of music. The generation before us also had a style. Today's generation has a style—a style that may cause you to switch the station on your radio—but a style nonetheless. Tomorrow's generation will have a music style specifically for them. Think of style as the way you like to have your eggs. Maybe you grew up with Denver omelets and can't eat eggs any other way. Maybe your kids prefer guacamole and salsa on scrambled eggs. Is either taste wrong? Of course not. We're talking about personal preferences, which are usually formed in our youth.

Sometimes your personal music style is determined by where you grow up. If you were raised in Texas twenty years ago, your radio was probably tuned to Merle Haggard and Dolly Parton. That's all changed now. Texas kids, for instance, have a broader spectrum to choose from today thanks to MTV, web access, and increased marketing from record companies. Country music is now popular north of the Mason Dixon line, not just in the South.

"I know there will be certain styles that parents don't like," said Randy, a House of Hope counselor. "There's certain music I don't like. The key is to find out what's happening with your teens, who they're hanging out with, and where they like to go. You've got to get a clearer picture and ask, 'Where is my child at regarding the pop scene? Where is my child going in his likes and dislikes with music?" Listen to the music, read the lyrics, do some research—and then talk to them.

The key question for parents is content, not style. My issue with popular music is not so much the beat but the lyrics. If you're zapping through channels with your family and stop on MTV long enough to say, "Look at those guys. They look like girls!" or "I can't understand the words," all you've done is reveal your prejudices or your age. What you need to do is understand those words. And that's a very easy chore these days. Nearly all CDs come with lyrics printed on small booklets; no artists bother trying to hide their sexist, anarchist or profane language.

CDs also come with parental notification stickers, not that these do any good. I think a "PA" sticker actually boosts sales because kids gravitate to material that pokes a thumb into the eye of authority. They are thinking, "If it's bad, then it has to be good."

Another problem in many households is concerts. What should parents do when their son wants to attend a Marilyn Manson concert? Let's listen to this conversation between a father named Robert, and Randy, a House of Hope counselor:

> **Robert:** My son wants to go the Marilyn Manson concert next month. He told me that he purchased tickets with his own money. I don't know much about Marilyn Manson. What should I do?
>
> **Randy:** You don't know much about Marilyn Manson? Then you need to take a cram course, and while you're at it, you need to bone up on other groups that your son is drawn to. Once you learn more about the groups and their music and lyrics, then you will understand what your child is being exposed to. Once you learn what Marilyn Mason is singing about—death, drugs and sex—you won't be so inclined to allow him to attend the concert.
>
> **Robert:** Does that mean I should tell him that he can't go?
>
> **Randy:** You will have to make that determination since you are the parent. But I will say this: you are responsible for what you allow your child to do.

Music Can Enhance Drugs

The need to listen to music to enhance the drug experience is a major reason why today's teens are attracted to rap, techno and a type of music called "house," "jungle" or "ace." They have steady, monotonous beats that appeal to kids high on drugs and keep them in a good mood. They want to dance and move around the whole time. When they're not on drugs, the songs have a way of taking them back to their formerly altered states. Kids tell me that fast techno music makes cocaine and crack a better experience, but teens on heroin are too zonked out to really care what's coming over the speakers.

> *"When I was at a night club, I had taken too many pills. I just lay down because I couldn't stand up anymore. There was speaker next to the couch that I lay down on, so the boom-boom of the bass kept me awake. I thought I was going crazy while lying on that couch. I had these weird dreams about elephants floating through the sky. Deer talked to me. Some friends took me home, but during the drive, I kept telling my friends not to hit the deer in the middle of the interstate. "The deer says he loves you," I said. My friends kept asking what I was talking about." —Rachel, age seventeen*

Frank, a House of Hope counselor, has some good advice regarding teens and music.

> *I don't think it does anyone any good for parents to throw up their hands and ban music that kids like. There are alternatives—great gospel and CCM artists—that you can plug your kids into. CCM, which stands for contemporary Christian music, has tons of groups and singers in nearly every genre—rap, pop, rock, metal, ska and techno. Some CCM artists are very "edgy," but you can count on positive lyrics that lift you up rather than bring you down.*
>
> *There's no question that music is the number-one influencer of teens. Just looking at a musical artist and his video*

tells you so much about the culture. There's a lot of sex-
megasex*. There are a lot of four-letter words. I guess you*
could say that music's gotten uglier in the last twenty years.

Music Is a Motivator

Music is a powerful medium, ranking right up there with cinema. You don't think so? The next time you're alone in the car, turn on an "oldies" station and sing along to an old favorite. Although you haven't heard the song in decades, you'll remember the words as if it were yesterday!

As with most art forms, music is extremely powerful with teenagers because it moves them to do something. Dr. Richard Pellegrino, a brain specialist who serves as a consultant to the entertainment industry, wrote in *Billboard* magazine that music interacts powerfully, often subconsciously, with receptors in the brain to produce "endorphin highs." He added that music triggers a flood of emotions and images that "have the ability to instantaneously produce very powerful changes in emotional states."

Concluded Dr. Pellegrino: "Take it from a brain guy: In twenty-five years of medicine, I still cannot affect a person's state of mind the way that one simple song can."[3] Music shapes attitudes, points teens toward certain behaviors, and molds their worldviews at a time when they lack experience and maturity.

As is typical for teens, their inexperience is compensated for by their emotions and energy. Music artists have learned to feed on that energy by producing faster and faster music: the guiding principle is the quicker, the better. Bands such as Linkoln Park, 50 Cent, The Pussycat Dolls and Marilyn Manson know how to push the right buttons.

Today's music reflects this gotta-have-it-now mentality prevalent in our culture. Everything has to be instant these days—instant food, instant drinks and instant access to the Internet. Have you noticed the foot race to increase bandwidth and download speeds off the net? Web surfing is too slow for today's teens. When a faster computer hits the streets, teens want to purchase a new one because faster is better.

They want a faster processor because songs can be downloaded from the Internet and passed from friend to friend. Your teens may be downloading music from MP3 or Napster and burning a CD without you ever knowing it. Anyone with a computer connected to the Internet can download any kind of music he wants, usually free of charge.

Groups and artists that we can recommend are Relient K, Nicole Nordeman, Grits, Kirk Franklin, Switchfoot, Fred Hammond and much more. You may not like the beat, but a least your kids won't be listening to dark music about rebellion, suicide and no hope for the future.

Have your teens listen to some positive alternatives at your local music store. Who knows? They may come back humming a new tune.

Gothic Culture

Kids caught up in the Gothic culture have their emotions running high. Also running high is the blood pressure of parents who are shocked the first time their son or daughter dresses in black from head to toe and empties a bottle of black nail polish on their fingers and toes.

When I asked Josh, one of our seventeen-year-olds, what parents should do if their son buys an all-black wardrobe and a pair of Doc Martens, he replied, "There's nothing you can really tell a parent because if kids want to do that, they will do it. My parents tried to stop me, but they couldn't."

"What did they do to try to stop you?" I asked.

"They took my clothes and threw them away. But I'd steal new ones from different people."

The first thing you—the parent—need to do is take a deep breath and think through a few questions. Why is your son or daughter dressing that way? Why is he feeling dark about himself? Are you spending enough time with your child? Are you fighting every day? Are you telling your child she is stupid?

Goth teens may appear happy on the outside, but the fact that they've chosen to step out of the mainstream is a signal that they feel lonely, unappreciated and unloved. Many carry suicidal thoughts, if for no reason other than because they listen to songs that glorify the "final solution" to their problems.

When teens arrive at House of Hope, they understand that the Gothic clothes don't come with them. "The kids that I've seen involved in Goth seem to have darkness about them," said Randy, a House of Hope counselor. "Initially, we just develop a relationship with them by loving them and caring for them. I said to one teen guy, 'Look, man, I don't know what's going on with you, but you seem dark. There's stuff going on here that seems very scary and out of character for you. I just want you to know that we're going to work with you and love you."

Another thing you should know is that the Gothic subculture is linked with many occult activities. The Goth scene is more common than occult behavior these days.

You may hope that their penchant for dressing up in Goth attire is a passing fad, but I would be wary of holding on tightly to that point of view. Gothic kids are a cause for alarm because their dress and their mannerisms are a symptom of a more serious, underlying problem. Goths are looking for experiences in other places because they are spending very little time with their parents. The relationship is not there.

Much of the Goth scene is about a sense of belonging, so if your teen is already hanging out with Gothic friends, it will be difficult for him to abandon them.

Look beneath her appearance and ask yourself if you are spending enough time with her. What changed in her life? When did she start dressing as a Goth? How and when did these changes start becoming apparent?

The answer is not banning those clothes. You have to get to the root of the problem, which could be feeling rejection from you, not spending enough time with her, dealing with hurts in her life, or trying to find an alternative way to get attention. It's really about seeking acceptance even if her dress shocks you, your friends and the people she comes in contact with.

Turning her around depends on how quickly you get to the root of the problem. Once kids feel love and acceptance here at House of Hope, and feel the security that comes with regular meals, unconditional love, normal school hours and healthy family interaction, their desire to dress Goth evaporates almost over night.

Conclusion

This chapter looked at the influence of movies, music and the Goth culture on today's teens. Another huge lure of the world is sex, the topic of the next chapter.

CHAPTER 9

Teen Sexuality

How do you keep kids clean in a dirty world? Can we even do that anymore? When media and music lures teens to do what feels good, there has to be some kind of hope given to motivate them to change. Most teens have had more sexual experiences by the time they are fourteen than most adult Christians have in their entire lifetime.

How do you define sex and how do most teens today define sex? How do you counsel them? How do you counsel their parents? What do we tell a teenager who sees nothing wrong with having sex before marriage, having multiple partners, attending sex parties or bi-sexual experiences?

Teens that do not look at sexuality from a sacred perspective pay a heavy price as they enter into adulthood and parenthood. In this chapter, I will share an insightful approach to sexuality. At House of Hope we use Scriptures to teach teens how to become pure again and how to forgive themselves for their poor sexual choices. In some of the testimonies you have read in this book, you will notice how the teens talked about being born-again virgins. We teach them that even though they may have lost their physical virginity, they can repent for that and then remain pure for the husband or wife that God has selected for each one of them.

Sex Education

Sex education begins before there is a birth in the family! What teens know about sex can be linked to how they were treated at birth and whether mom and dad treated sex as sacred or secular. Of course, there are other events that impact a teen's view of sexuality (i.e. abuse, incest, rape, etc.), but the responsibility of sex education clearly belongs to the parents. That being said, most parents have fallen short of this goal.

We know that most teens learn about sex from the Internet, TV/ media, peers, pornographers and in the public schools (not necessarily in that exact order). These people are not too interested in the spiritual or moral aspects that will impact a child's sexuality.

Sexuality is not the act of sex. It is how people view themselves, their gender and their respect for the opposite sex. In *Teaching Your Children the Truth about Sex,* Dr. Richard Dobbins explains:

> Believe it or not, healthy sex education begins as soon as your child is born. Your baby enters this world already wired for sexual plea- sure. A little boy's ability to become erect and a little girl's ability to lubricate are awakened by nature before they are born. They first begin to experience genital pleasure the first time they are diapered or bathed. (Lake Mary, Fla.: Siloam Press, 2006, p. 25)

Usually if Mom and Dad struggle with their own guilt, their own gender issues, and cannot even say the word "s-e-x" out loud, you can believe that the child is going to have some problems with their own sexuality. If Mom and Dad are not going to be the teachers, who will take over that role?

Of course we realize that most teens that come to us have already had sex and are no longer virgins—whether through a consensual act or molestation. While they cannot go back and undo that moment, God can restore their purity in their hearts. When we use the term "born-again virgin," that is exactly what we are referring to.

We do not allow the teens at House of Hope to date for many reasons. We do not want them to be distracted by boy-girl relationships, STDs, pregnancy, sneaking around and getting caught, how and where to have a "quickie," and all those other dating issues.

Adolescents can get into many kinds of trouble when they are permitted to have unsupervised time with members of the opposite sex. In many cases, we have found that dating or being alone with members of the opposite sex has been permitted by parents beginning at about twelve years old.

Sex with Girls at School: Kenneth, age 15

My name is Kenneth. I am fifteen years old and I was at House of Hope for almost ten months. I was adopted at birth, and my life began in New York. After my adopted father got fired from his job in a power plant, we moved to Florida. My two brothers stayed in New York to finish school.

My troubles began in elementary school. Life was fine until I started being sexually active with girls, and I began to steal from the kids in school. When I got tired of stealing from other kids, I looked for a challenge like shoplifting.

I became more and more sexually involved with girls in my school. I started using drugs and then selling stolen stuff to get money. My teachers began to think I was suicidal. Because of my behavior I had to go to counselors and crisis units.

When I got into high school, I was having sex with girls in school and stealing a lot more than before. When I got caught shoplifting, I was enrolled in a probation program. After seven months in that program, I got caught with a girl at school. To keep herself out of trouble, she said I raped her. She said that I took her over to this area, covered her mouth, and then penetrated her. So after that I was suspended.

When I came back to school, I hooked up with another girl. I got in trouble with more girls for sexual acts in school, and I was finally kicked out of school. When I went back to court, I had to go somewhere where I would be monitored, so I went to House of Hope.

Through deliverance prayers, I am free from the sexual perversion that was actually something that had been passed down from my father's generation. I have been improving relationships with my family and God, and I am finding the things in my life that I value. Just recently, I asked forgiveness and took a purity vow to God to stay pure until I get married.

Sexual/Emotional Maturity

Teens generally do not have the emotional maturity to successfully handle a boy-girl relationship—let alone twelve-year-olds. On top of that, boys and girls arrive at their maturity levels via different routes and times. The reason why there is such a mismatch of teens is because girls generally mature earlier than boys. How many times have you talked with a fifteen-year-old girl who is head-over-heels in love with a college-age guy? The boys in her class are babies! They are just a bunch of immature brats in her mind. What she doesn't realize is that she lacks the emotional maturity to recognize and stand against a nineteen-year-old male's sexual plots and advances.

Unfortunately, young teenagers are sexually active. To find out about their sexual activity and knowledge, a landmark poll of thirteen to sixteen-year-olds was conducted by NBC News and *PEOPLE* magazine. The results indicate:

> "In one of the first surveys of its kind, teenagers as young as 13 reveal how much they know about sex and how much they are doing. The poll, conducted by Princeton Survey Research Associates International, questioned 13 to 16 year-olds about their sexual behavior, relationships, oral sex, STDs, and casual sexual partners (what's now known as "friends with benefits")...
>
> "Nearly 3 in 10 (27%) thirteen to sixteen year-olds are sexually active and "have been with someone in an intimate or sexual way." Most of these sexually active teens have touched someone else's genitals and almost half had oral sex and/or had sexual intercourse."[1]

Another survey conducted by ABC looked at the frequency of unprotected sex:

"Among teens that have had sexual intercourse, nearly one in four say they or their partner don't always use a condom, and 14 % don't always use any reliable birth control. Two-thirds of them have had more than one sex partner. Seven in 10 say their first time was unplanned." [2]

The same survey said that teens will sometimes participate in sex when they don't really want to.

"More than a fifth of all teenagers — including a quarter of older teens, and about three in 10 older girls — say they've been in a relationship where "things were moving too fast sexually." And 12 % of teens, one in eight, say they've done something sexual they didn't really want to do — mainly because they were carried away, talked into it or too shy or embarrassed to say no. (Fewer say they were forced, or under the influence of drugs or alcohol.)"[3]

Unplanned Pregnancies

If we were doing our jobs, (i.e. teaching children how to respect their sexuality, talking about pregnancy, holding fast to morality issues, making godly decisions) would unplanned pregnancy even be a topic of discussion? The pregnancy centers are busy. Waiting rooms are packed. The women come and they go, but now it takes them a little longer to make their decisions because many of the centers are using high tech ultrasound machines that show the baby moving around. The teen sees that this "thing" is alive—swimming, kicking, moving—and she cannot deny it has life.

In the *Grassroots Abortion War* article in *Time* magazine, February 15, 2007, writer Nancy Gibbs offers this in an interview:

"They have been fed these lies, that it's just a bunch of cells, that's not worth anything," Nurse Joyce Williams says. "But those limbs are moving. That heart is beating. You don't have to say anything..."

"A woman goes into a center looking for information...and she doesn't get all the facts. That's taking someone's life and playing a really dangerous game with it."

A shocking number of unplanned pregnancies end in abortion. Here are the statistics.

Ž Just under 850 thousand women in the United States had an abortion in 2003. [4]

Ž Since 1973, there have been over 40,000,000 abortions in the United States.[5]

Ž Nearly half of all American women under the age of forty-five have an unplanned pregnancy, and more than one third of these pregnancies will end in abortion.[6]

It's sad to say that Christian women are included in these statistics.

Teenagers do not think about what would happen if they got pregnant or got someone pregnant. A *USA Today* article reported:

> Many teens say they have never really thought about what their life would be like if they got pregnant or got someone pregnant as a teen. Almost half of teens (48%) overall— including 50% of boys and 45% of girls—say they have not given teen parenthood any in-depth thought.[7]

Relative Truth

Across America tens of thousands of high school teenagers have taken pledges to be sexually pure until marriage. These types of teens participate in "True Love Waits," and they take a stand for the truth regarding their sexual purity. The problem is that most young people hear that truth through their own filter, which tells them that all truth is subjectively determined. In other words, premarital sex is wrong only if they personally believe it is wrong.

Most teenagers believe that all truth is relative according to their own circumstances. They do not believe there is a universal truth that is right for all people, in all places, at all times. They have been conditioned to believe that each individual has been given the right to say and do what that person thinks is best for him or her. If you question these comments, take a look at some of the Barna surveys and they will motivate you to action...after they break your heart.

This generation makes decisions based on their personal standard of morality and they justify their choices as acceptable under the circumstances. In other words, our young people have a distorted view of what makes things right and wrong. They have lost the universal standard for what is moral and ethical, and the result is a culture of young people vulnerable not only to wrong thinking but also to the destructive consequences of wrong behavior.

A *USA Today* news article observed that teenagers are making their own definitions of sex.

> "The generational divide between baby-boomer parents and their teenage offspring is sharpening over sex.
>
> Oral sex, that is.
>
> More than half of 15- to 19-year-olds are doing it, according to a groundbreaking study by the Centers for Disease Control and Prevention.
>
> Among teens, oral sex is often viewed so casually that it needn't even occur within the confines of a relationship. Some teens say it can take place at parties, possibly with multiple partners. But they say the more likely scenario is oral sex within an existing relationship."[8]

Unless we restore Christ—not their own opinions and choices—to His rightful place as the Standard, our kids won't have a chance.

Our job at House of Hope is to equip our teens to make good choices according to the truth of what the Scriptures teach, and our teens also take purity vows which are based on the God's Word, not their subjective views of reality.

Social Expectations about Sex and Being Sexy

The same *USA Today* article pointed out that both teens and adults believe that male teens are expected to have sex and female teens are expected to look sexy.

> Boys are expected to have sex... Most teens (58% of boys and 66% of girls) and adults (75%) believe that teen boys often get the message that they are *expected* to have sex.
> Girls are expected to look sexy... A distressing six in ten teens (61% of boys and 57% of girls) and fully three-quarters of adults (74%) believe that teen girls often receive the message that attracting boys and looking sexy is one of the most important things girls can do.
> ...And parents are sending different messages to both. Parents admit (61%) and teens acknowledge (65% of girls and 65% of boys) that when it comes to talking about sex, parents send one message to their sons and a different message to their daughters. "Teens define sex in new ways," by Sharon Jayson, USA TODAY, posted 10/19/2005, accessed at http://www.usatoday.com/news/health/2005-10-18-teens-sex_x.htm
> Virginity Three quarters of teens (73% of boys and 78% of girls) do not believe it is embarrassing for teens to admit they are virgins. A far smaller proportion of adults—just over half (54%)—agree.

Why would I spend so much time talking about sexuality? I believe that this generation is in serious trouble regarding values, morals and their health.

They lack respect for what God has fearfully and wonderfully made (Psalm 139:14). This is a concept that must be taught. If parents are not going to teach their children, who is going to pick up the gauntlet? As Christian counselors working with teens, we have a responsibility. It is vital that we go back to the basics and teach them what God's Word says about sexuality and about sex. Because our goal is to restore the family, we will need to teach the parents (yes, the adults) about sexuality and sex.

We may need to get comfortable with these discussions *prior* to counseling sessions. If you are not comfortable with using correct terminology for various body parts (i.e. penis, vagina, etc.) you will need to practice saying these words.

Setting a High Standard for Sexual Purity

At House of Hope, we do not allow teens to do any dating because they have their hands full already with learning how to submit to authority and dealing with past hurts, disappointments, bad memories and broken family relationships. When we remove the dating scenario, we are giving them a time out to learn how to respect their bodies and how to hear from God about waiting for their life-long spouse.

In most cases, the teens that come to House of Hope have not learned about sex in appropriate or healthy ways. Because of their intense desire to be loved, relational needs, peer pressure, drugs, alcohol and various other influences, most teens do not have a healthy view of their own sexuality.

Here are a few suggestions as to how we as counselors can help the teens and their parents.

Expect the teen to have high standards.

Don't allow the teen or parents to make comments like, "Boys will be boys!" or "Girls like to have fun." Those kinds of statements send a mixed message. Your goal is help them become pure, not semi-dirty!

Watch the vocabulary.

As a professional, it is important to set the standards of what you will accept during your counseling settings. Vulgarity should not be acceptable in your presence. Allowing cursing in your presence says that you are not able to set boundaries. I have heard parents call a child "slut" or "whore" during counseling sessions. This only compounds the teen's feelings of worthlessness and rejection, and you must stand against this kind of language. It embarrasses the teen and if you do not stand up for the child, you have lost the battle—not the war—but certainly the battle.

Teach responsibility.

It is vitally important for the teen and family to know that it is tough to control emotions but that *real* men and *real* women learn to control their actions and behaviors. When teens are tempted, we teach them to call on Jesus for help to give them the strength to make good choices and control emotions.

Everything has a consequence. Some consequences are good and some are not good. Taking responsibility for behaviors and facing consequences are part of teens maturing and growing into the people that God wants them to be.

It is important for the counselor to be proactive when dealing with teens on the issue of sexuality and sexual purity. It is important to set boundaries and limits and hold them accountable for their behaviors, and even their thought lives. We must back up our boundaries with the Word of God. Purity does not start with the body, it starts in the mind. Treating themselves and others with respect regarding sexuality is required by God.

At House of Hope our boys and girls take Purity Vows to remain sexually pure until they are married. It is thrilling to see these teens with a passion for purity and an excitement about saving themselves sexually for the spouse God has prepared for them.

From a Mess to a Miracle: Marie, age 14

My name is Marie, and I am fourteen years old. I was born and raised in Florida in a safe and secure home. My mom started working when she had her first child, which was my older sister. Then my brother came four years later. I was born when he was two.

My dad was the provider for the family, and Mom stayed at home with us. My sister started hanging out with the wrong crowd, and I followed soon after. At the age of thirteen, I was a mess. I started smoking weed, was disrespectful to my teachers, skipped school a lot, stole what I wanted and even brought alcohol onto school property. I lost my virginity that year to a guy who did not even care about me.

I was full of anger, and my family never saw it. I was finally kicked out of school because of my disrespect. I was sent to the Juvenile Detention Center for several hours.

Through all this, my mom and dad were not doing well. He actually left for several months and was never there for me. Mom tried to be, but she was clueless as to what was really going on. I hated her because she read my journal; I thought she was just trying to make my life miserable.

I found myself in the Excell program, which is for kids who are not allowed to return to school. That did nothing for me, and I was kicked of there, too. I did not care.

Finally Mom found House of Hope, and I really feel a change on the inside. I want to save myself for the man God is saving for me. I am a born-again virgin, and I can't wait to see what God has in store for me.

Conclusion

God's forgiving love gives the freedom for those who ask to be born again virgins.

CHAPTER 10

Drugs

IN MANY RESPECTS, THERE'S NOTHING NEW UNDER THE SUN regarding teenage drug use. What's happening is that kids are being introduced to many different things at a much earlier age. Thirty or forty years ago, there was a rather orderly progression: teens smoked cigarettes, discovered beer, and moved on to Jack Daniels. Then they started smoking pot, which was an entryway to acid. For most teens back in the sixties, and seventies, this is where their drug use leveled out.

Today's teens also follow a progression, although they are prone to skip over several steps. They may start smoking in grade school before ditching the Marlboros for a cigarette with some punch—marijuana. Once that loses its thrill, it's time to experiment with pills such as Valium and Seconol, and then their drug use becomes serious. They turn their attention to several new "designer" drugs, the most popular being MDMA (methylenedioxymethamphetamine), otherwise known as XTC or "ecstasy." Painted like candy canes or imprinted with Nike swooshes to appeal to adolescents, ecstasy pills are sold on the street for prices ranging from $15 to $25.

Ecstasy has components that break down communication barriers, which is why it has been so popular in raves. Ecstasy causes you to ignore the body's warning signals that it needs rest and water. You can literally dance yourself into a heat stroke by combining ecstasy with alcohol, because the diuretic in the alcohol drains your body of fluids quickly.

When a teenager comes to House of Hope and is on drugs, a counselor prays with them, has them name each drug they've taken and pray against the stronghold these drug represent. Many teens are hooked on cocaine, ecstasy, marijuana and alcohol. In twenty-two years I know of no teenager who went through withdrawals at House of Hope Orlando, and we make sure, of course, that teenagers have no access to drugs during their stay and receive any medical attention that may be warranted.

A Drug Expert

I first saw Scott, a local policeman, being interviewed about his work on an Orlando TV program. "Parents don't have a clue which disguised drugs their kids are bringing into their homes," said Scott, and I nodded my head in agreement. I knew right away that I had to get in touch with this streetwise cop and bring him to House of Hope to educate our staff and talk to the teens about the dangers of going back on drugs.

We immediately liked Scott, a friendly, outgoing and approachable fellow in his mid-thirties. As he regaled us with stories from his under-cover days, we soon realized that he was a brave guy who stayed alive by employing his street-savvy wits. I asked Scott to be my expert on the teen drug scene because he worked undercover for six years—a long time in that dangerous line of work. He regularly comes to House of Hope to talk to the teenagers.

He certainly has a way of grabbing the kids' attention. All he needs to do is start telling a few stories about taking down the bad guys, and our House of Hope kids want to hear more. Our kids recognize courage when they see it.

Throughout much of the 1990s, Scott's job was to infiltrate Orlando's burgeoning rave scene and discover who the drug dealers were. He witnessed their handiwork every weekend at the raves. "I saw it all." he says. "Kids experienced seizures and blackouts. Kids became uncontrol-lable due to the various 'designer' and 'club' drugs they were ingesting at rave parties. One time I saw a kid shuffle out of the Warehouse, drop to the ground and start flopping like a fish," said Scott. "Then he vomited and spit up foam. It was bad, man."

Scott speaks in the matter-of-fact manner of one who has seen too many drug overdoses, or ODs, through years. He has been in too many

Orlando hospital emergency rooms, trying to comfort inconsolable parents who have been asked to identify their dead son or daughter.

Scott explains that raves began as nirvana-like parties in which the zonked-out participants promoted peace, love, unity and respect. Organized drug dealers discovered that raves are easy places to sell heroin, GHB, crystal-meth and other deadly drugs. Remember: the effects of drugs enhance the intensity of the music and lights in a club. If someone comes along and says that ecstasy or GHB is the ticket to ride, who's going to say no in such a free-for-all, chaotic atmosphere.

Here's how the teens explain the appeal of trying new drugs.

> *Smoking weed and doing acid was boring, I didn't like it. Then one of my friends showed me ecstasy and said I would love it, that it would feel as though my skin was flying off. Ecstasy sounded like fun, so I took it. Most kids have a drug of choice. My drug of choice became ecstasy. —Kelly, age fifteen*

> *I can tell you why kids take more and more drugs. It goes like this: if speed and crack take you up to the fourth floor, then why not go all the way to the twelfth floor and take a chance with harder drugs? Either way, the fall will kill you.— Curtis, age sixteen*

Teachable Moments about Drugs

At House of Hope, we work to educate parents about drug use among youth today. Unfortunately, the parents of our teens usually had no idea about how to talk with their children about drug use.

I encourage parents to look for teachable moments to talk about drugs. Talking with children is not as difficult as people think. Children begin learning about the dangers of drugs in elementary schools through the DARE programs, and depictions of drug use are pervasive throughout the entertainment media. Kids often think *their* knowledge about drugs is rather sophisticated.

Parents can jump start a conversation about drugs by watching a news segment on TV, hearing drug-related lyrics on the car radio ("Lucy in the sky with diamonds..."), or reading the sports page and learning that yet another high-profile athlete was busted for drug use.

Parents need to tell teens where they stand. They should talk about their future, reminding them how drug use can ruin their chances of being accepted into a good college or limit their career choices. If the teens retort that taking drugs is a "victimless crime," parents can remind them that there is a victim—the teen taking the drugs.

Parents should ask these questions as they consider whether their teens might be among those who use or experiment with drugs:

- On Friday and Saturday evenings is your teen out with friends past 10 PM or a reasonable curfew?
- Do you go to sleep on weekend nights without witnessing their arrival home?
- Are you unfamiliar with their friends?
- Do they constantly ask you for more allowance?
- Have you noticed money missing from your purse or billfold?
- Does your teen sleep half the day away on Saturdays and Sundays?
- Has your teen's grades taken a nose dive in the last semester?
- Have they become more uncommunicative recently?
- Have our teens started dressing different?

If the parents answered 'yes' to two or more of the above questions, I suggest that they take their teen out to a restaurant for a meal where they can have a family discussion. Here are some starter questions we suggest for parents to ask their teens.

- Why do you think kids take drugs?
- Do drugs harm the body? If so, how?
- What's the drug of choice these days?
- Do many kids take drugs at school?
- Do you know kids who sell drugs at school?
- How much peer pressure is there to do drugs at your school?

⅄ What kind of drugs can you buy at school?

⅄ Are there any long-term side effects to taking drugs?

⅄ What are some of the slang names for drugs that you've heard?

⅄ How much does it cost to buy drugs these days?

⅄ Is alcohol a drug?

⅄ Are drugs popularized in today's TV shows or movies? If so, can you remember a show?

Parents should not delay such a conversation. Helping their child as soon as possible may prevent some agonizing times down the road— including expensive "rehab" programs, many of which are not covered by regular medical insurance.

Obvious Signs of Drug Use

Parents often fail to see the obvious warning signs that their child is using drugs. Many times teens believe they are sending clear signals to their parents that they are taking drugs. Listen in on this conversation I had with a teen named Kevin:

Sara: How did you start getting into trouble and doing drugs?

Kevin: I started getting into trouble when I was eleven years old. I became rebellious, stopped doing what my parents told me to do, and began smoking pot with my friends. My parents didn't really know what was going on for a long time.

Sara: But couldn't they tell you were on drugs?

Kevin: I'm really surprised that they didn't. I guess they didn't want to know. I basically told them. I told them without saying words. I showed them through my actions. Anybody who knew about drugs knew I was taking them.

Sara: So they made a mistake by not being educated on what kids are like when they're high on drugs?

Kevin: Yeah. They should have been educated.

"I showed them through my actions"—a very telling admission for both generations. If anything, parents should be keeping a closer eye on children when they reach adolescence. Just because their voices change or they begin filling out a bikini doesn't mean that your parental role is over. It means it just got tougher!

If parents suspect children may be taking drugs, they should look for the root reasons. Parents should ask themselves

- Why are our teens experimenting with drugs?
- What's the attraction?
- Is our family spending quality time together in a way that allows all members' needs to be met?
- Why do they want to escape reality?
- Who are their friends? (Remember peer pressure from your teenage days? Human nature hasn't changed in one generation!)
- Do our teens get enough of our positive attention?

Parents could learn many lessons by reading the story of Mike, who was heavily medicated for ADHD and depression, suffered painful verbal abused from his dad, and quickly got hooked on illegal drugs while his parents were gone from the home for a weekend trip.

The Steps to Getting Hooked on Drugs: Mike, age 14

My dad is Arabic; his ancestors are Arab Muslims from Lebanon. He grew up Muslim, but he didn't kneel down on a prayer rug and pray five times a day or fast during Ramadan like most Islam believers. Nonetheless, he didn't eat ham or other pork products, and he still doesn't to this day.

My mom grew up as an Italian Catholic, so you can see how they had a mixed marriage. Then my mom converted my dad to Christianity, so I've been raised in the church all my life. I always had to go to church on Sunday morning. Even from a young age, though, I dealt with much depression. That's because doctors said I was born with ADHD—Attention Deficit Hyperactivity Disorder. They put me on Ritalin and Adaril when I was three years old (and I've been taking it ever since). If I didn't take my medicine and chewed on a piece of gum, for instance, I would go nuts. A little bit of sugar, and I bounced off the walls. Bottom line: I grew up medicated.

Around the age of twelve, I started realizing what else was out there. Mom, who sensed these changes in me, pulled me out of school and started home schooling me. I didn't have any friends when I was schooled at home, and my relationship with my sister Stephanie, who was three years older, was terrible. We fought a lot and argued.

I would always hear my dad say do this, do that, and you need to do this right now, and I remember what the Bible said about obeying your father and mother, so I did what I was told to do. But I always resented the way he raised his voice and the way he spoke to me, which was usually in a yelling manner. He liked to push me up against a wall or slap me in the face with his open hand. Deep down I wanted to hit him back, but I remembered what God's Word said.

The way he treated me made me feel even more depressed, so I would walk around my neighborhood or sit in my room and listen to music. When my mom noticed how glum I was, she put me on an anti-depressant called Wellbutrin, which I had to take along with my ADHD medicines.

One night, Dad was going at me as usual, so I fought back the only way I knew how. I said, "If you touch me again, I'm going to kill myself."

"What?" he asked.

"You know you heard me," I answered. "I have this pill that can kill me in three minutes." I didn't really have such a pill, but I wanted to scare him.

He called my sister to the room, and said, "Watch him for a minute." Then he told Mom what had happened. The next thing I knew, Mom drove me to the hospital, where we had to wait until four in the morning for a room in the psych ward to open up. The only good thing was that they didn't put me in a straightjacket and a padded cell. Instead, I was placed in a watch room, where people watched me from behind a mirror.

I liked the psych ward because they didn't yell or scream at me. They let me out after five days of observation and put me on a higher dose of Wellbutrin. Not long after I arrived home, my parents left Stephanie and me home alone for the weekend. They were doing that a lot because my dad won trips for being a top salesman in his company. Stephanie told me that she would have a few friends over for a little party. I said that's cool.

"You won't tell Mom and Dad will you?" she asked.

"No," I promised. "You just have to give me some space."

The party started mellow. My sister and her friends were drinking beers on the back porch, and her friends were getting really messed up. I got messed up, too, and after that party, I got into drugs. I knew what God's Word said, but I would do what I wanted.

The stuff cost money, though. One time, Mom drove me up to an ATM and handed me her card and told me her PIN number so I could get her some cash. It was easy to get her ATM card whenever she went out of town. I went to a nearby 7-11, stuck the card in an ATM machine, typed in $260, and collected thirteen Andrew Jacksons.

My friend and I got some drugs that I thought were good, but they really messed us up. I promised myself that I would never do that again.

A week later, I took out another $260. Again, I told myself this would be my last time. We bought some hash—that's like 100 % THC, pure weed, straight up, one of the best types of weeds.

The next time I took $500 out of the ATM machine, which was linked to my parents' savings account. That's why my parents weren't on to me. The money was coming out of savings, not their checking account.

I stole because drugs hooked me. I went out with my friend one time and got really drugged up, but my friend had a reaction to it and almost died. That's when his parents called my parents. Mom and Dad went through my room and found some weed, pipes, drug paraphernalia, and a wad of cash. Dad called my school, and before I knew it, I was meeting with them and the counselor. I was pretty much shocked that they found out, and my parents were shocked this could happen. Mom always thought I was a good Christian boy. Now she thought of me as a liar.

My parents had heard about House of Hope, and as soon as there was an opening, they brought me here. I was mad that I had to leave home. I had gotten saved when I was a little kid, but it didn't mean anything to me. My salvation finally meant something to me during a House of Hope chapel service one morning on December 10, 2002. As I cried out to God, I felt as though I received a warm hug in return. I put down all the drugs after that. Now I can talk to my dad without arguing. I have a better understanding of him now. I learned that he yelled at me because his dad always yelled at him when he was growing up.

The Lord is teaching me who I am in Christ. I know that someone put the label on me that I was ADHD. I refuse to believe that curse. I know I am a child of God, and I have the potential to be the youth pastor I want to be.

If you have been labeled like I was, don't go for it. What the devil meant to destroy, God is using for good in my life. He will turn your life around, too!

But the fruit of the Spirit is love, joy, peace, patience,
kindness, goodness, faithfulness, gentleness and self-control.
Against such things there is no law.—Galatians 5:22-23,
NIV

Kids Still Smoke up a Storm

I would be remiss if I didn't say anything about smoking. Most teens at House of Hope arrive as smokers. Cigarettes are their companions to help pass the time. They drag on cigarettes while watching TV, going to the mall to shop, or hanging out on the street corner and watching life pass by. Smoking is a coping.

Smoking is a coping mechanism for insecurity, which can mean that teens feel insecure due to not spending enough time with their parents. But let's say the parents are spending time with their teens or that they have made the commitment to do so after reading this book. However, the teen still smokes, and he or she needs to quit this vile habit. The first step is to educate the teen on the dangers of smoking. If the teen is living at home, parents need to explain: "We're going to start a new rule here. I know you're smoking, and that scares me for you. Because I love you, these are the boundaries: You're not allowed to smoke in the house, nor when we are doing things together as a family." Parents do not need to defend their position against smoking. They simply explain the guidelines that the teens are required to respect.

To encourage the kids at House of Hope to stop smoking, we take a yellow Post-It note and write on it, "I love you and want the best for you." We stick this note on the bathroom mirror so the teen can see it every morning when he washes up. This note is a reminder of our love, and it starts to soften his attitude (at least, we hope it will). We encourage each small step the teens take in kicking the habit.

At House of Hope, we have great success in helping our teens quit smoking. I attribute that to positive peer pressure. When a smoking teen is around a couple of dozen teens who don't smoke, he finds that he doesn't need that cigarette as much as he thought he did. Teens listen with big ears when a peer says he quit two months ago and his lungs are totally clear now.

If teens continue to hang out with buddies who smoke, it's going to be very difficult for them not to puff. They may need a change of scenery!

Conclusion

When teens are hurting, drug use is a common form of escape. At House of Hope, we find that with love and counseling, we can lead teens to pray against the stronghold of drug use. We look for the root causes of the wounds that a teen manifests, which takes us to Step 3 of our Triage Approach to Counseling—assessing the family history.

STEP III

ASSESS FAMILY HISTORY

CHAPTER 11

Generational Curses
and Sinful Patterns

LET'S GO BACK TO OUR ANALOGY OF TRIAGE COUNSELING. WHEN the EMT has taken care of life-threatening situations and treated the visible wounds, he will put a green tag on the patient. This means that the patient is stable for the moment but requires watching. At this point, the medical team can take a closer look at the patient and gather the medical history. The medical history will help doctors to design the most effective treatment to help the victim recover.

As counselors, we also need to learn the histories of our clients—their family histories. This is where we can find the spiritual and emotional roots of problems in individuals and families.

This chapter will deal with generational patterns, or as some refer to as generational curses and the sins of the father. I will show you specifically how to lead the client in prayer to break the power of these curses and patterns.

Roots in the Family Tree

We look at the generational sin process in a family by identifying recurring patterns of tragedies, sickness, early death, abortions, divorce, financial problems, abuse, abandonment, anger, control, occult, pornography, rebellion, and depression in their families.

Our goal is to break sinful generational curses and patterns that started from deep roots in the family tree. I know I have personally dealt with things in my immediate family that were the results of generational curses and patterns. Even though I don't know exactly what happened in my relatives' lives three or four generations ago, I could recognize the effects in my family today. Exodus 20:5 says, "I, the Lord your God, am a jealous God, visiting the iniquity of the fathers upon the children to the third and fourth generations of those who hate me."

After a counselor has identified a generational pattern, he or she leads the counselees in a specific prayer, asking God to forgive the sins of the fathers and to remove the effects of these sins in their lives.

We focus on two types of generational patterns:

1. Spoken curses and blessings
2. Sins of the fathers

Spoken Curses and Blessings

Blessings or curses spoken into a person's life can have a powerful, long-lasting effect upon them and even generations after them. James 3:10 says "Out of the same mouth proceed blessing and cursing."

The first thing we need to understand is the nature of blessings and curses. They can be defined as "words that have spiritual authority to set in motion something that will continue to have an effect from generation after generation." (See Deuteronomy 28.)

A curse empowers a person to fail. A blessing empowers a person to succeed. Blessings and curses are words that give power to either God or Satan.

With that in mind, we all need to consciously choose to bless and not curse with our mouths.

The good news is because of Jesus Christ, we have been given authority (Luke 10:19) the things that have been spoken against us (such as those found in Deuteronomy 28:15-45). Isaiah 54:17 says, "No weapon formed against you shall prosper, and every tongue *which* rises against you in judgment you shall condemn. This *is* the heritage of the servants of the LORD, and their righteousness *is* from Me," says the LORD."

Curses directed against a person can come from three sources:

1. Others
2. Themselves
3. Disobeying God

Many people I have counseled are not only the victims of these sinful generational patterns; they are also the perpetrators. In other words, not only have they received curses, but they have also spoken curses against people in their lives. So at the same time you address the curses the counselee has received, you will also deal with the curses they have given.

Below are examples of prayers that will help you in breaking curses.

Prayer for the Counselor

Before you as a counselor can lead anyone to pray for release from a curse or to repent for speaking a curse, you need to repent for any words from your mouth that have caused harm. We are all human and make mistakes. The key is to obey God's Word and repent for what we do wrong. Ask the Lord to reveal to you any curses that you have said against others, and you can use the following prayer as a guide to repent.

> Dear Lord, I ask for forgiveness for my curse, _____, [name the negative statement] against _____ [name the person].
>
> I forgive myself. I cancel and remove all power I gave to negative spiritual influences to carry out the curse. I release God's healing and freedom to _____ [name the person you cursed].
>
> In Jesus' name I pray, AMEN.

Prayer about Curses from Others

Ask the counselees to list curses that other people have spoken against them, such as, "You'll always be stupid." "You'll never amount to anything."

Lead them in prayer:

> Dear Lord, I forgive _____ [name the person] for cursing me with the spoken word of _____ [name the negative

words]. I ask You, Lord, to forgive me for receiving this curse and giving it authority in my life.

I break its power. I am no longer in agreement with this curse. I appropriate the blood and the power of the cross to stop all negative spiritual influence and judgments connected with this curse.

I receive and affirm God's blessings of _____ [name the blessings God promises to his children].

In Jesus' name I pray, AMEN.

Prayer about Cursing Ourselves

Many people have such a poor image of themselves that they speak curses into their own lives. List any of the ways your clients have spoken curses against themselves. For example, "I have no memory," "I am so stupid," etc. We speak defeat and failure over our lives when we say, "I can't," "I have not," etc. We need to pray:

Dear Lord, I forgive myself for my words against myself and saying _____ [name the negative words].

I ask You to forgive me, Lord, for receiving this curse and giving it rule in my life.

I break its power. I am no longer in agreement with this curse. I appropriate the blood and the power of the cross to stop all negative spiritual influence and judgments connected with the curse.

I receive and affirm God's blessings of _____ [name the blessings God promises]

In Jesus' name I pray, AMEN.

Prayer about Curses Caused by Disobeying God

God's will is to bless us above all that we could ask or imagine. If we obey, God will bless us.

Now it shall come to pass, if you diligently obey the voice of the LORD your God, to observe carefully all His commandments which I command you today, that the LORD your God will set you high above all nations of the earth. And all these blessings shall come upon you and overtake you, because you obey the voice of the LORD your God:

"Blessed *shall* you *be* in the city, and blessed *shall* you *be* in the country.

"Blessed *shall be* the fruit of your body, the produce of your ground and the increase of your herds, the increase of your cattle and the offspring of your flocks.

"Blessed *shall be* your basket and your kneading bowl.

"Blessed *shall* you *be* when you come in, and blessed *shall* you *be* when you go out."—Deuteronomy 28:1-6

However, God cannot bless those who rebel against His commandments. Deuteronomy 28:15-19 (MSG) tells what will happen if you don't obediently listen to the voice of God and diligently keep all his commandments and guidelines: "All these curses will come down hard on you."

The curses are visited on the third and fourth generation of those who hate Him. (See Deuteronomy 5:9). As it says in Joshua 24:15: "Choose for yourselves this day whom you will serve."

A simple prayer to break the curses that come from disobedience to God would be one of repentance, asking God's forgiveness for the rebellion and praying for the curses to be lifted, naming each one specifically.

Prayer about Curses Spoken Against Others

Just as you repented for any curses you have spoken into other people's lives, you need to lead your clients in the same kind of prayer. They need to acknowledge their sin, repent, and pray for the power of the curse and any negative spiritual influences to be broken.

Dear Lord, I ask for forgiveness for my curse, _____, [name the negative statement] against _____ [name the person].

I forgive myself. I cancel and remove all power I gave to negative spritiual influences to carry out the curse. I release God's healing and freedom to _____ [name the person you cursed].

In Jesus' name I pray, AMEN.

Sins of the Fathers

In addition to curses, the Bible also talks about the sins of the fathers. These are acts of rebellion against God's laws that result in curses that are passed down generation after generation (Leviticus 26:40). One only has to examine society to see this operating down the family line.

God loves the family and has made every promise for the family to be free from the sins of the fathers by giving His Son Jesus to die and shed His blood for the remission of all sins. (Colossians 2:14) We can choose to receive Jesus' blood which removes the sins of the fathers. He became a curse for us that we may be free. (Galatians 3:13)

We can't allow the negative spiritual influences that came down through past generations to continue to our children. The buck needs to stop with our bloodline. The story you are about to read is a strong example of how sins from a grandmother and mother were passed down to the next generation. However, I am so proud of Patti and her family for putting a stop to the "sins of the fathers" in their family.

Witchcraft Passed Down: Patti's Story

My precious daughter, Patti, started off difficult, being born in a breach position. She was always a strong-willed child, but sadly I didn't realize it until she was around twelve years old.

Then I realized that I had not been strong enough as a single, working mother to deal with the challenges I was about to face.

I was divorced from my husband when Patti was only seven years old. Her brother was five at the time. I had no one to help me, so I had to work long hours to make ends meet. I also decided to further my education as much as my schedule permitted, and I went to vocational school during that time.

I had come out of drug abuse myself and was far from an ideal parent and certainly did not provide the best atmosphere for my children to grow up in. My own mother practiced witchcraft and lived with a warlock.

I was twenty-five when I was divorced and by the time I was thirty-one, I realized that I really, really needed God in my life. I was wonderfully saved and delivered. Up to that time, Patti did quite well in school and I really didn't have any problems with her. But it seems that right after my life was turned around, things got really difficult. She rebelled terribly and got into the skinhead movement.

It was so hard for me because I had found God, and the devil seemed to manifest through her. It got worse and worse at our home. She would leave for days and not let me know where she was. I would have to call the police and they would tell me that I was responsible for whatever she did because she was a minor.

She was very violent and destructive during those years prior to House of Hope. We had many bouts with the law. I really became a desperate woman. Even the youth pastor at our church didn't know what to do with her. When we went to visit him, she went into a trance state, with her Mohawk hairdo, face painted white, black lips, black clothes, boots and tattoos.

Well, after trying for almost two years to get help from every organization I heard about, I finally received a glimmer of light from House of Hope. They sure are named appropriately, for I had almost lost hope. I went there, and even though I couldn't possibly pay them, they took in Patti.

Actually, she didn't want to go at all but she didn't have a choice. She had been before the judge so many times that he was fed up with her, and he told her to go try this program or else get locked up until she was nineteen. She was fifteen at the time. I was not living near the Orlando House of Hope, but that two-hour drive was worth it to see what was happening to my daughter.

I had to go there and receive counseling myself and participate in the program. I too received much healing from these times, and our home began to be reconciled at long last. Patti had to be delivered from a generational curse of witchcraft that came through my mother's involvement. She also received healing from the hurts of rejection she received from her dad not being there for her.

Patti eventually became an example for other girls coming out of their difficult times. Now Patti is thirty-five and graduated from college and is studying for her master's. She has beautiful long blonde hair with olive skin and red lips and tattoos removed. She is very busy working and raising three children and lives with me.

I am so proud of her. I am really eternally indebted to House of Hope. They never made me feel bad for not being able to pay. And to this day they are very much a part of our lives, and I suppose always will be. I thank God in Heaven for Sara Trollinger [our counselor] and her lifelong commitment. When no one else was there, she was. May the Lord above grant her eternal rewards for what she has done in our lives alone, not to mention all the others that have been changed through House of Hope.

Inheriting Anger: Zeke, age 15

I was seven years old when my parents got a divorce. My mom and dad fought a lot, and I'd hide in the closet to get away. My dad would yell and verbally abuse me, calling me "stupid, dumb, screwed up." He made me feel rejected, and we were falling apart. People that I loved seemed to go away—my brother, my dad and my grandmother. I was taught never to show weakness and to never back down, so I always carried these false burdens.

I didn't see my dad for a long time. When I did see him, he was always in a bad mood and made us feel like we were guilty and caused their problems. I was afraid of him because he would beat me and tell me that I didn't know how to do anything. He would go into a rage of anger. I was mistreated by my dad, and I also had a fear of crying. My dad slapped me across the face and told me not to cry.

When I was thirteen I began getting into fights. My anger was just like my dad's. I rebelled against everyone in authority. The wrong friends made me feel accepted. We would start fights and be destructive. I got into so many fights that I got arrested and wound up in a detention center. After that I got involved with even worse friends. I started taking and selling drugs.

When I came to House of Hope, I got involved in anger management classes. I also began counseling with my dad, and he asked for my forgiveness and I forgave him. I've also had the generational curse of anger broken from my life. I have been healed of the ungodly vows that I have made, like "I'm never going to be like my dad."

Prayer for Healing from Curses and Sins of the Fathers

As a counselor, you can help teenagers like Patti and Zeke and their parents deal with their spiritual and emotional histories. First, identify specific sins committed by their fathers and any spoken curses. Look for recurring negative spiritual influences and patterns of tragedies, sickness, early death, miscarriage, abortions, divorces, financial woes, etc.

Here are some examples to help you identify the ones specific to your client.

- ⋏ Abandonment, insecurity, desertion, rejection
- ⋏ Abuse—sexual, emotional, verbal or physical
- ⋏ Addiction, compulsion
- ⋏ Anger, bitterness, rage, criticism, cursing, judging
- ⋏ Control, passivity, people-pleasing
- ⋏ Deception, family secrets, lying, hatred, violence
- ⋏ Depression, hopelessness
- ⋏ Divorce, unfaithfulness
- ⋏ Fear, shame

⅄ Financial patterns, such as cheating or stinginess
⅄ Idolatry
⅄ Neglect
⅄ Occult, witchcraft, blood oaths
⅄ Premature death, murder, suicide, abortion
⅄ Rebellion, pride, lawlessness
⅄ Sexual sins, pornography, abuse, illegitimacy
⅄ Unbelief

Next, the counselee needs to go before God with these issues in his or her life and ask for healing. Ask him or her to repeat the following prayer after you.

> Dear Lord, I confess that my ancestors and I sinned, both knowingly and unknowingly, and opened doors of ungodly generational patterns of sin into my life.
>
> I forgive the sins of my father and my own and name each ancestral sin: _____. [List the sins and curses that you discovered.]
>
> I release and forgive my ancestors of these sins and the curses and how they have affected my life by _____. [List how these sins and curses have affected you.]
>
> I ask for forgiveness for these sins in my life. I destroy these sins and sin patterns in Jesus' name.
>
> I forgive myself for all participation in these sins and curses. I place them with Jesus on the cross, where He became a curse for me so that I could be free.
>
> I break their power in my life and close all doorways in my body, soul and spirit. I receive Your forgiveness and empowerment now in Jesus' name.
>
> I declare I have a new bloodline where there are no sins of the fathers. I ask that You bring healing and freedom to every area mentioned above. I declare that the generational blessings of my generation shall come into my life. AMEN and AMEN!

After you lead your clients in this prayer, it is a good time to receive the Lord's Supper. Explain that the shedding of Jesus' blood ensures a new bloodline where there are no sins of the fathers.

Victory over Generational Hurts: Tammy, age 15

My daughter had always been the "good one." Tammy did well in school, was obedient, trustworthy and seemed to be fairly happy...until she turned fifteen. There were signs before, but I hadn't realized how serious the situation was. Her brokenness and woundedness came out as anger and rebellion. She wasn't going to school. She was using drugs, sneaking out at night and completely falling apart. Her depression was terrifying. She had tried to kill herself and nothing anyone was doing was helping.

Three years before, we had moved to Florida from New Mexico—a transfer with my job and God's perfect timing to get me out of another unhealthy relationship, I thought. As a family, we had no idea what the Lord had planned for us.

I had been an alcoholic, and even though I had been sober for over five years at this time, the damage had been done to my children who were products of generational curses. I was a wounded person creating broken people. I had accepted Jesus as my Savior, and He was turning my life around, but the destruction of my past was enormous.

Memorial Day 1996, I drove to House of Hope, a Christian residential program (and so much more) that my mail carrier had told me about. My son, Cory, sat in the backseat with Tammy to keep her from jumping out of the car into the traffic on the turnpike. She had been on the waiting list for a very short time, but didn't know exactly when she was going in until the night before. She was livid!

The last year in our home had been a time of horror, never knowing what would happen next. I spent my time on the floor of the bathroom on my face crying out to God for help. I know now how perfect God's timing is. We left her at House of Hope with her hating me, crying, her brother crying, and everyone else in the family hating me. There are times when you know that you know what the Lord wants you to do, no matter what anyone else says or does.

Tammy didn't speak to me for the first few months she was there, unless she was made to, out of respect. I kept asking Sara and the staff if I could come live there, saying, "This is where I need to be." At one point, Tammy said she didn't want me there. I was going for counseling, parenting classes, and coming for all visitations. I finally had to tell my daughter that her anger was not going to push me away or make me stop loving her and that I was coming there for me!

I knew this was not just her problem, but the whole family's. I had to be willing to be teachable and to do whatever it took. I decided that whatever Tammy was doing at House of Hope, I would do at home, memorizing Scriptures, reading, devotions, studying and being willing to allow the Lord to do what He wanted to do in me.

Tammy was in the program for twenty months. She led her father, who was in California, to the Lord over the phone. After graduation, she got her GED, at seventeen entered Bible school, graduated and returned to House of Hope as a house staff, a mighty woman of God!!

Today at twenty-seven, she is absolutely beautiful. She's still clean—eleven years now—and holds a high management position at one of the city's finest resorts. Did I mention that she is my best friend? God did that.

The Lord is still healing us, restoring our family, tearing down strongholds, breaking generational curses, and He has even redeemed the time that was lost. Malachi 4:6 is a reality in our family. Praise God!

CHAPTER 12

Soul Ties, Vows, Judgments, Ungodly Beliefs

AFTER WE HAVE ADDRESSED NEGATIVE SPIRITUAL INFLUENCES generational patterns and sins of the fathers, we can move on to other circumstances from the past that may have created strongholds in your client's life. These circumstances may include:

1. Soul ties
2. Vows
3. Judgments
4. Ungodly beliefs

This chapter will describe each issue and how to address it in counseling.

Soul Ties

More people than I care to acknowledge are bound because of soul ties. Soul ties can be with friends, parents, siblings, former spouses and sexual relationships.

What are soul ties? Simply put, soul ties are unhealthy connections between people. They are covenants hindering or interfering with our lives, particularly with relationships and marriage. These ties can be spiritual or emotional, such as we might find when there has been a perverted parent/child relationship or in fornication (sex outside of marriage). They can also be found in codependent relationships.

Most teens that come to House of Hope have been involved in one or many sexual relationships, and codependency is typical. These ungodly alliances, ties and beliefs must be broken for wholeness to be evident.

Journey to Wholeness: Mackenzie, age 17

Hi, my name is Mackenzie and I'm seventeen years old. When I was six years old in Thailand, I was sexually molested by a group of men in the village. I ran home and cried to my mom, and she prayed for me, but I didn't accept it. I wondered why God let this happen.

I was raised in church. My dad and mom were missionaries, and I knew about God and could fake it on the outside that I had it all together, but inside I was hurting. My grandpa died, and my brother was taken from us, so I was furious with God.

We moved to Florida when I was in high school and that is when it all went downhill. I began to hang out with the wrong crowd, drinking, doing drugs, smoking daily and partying. As I was partying, I was introduced to a lot of different guys and started doing things with guys at the age of fifteen sexually. I had no remorse for it, because I was drugged up or so drunk, and I was just doing it for pleasure.

I met a guy I had really liked, and to be accepted I forced him to have sex with me. I felt very weird because I had also ruined a friendship. I had no self-respect.

My mom began to notice that I was out of control. She found House of Hope. At House of Hope, I was prayed over to be healed of soul ties. I realized I couldn't have a healthy marriage if I was in bondage to these spirits.

Now, I am a born-again virgin and saving myself for my husband. Because of all the sexual abuse and hurts in my past, my counselor prayed for healing from my broken past that I had stuffed in, and never dealt with. I received healing from the addictions, fear of failure, and hurts from the things I did when I was on drugs.

My goal is to go back to Thailand and help others.

Prayers to Confess and Break Soul Ties

Soul ties cause us to be connected wrongly and live a fragmented life. God is a covenant-making God and hates ungodly alliances, ties and beliefs in our lives. Lead your client in the following prayers:

Prayer to Confess Soul Tie

Father God, I submit myself completely to You. I confess all of my emotional and sexual sins that resulted in ungodly soul ties. I choose to forgive and release each person that I have been involved with in any wrong way. Forgive me for my sin that has resulted in ungodly ties. I receive Your forgiveness. Thank You for cleansing and forgiving me. I choose to forgive and release myself from all anger, hate and punishment as a result of the ungodly soul ties. In Jesus' name I pray, AMEN.

Prayer to Break Soul Tie

Father, I break my soul tie _____ [Name persons.] I release myself from him/her and her/her from me. I pray that You will cause him/her and me to be all You want us to be. Father, cleanse my mind from all memories of ungodly ties and unions so that I am totally free to give myself to You and to my mate. I renounce and cancel all negative spiritual influences attempting to keep these ties. I thank You, Father, for restoring my soul to wholeness. Please let me walk by Your grace. In Jesus' name I pray, AMEN.

Vows: A Form of Curse

A vow is a form of putting a curse on ourselves. The question is, how much of our lives will we let God control and how much will we take back as a vow and curse ourselves?

To say "I will never" produces two effects:

1. It causes our self-will to rule. These words give our will authority and power, rather than depending on God's authority. Our will does battle against God's will.

2. It is also a contract with the enemy of our soul to bring about the very thing that we vow we will never do, say, be, etc.

For examples, as a teenager, I remember a few of my friends' mothers stating, "My daughter will never get pregnant and have to get married." Sad to say, every mom who made that vow or curse had a daughter who got pregnant and had to get married. It has stuck in my mind all these years as I remember to avoid saying "never." Other examples of vows are, "I'll never be like my mother," or "I'll never get a divorce."

To deal with vows like these, lead your clients in the following prayer:

Prayer to Renounce Vows

> Dear God, I renounce and break the power of the following vows: _____ [List vows made.]. I rebuke all negative spiritual influences assigned to bring this vow to pass in my life in Jesus name. Forgive me, Lord, for making this vow. I forgive myself for making this vow. I now release my will, authority and power over this part of my life and give it to You God

to be under Your will, authority, and power. In Jesus' name I pray, AMEN.

Judgments

Many of us have judged and made judgments of others, even knowing that the Scripture says:

> "Judge not, that you be not judged. For with what judgment you judge, you will be judged; and with the measure you use, it will be measured back to you."—Matthew 7:1.

God's Word tells us:

> Do not be deceived, God is not mocked; for whatever a man sows, that he will also reap.—Galatians 6:7

When I sow seeds of judgment toward others, I am without excuse. When I judge another, I am guilty also.

Many children judge their parents, saying, for example, "My mother and father are no good." Even with ungodly parents, the child must show honor, as it says in Ephesians 6:1–3 (NIV): Children, obey your parents in the Lord, for this is right. "Honor your father and mother"—which is the first commandment with a promise— "that it may go well with you and that you may enjoy long life on the earth."

At the same time, many parents judge their children. God is hindered and cannot work when an individual refuses to forgive children, friends or family members for ungodly ways. It is much faster and more effective to believe and trust God's word than to judge them and allow roots of bitterness to spring up. Here is a sample prayer to pray.

Prayer to Renounce Judgments

> Dear God, I now renounce all judgments I have made concerning _____ (Describe the judgments specifically.) I

repent, Lord, and ask You to release me from reaping what I have sown. I forgive and release all those who have caused me hurt in any way and contributed to my forming these judgments. I declare dead on the cross all flesh that identifies me with these judgments. Make me like You, Jesus, and fill me with love and mercy. I now reclaim all spiritual blessings that I and my family have missed, and I ask You, God, to restore all the years that I have been in bondage to these things. In Jesus' name I pray, AMEN.

Ungodly Beliefs

Ungodly beliefs are defined as attitudes, judgments, agreements, beliefs, and decisions that do not agree with the Scriptures. Many ungodly beliefs are formed from trauma—negative experiences, words and hurts inflicted upon a person. The bottom line is that ungodly beliefs are lies—lies about others, ourselves, or God. They are often formed in childhood.

Any beliefs that do not line up with the truth of God's word must be written down and renounced. In order for the counselee to fulfill his or her destiny, new, godly beliefs must be created. Teens that do not root out ungodly beliefs are held back from maturing.

Many times a counselee needs help in identifying his/her ungodly beliefs because the beliefs have deep roots in experiences that may continue to be reinforced. For example, a counselee may have had a traumatic experience of rejection. Because of that experience, this person expects to be rejected. He believes he is rejected and behaves as if he were already rejected. Therefore, he experiences more rejection, thus confirming his ungodly belief.

When a person has accepted an ungodly belief, the mind is renewed by breaking any agreement with the enemy and declaring a new belief that is in agreement with God's Word. This step must be taken in order for the counselee to fulfill his destiny and be a complete person. (See Romans 12:2.)

In one's natural strength, breaking a habit takes usually twenty-one to thirty days. Replacing an ungodly belief with a new belief takes at least as long. The new belief must be acknowledged and spoken by the counselee for thirty days audibly for their ears to accept it.

Counselors will work with the teen or parent to form a list of ungodly beliefs, which may include:

- false guilt
- false identity, resulting from lies spoken over them by others
- not belonging
- rejection
- low self-worth
- shame
- unworthiness, etc. ("I will always be left out" … "it is my fault" … "no one likes me")

Our counselors and teens find Scripture to replace the ungodly beliefs with godly beliefs. For example, instead of saying, "I don't belong," the teen will say, "I fit in. With my healing, acceptance, and trusting God, He is putting people in my life who like me."

The following is a sample prayer based upon Romans 12:2:

Prayer of Repentance for Ungodly Beliefs

> Dear Lord, I forgive anyone who helped me form this ungodly belief of _____ [Name the belief.] Forgive me, Lord, for living my life based on this wrong belief by _____ [Name the behavior that resulted from this belief]. I forgive myself for believing that way.
>
> I renounce this ungodly belief and how I gave it place in my life. I break its power over my life now. I now choose to accept my new godly belief of _____ [List the new belief to replace the old belief.] In Jesus' name I pray, AMEN.

Conclusion

We have just finished reviewing the main areas which are part of the family history. Now it's time to go to Step 4 of our Triage Approach to Counseling: performing any essential surgery, i.e., prayer for people to be set free.

STEP IV

PERFORM
ESSENTIAL
SURGERY

CHAPTER 13

How to Help Someone Live in Freedom

IF YOUR CLIENT GOES THROUGH ALL THE NORMAL CHANNELS OF prayer, spiritual discipline, applying the Word, and he or she is still struggling, you may need to deal with oppression and other negative spiritual influences. You may discover the person urgently needs to experience freedom in Christ, or it may be delayed, depending on the individual case. So in EMT terminology, in Step 4 the teen can be tagged as either yellow (urgent) or green (OK to wait).

Understanding Negative Spiritual Influences

The same Bible that tells us about God and His holy angels also tells us about Satan and his fallen angels. These fallen spiritual beings are often referred to as demons or spiritual entities that are seen as "demonic" and which are in league with and under the control of Satan. They are out to do his bidding and to torment people. Once a person is born again, Satan attempts to unleash the forces of hell and does anything to keep a person from maturing and being an effective witness and minister for Jesus Christ.

People always debate: Can a Christian have a demon? My personal belief is that we can have anything we want to have, but that a Christian can only be oppressed, not possessed, because a Christian's spirit is already possessed by the Holy Spirit.

Believers can experience spiritual oppression because of open doors where Satan has a legal spiritual right to enter into peoples' lives and to torment and oppress them because of sinful choices. We open the door to sin when we choose to do something that is contrary to God's Word. As Christians, sometimes we have destructive or unhealthy behavior patterns where we've allowed negative spiritual influences to oppress us. Some see the concept of negative spiritual influences entering through an open door. Originating from Genesis 4:7 when God spoke to Abel and said, "If you do what is right, will you not be accepted? But if you do not do what is right, sin is crouching at your door; it desires to have you, but you must master it"

Demons are liars and usually lead to self-deception. Their purpose is to prevent or hinder salvation and sanctification.

There are many possible indicators of spiritual oppression. Be aware, however, that these behaviors may also indicate other disorders besides spiritual oppression. (Some examples of are: physical dysfunction, personality disorder, developmental delay, a lack of sound teaching, etc.). A list of indicators demonstrating possible spiritual oppression includes:

- Abnormal emotions: intense, exaggerated, out-of-control
- Abnormal sex life: little or demanding too much
- Breakdown of marriage and family: separation, divorce, abandonment
- Deception about normal personality: "This is just the way I am."
- Extreme bondage to sin: can't stop, even when trying hard
- Financial insufficiency
- Incapacity for normal living: inability to feel joy or satisfaction in life
- Inner anguish: turmoil, depression, mental lapses
- Rapidly changing personalities
- Reporting of demonic torment
- Restlessness and/or insomnia
- Self-inflicted injury

⅄ Tragic happenings and being overly prone to accidents
⅄ Trances
⅄ Violence; super-human strength

Let me say here that I know this is an area of ministry and counseling where there has been some controversy within the body of Christ and that there are a variety of opinions and teachings among sincere believers. I am attempting to share with you out of my own life and experience. It is essential that we are always praying for God's discernment so that we can accurately see and understand what is going on with a client; and secondly, we need His wisdom to know what to do with what He just showed us.

Questions to Ask About Oppression and Negative Spiritual Influences

If you suspect that a client needs significant freedom in an area of their life, you should schedule a time to talk with him or her about possible occult experiences from the past because these may have created an open door for oppression.

The following are questions that can assist in determining a client's previous involvement with occultic activities.

Has there, to the best of your knowledge, ever been involvement by you or anyone in your family history in any of the following? Have you ever:

⅄ Been involved with, read about, or possessed literature about cults such as Armstrongism, Christian Science, Jehovah's Witnesses, Mormonism, Rosicrucianism, Unitarianism, Unity, Buddhism, Silva, or any other cult?
⅄ Read or possessed false teachings on reincarnation?
⅄ Read or possessed occult or spiritualist literature such as books on astrology, metaphysics, scientology, magic, fortune telling, ESP, clairvoyance, psychic phenomena and other occult books

by such authors as Jean Dixon, Edgar Cayce, Arthur Ford or Ruth Montgomery?

⋏ Read or followed horoscopes?

⋏ Had your fortune told by Tarot cards, tea leaves, palm reading, crystal ball, 8-ball or I Ching?

⋏ Attended a séance or spiritualist meeting or consulted a medium?

⋏ Tried to contact the dead?

⋏ Consulted an Ouija board for fun, out of curiosity or in earnest?

⋏ Played with so-called games of an occult nature, such as ESP, Telepathy, Kabala, etc.?

⋏ Sought healing through magic conjuration and charming by anyone who practices false spirit-healing for such things as wart removal, burns, etc.?

⋏ Sought to locate missing objects or persons by consulting someone with psychic powers?

⋏ Practiced table-lifting, levitation, water-witching, or used a pendulum or wedding ring to predict the sex of an unborn child?

⋏ Practiced automatic writing or had your handwriting analyzed?

⋏ Used any kind of charm or amulet for protection—metal or otherwise—thus not putting your full trust in Jesus?

⋏ Sought psychic experiences or cast a magic spell (hex or curse)?

⋏ Possessed any occult or pagan religious objects—occult jewelry, idols, voodoo masks, etc.?

⋏ Practiced astral travel (attempts to project your spirit out of your body), telepathy, telekinesis, or any other forms of extra-sensory perception?

⋏ Been dependent on superstitions?

For each thing the client has experienced, the counselor should lead them in a prayer of freedom (which will be described later in this chapter).

A Christian's Authority over Negative Spiritual Influences

The ministry of deliverance was part of the ministry of Jesus, and He never sent out His workers to preach without giving them authority over Satan. "And these signs will accompany those who believe: In my name they will drive out demons; they will speak in new tongues." (Mark 16:17, NIV) Remember, Christ is the Deliverer, and the Holy Spirit is the Power of our ministry. "For this purpose the Son of God was manifested, that He might destroy the works of the devil." (1 John 3:8)

We cannot help people unless they want to be helped. Their willingness to be helped will be determined by their willingness to submit, to be honest with us, and follow our suggestions in counseling. "Therefore submit to God. Resist the devil and he will flee from you" (James 4:7).

We shouldn't look for oppression-based strongholds everywhere, but when we encounter them attacking us or the lives of those to whom we are ministering, we must deal with them.

Our Defensive Weapons

- ⅄ Renewed mind (2 Corinthians 10:3-5; Romans 12:1-2; Ephesians 4:22-24)
- ⅄ Spiritual armor (Ephesians 6:10-18)
- ⅄ Submission (James 4:7; 1 Peter 5:5-9)

Our Offensive Weapons

- ⅄ Name of Jesus (Mark 16:17)
- ⅄ Blood of Jesus (Revelation 12:11)
- ⅄ Holy Spirit (Matthew 12:28)
- ⅄ Word (Ephesians 6:17)
- ⅄ Prayer, praise, and a positive confession (Matthew 18:18-19, Psalm 149:6-8)

Both the counselor and the counselee must be prepared.

Counselor's Preparation

There needs to be a time of counseling/prayer before beginning a ministry session of this nature. We should pray for the Holy Spirit's leading as to whether this is truly a case of spiritual oppression or whether this person's problem is in the soul (psyche and emotions), rather than the spirit. For an overview on spiritual oppression, please see the "Glossary of Terms" in Appendix B.

We must pray for the gift of discernment. Many problems are branches from the main trunk. We must learn to identify the trunk when we see the branches. For instance, gluttony could be a branch growing on the trunk of frustration.

We cannot overemphasize the importance of prayer, fasting and faith. At times, it may be necessary to trust – to accept by faith that Jesus' Word is true and that a work has been accomplished in the individual's life. As Jesus said, "In My Name, they will cast out demons" (Mark 16:17).

We suggest fasting at least one meal as spiritual preparation, but we shouldn't do all the fasting. Let the person who needs to experience freedom do some fasting, too. Many times, spiritual oppression will work one of two ways as we approach the session – either there might be a temporary relief so that the person will actually wonder whether he or she needs this type of session at all, or there might be such internal conflict in the person that they appear to be in a lot of torment.

We must not be surprised if the person seeking freedom may feel intense anger or even hatred toward us. We have to remember that may be the spiritual oppression within them causing this.

We must be very approachable and treat people with love, kindness and tenderness. We shouldn't condemn them or appear shocked at what they have to say. We should ask questions and let them respond, be good listeners, and pray with them.

Counselee's Preparation

Before planning a session like this, you need to make sure that the counselee wants to experience freedom from *all* negative spiritual influences, not just certain ones.

I tell teens that they must "hate sin and mean business." Before the session, they should:

⅄ Repent and confess sins.

⅄ Start renouncing negative spiritual influences

⅄ Rid themselves and their surroundings of all reminders of involvement with negative spiritual influences (charms, books, records, friends, places).

⅄ Pray and fast for at least one meal (just as the counselor does).

⅄ Call on the name of the Lord (Joel 2:32).

⅄ Pray and read the Bible daily.

⅄ Read about spiritual warfare (if time allows). Ask forgiveness for sins. One of the biggest hindrances is an unforgiving spirit. I tell teens, "Forgive all, including yourself, and hold no grudges. Will yourself to forgive. (Forgiveness is not primarily a feeling but an act of your will). If you do not forgive, God cannot forgive you...nor deliver you. Here's how to ask forgiveness. If you have only thought wrong of another person, and it has not affected your behavior toward that person, you need only to ask God's forgiveness. If you have talked or acted in an un-Christlike manner toward another person, apology, restitution and restoration are necessary.

Other conditions that must be considered include:

⅄ Dominating spirit of one person over another

⅄ Excessive lying, stealing, coveting, any deceptive practices, etc.

⅄ Occult and cult involvement

⅄ Abortion that has not been confessed

⅄ The secret of fornication or adultery

⅄ Homosexuality

These things will also hinder experiencing freedom from oppression if the counselee does not renounce them. Prayers of confession could sound like this:

Prayer of Confession

Thank You, Lord Jesus, for dying for my sins, for Your glorious resurrection, and for making me a new creature in Christ by faith in Your precious blood.

Dear Lord, I have confessions to make. Through ignorance, stupidity, or willfulness, I have sought supernatural experiences apart from You. I have disobeyed Your Word [Deuteronomy 17:2-5; 18:10-12], and I ask You to help me as I renounce all these things. Cleanse me in body, mind, soul, and spirit, I pray. I am closing any door which I may have opened through contact with the occult.

I renounce all contact with witchcraft, magic, Ouija boards, tea leaves, and other occult games.

I renounce all kinds of fortune telling, palm reading, crystal balls, and Tarot cards.

I renounce the heresy of reincarnation and all healing groups involved in metaphysics and spiritualism.

I renounce all music which is not pleasing to my Heavenly Father and damaging to my soul and spirit.

I renounce all transcendental meditation, yoga, Zen, and all eastern cults and religions and idol worship.

I renounce all water witching or dowsing, levitation, table tipping, body lifting, psychometrics (divination through objects), and automatic writing.

I renounce, in the Name of the Lord Jesus Christ, all psychic heredity that I may have; and I break any demonic hold on my family line on both sides of my family.

I renounce and forsake every psychic and occult contact that I know about and those which I do not know about.

I renounce every cult that denies the blood of Jesus Christ, and every philosophy which denies the Deity of the Lord Jesus.

Lord, I have another confession to make: I have not loved, but have resented certain people; and I call upon You to help me forgive them [Matthew 18:22-35, Mark 11:25-26; Hebrews 12:15; 1 John 4:7-12].

Lord Jesus, now I forgive the following people for anything they have ever done to hurt or disappoint me: _____ [Insert here the names of persons living or dead who come to mind and how they hurt you.] In Jesus' name I pray, AMEN.

Helping Someone Take the Steps toward Freedom

Setting up the Session

- ⋏ Choose an area where you can be alone with no interruptions.
- ⋏ It is always best to have another Christian in the session for prayer support.
- ⋏ The counselee must not dominate the counseling session or any situation. We are in charge and should be kind but firm.
- ⋏ Most people have a poor self-image, and in the counseling session that self-image will be destroyed even more. It is our job to build this self-image.
- ⋏ Counseling sessions should not last more than one hour at a time.

Step 1: Set an Atmosphere of Praise

We have victory over spiritual oppression through praise (Psalm 149:6–9), so we should set the atmosphere with praise.

Step 2: Give Instructions to the Counselee

Before we begin, we must be sure the person understands what we are going to do *and* get their consent. Also give them the following instructions:

- ⋏ Be humble and acknowledge your need for help.
- ⋏ Be completely honest when you answer questions, but details are not necessary. (God already knows them, but you can speak them if speaking will help remove the internal darkness for healing purposes).

   ⅄ Be confident that your counselor is "unshockable" and trustworthy.

   ⅄ Don't pray at the same time the counselors are praying for you.

   ⅄ Be aware that some of your thoughts, attitudes, actions, etc., may be coming from negative spiritual influences.

   ⅄ You may experience some physical manifestations. Do not feel like you have to repress them

   ⅄ The Greek word for spirit is *pneuma*, which is also the word for "breath." -

Step 3: Pray for Protection

We pray protection for everyone involved and plead the Blood of Jesus Christ over everyone on the premises, members of our family, their family, etc.

Confronting spiritual oppression involves team effort. When we minister, we explain to the counselee that he is to minister as well and that we are praying together, agreeing in prayer. . In praying, we quote from the Holy Scriptures to counter the attack of the devil.

Step 4: Deal with Possible Blockages

Before the session begins, we must go over all areas that could block a person from experiencing freedom. Have we, along with the counselee, forgiven all who have hurt us? Have we renounced occultic practices? Have we confessed and received forgiveness for our sins?

It is good to make sure the person receives Jesus as their personal Lord and Savior before walking someone through the session. To ensure this, we have counselees repeat the sinner's prayer after us. For example:

> Dear Lord Jesus, I believe that You are the Son of God, that You died on the cross for my sins, and that You rose again from the dead. I confess You as my Lord and Savior. I repent of all my sins.
>
> I repent of all my contacts with Satan and all his evil works. I renounce any involvement with the occult. I repent and renounce all negative spiritual influences that I have allowed to enter into my life.

Lord, I forgive all others who have wronged me or harmed me. I lay down all resentment, all hatred, and all rebellion. In particular, I forgive _____ [Name key issues of forgiveness for this person.].

Lord, I ask you to forgive me and to cleanse me by Your precious blood. I accept it now. I accept your forgiveness, and I forgive myself.

Now, Lord, I loose myself from every negative spiritual influences in the name of Jesus, and I command them to leave me.

Lord, You said: "Whosoever shall call on the name of the Lord shall be delivered." I call on Your name right now, and I recognize You as my Savior and as my Lord

AMEN.

Step 5: Proclaim Freedom Over Strongholds and Negative Spiritual Influences

Next we claim Joel 2:32: "And it shall come to pass *that* whoever calls on the name of the LORD shall be saved." We name the demonic spirits and renounce them in the name of Jesus. We try to name strongholds and negative spiritual influences as specifically as possible. Be sure to refer to Appendix C of this book, which lists these things according to their specific groupings. After each proclamation, we praise the Lord.

Ask the Holy Spirit to show you the areas where freedom is needed for the person. You may pray:

I renounce and break agreement with the stronghold of _____ and its symptoms _____ [name the symptoms] In Jesus' name, I I proclaim freedom over. _____ I am free in Jesus' name.

Do this for every stronghold and related area of oppression until completed!

During the prayers, if the person becomes violent, we do not involve ourselves in a wrestling match. We simply pray for the peace of God in the name of Jesus. If additional sessions are necessary, we don't leave the sessions with too great an interval between them.

Step 6: End with Praise

At the end of the session, we should have a time of praise together and pray to the Father in the Name of Jesus.

Follow-up after Prayer Session

After Satan finished tempting Jesus in the wilderness, he planned to renew his attack on Jesus at a more "opportune time" (Luke 4:13).

Make sure the counselee understands that spiritual oppression can return, but he or she will be able to resist it with God's help. To retain this new found freedom, the counselees should continue to:

- ⅄ Yield every area of life to the Lordship of Christ (John 1:11-12; Matthew 7:21-23).
- ⅄ Be continuously filled with the Holy Spirit (Ephesians 5:18; Romans 8:13).
- ⅄ Live by the Word of God (Luke 11:13; Matthew 4:4, 7; Ephesians 6:17).
- ⅄ Wear the whole armor of God (Ephesians 6:10–18).
- ⅄ Cultivate the renewed mind. (Romans 12:1–2; 2 Corinthians 10:3–5; Romans 8:5–7; Colossians 3:1–2)
- ⅄ Pray in the Spirit (Romans 8:26–27; 1 Corinthians 14:2, 14–15; Jude 20).
- ⅄ Practice praise (Isaiah 61:3; 60:18; Hebrews 12:15).
- ⅄ Cultivate right relationships (Matthew 18:15–20; 1 John 1:7; 1 John 2:9–11).
- ⅄ Develop a strong, dynamic faith (Romans 10:17; Mark 4:24; Luke 8:18).
- ⅄ Practice confessing the Word of God (Hebrews 3:1; 4:14; 0:23).
- ⅄ Seek to obey the Lord in every area of life. If there is a failure, confess immediately (1 John 1:9). Conviction comes from the Holy Spirit; condemnation comes from Satan.
- ⅄ Make Jesus Christ central to all of life (John 12:31–32).
- ⅄ Learn how to crucify the flesh and resist the devil (Romans 6:6, 11; James 4:7, 1 Peter 5:8–9).

⅄ Avoid those people who become a bad influence on life (James 4:4).
⅄ Submit to the Lord, and to one another, in love and humility (James 4:7, 1 Peter 5:5–6).
⅄ Maintain a daily prayer life (Matthew 6:11–13).
⅄ Use the weapons of defense (2 Corinthians 10:3–5; Ephesians 6:13–17).
⅄ Use your weapons of attack: the Word, the blood, the name of Jesus, the Holy Spirit, prayer and praise, and a positive faith confession.
⅄ Maintain a disciplined life (Romans 12:1–2; 1 Corinthians 9:27).
⅄ Fast regularly to keep on the "cutting edge" in your spiritual life (Matthew 6:16–18).

Unsuccessful Prayer Sessions

Experiencing total freedom may not be completed due to:

⅄ Lack of true repentance. Repentance means a change of attitude and behavior.
⅄ Failure to confess sins (1 John 1:9; 5:16)
⅄ Failure to forgive others (Mark 11:25–26; Matthew 18:21–35)
⅄ Failure to break with occultic practices (Acts 19:13–19)
⅄ Unwillingness to be completely honest with God

If you feel the session was not a complete success, work with your client more on the areas that were lacking and then conduct a new session.

Conclusion

In this chapter we discussed:

⅄ How spiritual oppression operates
⅄ What symptoms it can cause
⅄ The six steps to leading a prayer session
⅄ How to maintain deliverance

In the next few chapters we will look at specific areas where freedom from negative spiritual influences is often needed in order for counselees to achieve victory in their lives. The first area we discuss is false religious beliefs.

CHAPTER 14

Confronting False Religious Beliefs

AMERICAN TEENS YEARN FOR THE SUPERNATURAL, BUT THEY SEEK it in the wrong spiritual world. Harry Potter, in the last ten years, has made a huge impact in this area and has been a fantasy escape that has led many teenagers into witchcraft and other occult oriented practices with devastating results. As counselors, teachers, parents and youth leaders, we find ourselves in a critical time for this generation. They are crying out for help! We don't want to be charged as guilty because of our lack of initiative commitment to help them. We cannot afford to allow this generation to continue to be enticed and lured by negative spiritual influences that capitalize on their fears and need for excitement and produce hopelessness, self-destruction and violence.

Being involved in occultic practices opens a person up to spiritual oppression. Heavy penalties come with occult activity (See Jeremiah 27 and Acts 16:16–18.)

As our nation slides back toward paganism, God's people need to understand the increasing influence, trickery, and cruelty of the evil one—while always thanking and following our God, whose power is far greater. Therefore, I plead with all of you to exercise great caution when confronted with any sign of Satan's work.

In the following testimonies you will read how teenagers became ensnared in the occultic practices but were restored through counseling, prayer and deliverance.

Going to the Occult for Answers: Amber's Story

I was born when my mom was sixteen—that's when my problems started. She was in and out of marriages, and I never got along with any of her husbands. One of my mom's husbands kidnapped me for a short while. One stepfather sexually abused me and my brother in the middle of the night. He is now in jail serving fifteen years. I saw some of his gross pornographic pictures.

My mom married again. I was miserable and started rebelling—getting into fights, drinking, sneaking out at night, skipping school. Then I began taking hard drugs: alcohol, marijuana, cocaine, other uppers and downers, including crack. My life got worse. I was looking for answers; I wanted to be accepted.

Next, I got involved in the occult, attended séances, drank animal blood and sacrificed a cat to a demon. Things kept getting worse. I tried to commit suicide eight different times. I thought there was no reason to live.

My mom was as desperate as I was, and she found House of Hope. At House of Hope, I found the acceptance and love I have always needed. I was delivered from the occult involvement and drugs, and healed from the pain of my past.

Started Occult at Age 7: Tiffany's Story

My name is Tiffany. I'm seventeen years old. When I was little, my mom and dad broke up after a violent fight. At that time my mom was a prostitute and a stripper, and was never really around for my sister and me. She was addicted to several drugs and had many boyfriends. At the age of two I was molested by my mom's boyfriend and developed a sexually transmitted disease that could have killed me. But thanks to God, I am cured.

When I was seven, I was pulled into a satanic cult. I started to see and hear strange things I thought were monsters. One night I was home alone watching the 700 Club and the lady asked, "Does anyone watching want to pray?" I had never even heard anything about Jesus Christ before. I accepted Christ and told my mom that she needed to go to church. I was only seven. I was surprised that she went, and shortly after that she became a Christian. She stopped stripping, prostituting and doing drugs.

In fifth grade, my grandmother died. I was so hurt that I began to cut my arms with sharp objects. My mom noticed blood on my sheets and clothes. She blamed it on my friends. Soon after, she took me to House of Hope.

I have been in House of Hope for a year now, and God has really done a turn-around in my life. My relationship with God has grown, and I'm learning to follow and listen to His voice.

I thank God for putting me in House of Hope where I received deliverance from a Satanic cult and healing from hurts in my past. There are so many people that love and care for me.

My favorite Bible verse is the twenty-third Psalm, even though I have walked though the valley of the shadow of death, I am not afraid for God is with me. The Lord is my Shepherd.

Note: At this time, Tiffany is happily married and is expecting her first baby.

Gangs, Witchcraft and Porn at 11: Joann's Story

My name is Joann. My life was pretty good until I was ten years old and my grandpa died. I would cry myself to sleep. After that, my parents got divorced, and because of that I had to switch schools a lot. My grades dropped from As to Fs. I didn't know how to deal with the grief.

Then at the age of eleven, I started smoking marijuana, dating older guys, drinking and going to clubs. Then because I wanted to look like my friends, I started selling my body to afford clothes. What I didn't buy, I shoplifted. I got involved in gangs and pornography. I ran away several times and was arrested. Finally, I was brought to House of Hope.

Soon after I got to House of Hope, I accepted Jesus Christ as my Lord and Savior. Through counseling, I was taken through a grieving process because of all the losses in my life. I'm a born-again virgin. My family is being restored, which I thought would never happen, and I learned that Jesus Christ is going to love, accept and forgive me — no matter what.

I was reading the book of Esther in the Bible and I want to be like Queen Esther. She was always brave and courageous. I am taking the chance of losing popularity, just as she did, to help others and to help save my generation. I want to tell my friends about the Jesus I've found and how He has helped me process my hurts.

In Philippians 4:19, it says that I can trust God to meet all of my needs because I have learned to pray and seek Him first. I don't have to steal or sell my body because Jesus has promised to provide for all of my needs.

Occult Symbols

Occult symbols are fast replacing Christian symbols in our culture. Go to www.Radioliberty.com to find a well-defined and illustrated list of occult symbols. We encourage you to use this list to warn others. (Click on the link titled "Symbols and Their Meanings.") Many Christian kids are inadvertently wearing and displaying these symbols because they are popular.

Some of these symbols have double meanings. For example, the pentagram has been used to transmit occult power in all kinds of rituals for centuries, but to Christians the same shape may simply represent a star—a special part of God's creation. The image of a fish may mean a sign of the zodiac (astrology) to some, but to Christians it has meant following Jesus and sharing the message of His love. We will continue to delight in the cross, while recognizing that others use the same image to represent their dark forces.

Please don't pass judgment on those who happen to wear these symbols. Instead, let us seek God's will and discernment so that we might all honor Him with our lives and understand that He is first concerned with a person's heart. Remember, "So then each of us shall give account of himself to God. Therefore let us not judge one another anymore, but rather resolve this, not to put a stumbling block or a cause to fall in *our* brother's way." (Romans 14:12-13)

Definition of a Cult

Rather than getting involved with the *occult*, some of our teens and parents have been ensnared in *cults*. A cult is a perversion, a distortion of biblical Christianity and as such, rejects the historic teachings of Christianity. In practice, it usually denies the divinity of Christ, the blood atonement, or His bodily resurrection. According to Walter Martin, a cult is a group of people polarized around someone's interpretation of the Bible. It is characterized by major deviations from Orthodox Christianity relative to the cardinal doctrines of the Christian faith, particularly the fact that God became man in Jesus Christ. A cult is characterized by the following:

1. **New truth.** Many cults promote the false idea that god has revealed something special to them.
2. **New interpretations of Scripture.** They believe they alone have the key to interpreting the mysteries of the bible.
3. **Non-biblical source of authority.** Some cults have sacred writings as a source of authority that supersedes the bible.
4. **Another Jesus.** All cults have false teaching about the person of Jesus Christ in light of historical biblical Christianity.

5. **Rejection of orthodox Christianity.** Many cults argue that the church has departed from the true faith.

6. **Non-biblical teaching on the Trinity.** Cults tend to either outright deny this or have an inadequate view.

7. **Salvation by works.** One teaching totally absent from all cults is the gospel of the grace of god.

8. **False prophecy.** Cults often make bold predictions of future events, supposedly revealed by the inspiration of god.

9. **Reincarnation.** Some cults claim that each person must continue to be reincarnated until the spirit is purified of fleshly attachments.

Just as teenagers fall into the lure of drugs, sex, Goth and peer pressure to meet unfulfilled needs in their lives, so are we seeing them lured into cults in great numbers. Increasingly today we see a large number of teen converts to cults such as Hare Krishna, The Way International, spiritualism and much more. Most Christians also believe that Jehovah Witnesses and Mormon are cults.

These teenagers may have attended church regularly with their parents and were met with sermon after sermon on Christ but were left missing something. The cults are offering fascinating rituals plus promises of spiritual experiences and miracles. These are all things that Christ spoke of, but sometimes they are missing from the teachings at church. Or the teens may have looked to their parents and noticed they were not walking out what was discussed week after week at church. In contrast, in the cult, the teen sees every person passionately living out what is preached.

Teens who have gone through trauma—which includes almost all our clients—are particularly susceptible to cults because the cults offer the things they need and want—a listening ear and a feeling of belonging. Cults offer intense interaction and involvement in each other's lives—things a hurting teen is desperately seeking.

For us to assist parents and the teens that have been tangled in the web of a cult, we need to be knowledgeable of the Word of God. The cults claim to have the answers but really don't; the answers are found in the Bible and in the Lord Jesus Christ.

CHAPTER 15

Freedom from Sexual Perversion

MANY TEENS COME TO HOUSE OF HOPE IN BONDAGE TO SEXUAL perversion and find freedom through our prayer ministry.

Society creates sexual perversions among teens by interrupting their social development with sexual activity. The expected norm among teenagers in America today is to be sexually active. By tenth grade, more then half of American teenagers have had sex. By the time the teens graduate from high school, the number who have had sex jumps to two-thirds.[1]

Many adults in sexual addiction programs today are suffering from their adolescent issues. Some never stop acting like teenagers because they have never finished their development from teenager to adult. They have not discovered their identity.

This interruption of the development process may result in highly self-destructive sexual behavior, causing physical and emotional trauma. Those teenagers who have been the victims of sexual abuse usually reenact their traumas in sexual perversion.[2]

Some teenagers never learn how to receive love from their peers through social interaction. Sex becomes the only form of love that they know how to give and receive. Teenagers long to be intimate and have deep emotional needs, but if they never learn how to be close to others, they have to rely on sexual activity to make them feel loved.

This type of arrested social development is not something that begins in adolescence. Learning how to be socially well adjusted is a skill that is developed throughout a lifetime, beginning in early childhood. Teenagers with the emotional capacity of children are confused and unprepared to handle the adolescent feelings of sex and intimacy with others. In turn, these feelings of confusion lead to poor cognitive understanding of sex. When a teenager does not understand sex, it often results in addictive or compulsive sexual behavior.[3]

Prayer for Freedom from Perversion: Drew's Story

When I was twelve years old, my friends introduced me to pornography. They showed me how to steal magazines with pictures of naked women from the convenience stores, and then they taught me how to find pornography on the Web sites.

My problems with pornography started small, but they soon got bigger and bigger. I didn't know how addictive this stuff was to look at. I prayed for God to get me out of it, and that seemed to work for a while. I still got depressed a lot, though. I didn't want to talk to anybody, and whenever my friends tried to say something to me, I would hang up on them or cuss them out.

I was even depressed on my birthday. I sat there like a lump of coal at family outings. Sometimes I would laugh and play around when I felt like it, but most of the time, I moped.

I wanted to take drugs, but there was no way for me to get drugs because I was a PK—a preacher's kid. My friends gave me some drugs, but they also showed me how I could crush up over-the-counter drugs, like Motrin and Advil, to get a little buzz going. I took those pills from bottles in the family medicine cabinet. I replaced the pills I stole with sugar pills. Motrin and Advil really didn't do anything, but it was kind of a thrill to get away with it anyway under my parents' noses.

Another six months went by, and I just went downhill. Some new kids at school showed me Web sites for paintball guns, real guns and Airsoft rifles, which shoot pebbles and BBs. It did not take long to get from one Web site to another.

I got right back into pornography when my friends brought it to school. They had it in their lockers, and each time they showed me a picture of a naked woman, something inside me was stirred up. I couldn't stop myself from looking. I started downloading all kinds of stuff on my computer until my dad found out. He discovered that I had visited over four hundred porn sites.

My dad and mom prayed with me about what was best for me. My dad then called Sara and said the best thing I could do was go to House of Hope and get some help. My father said it would be fun, and I would learn a lot.

My first day at House of Hope was a Monday. I sat in the front office while my parents were getting counseling from Sara. The people that work here said everything would be all right, but I cursed at them.

I still wanted my pornography. My counselor prayed for deliverance from sexual perversion and pornography. I had to close the door to demonic spirits.

I would like to tell you it was magic and that I was never tempted. I have been out of House of Hope for four years, and I often have to make the choice not to go to the wrong places online. I have learned to overcome temptation. God always provides a way of escape when we ask Him.

CHAPTER 16

Freedom from Eating Disorders

IF I HAD TO GUESS, I WOULD SAY THAT HALF OF THE GIRLS ARRIVE AT House of Hope's doorsteps with an eating disorder. It's that prevalent.

Prayer for freedom may be a necessary part for a client to achieve victory over an eating disorder. In cases where freedom is needed, the spiritual power is broken and the ability to choose food wisely is returned. But I do want to be clear that not all eating problems have a demonic root. Psychological causes can also cause serious eating disorders.

Obsession with Food

At first glance, we can't tell whether our newly-arrived teen girls are anorexic or bulimic, but they give us hints in the first week or two. We notice that they always raise the subject of food and have an unbelievable focus about the subject. They ask us questions like: What kind of meals do you have here? Are there snacks? Are the apples organic or regular? Is this yogurt low fat or nonfat? How many fat grams in the lasagna? Do you know how many calories this cake has?

We are fortunate that House of Hope teens eat well, thanks to donations from local supermarkets. I remember the early days when lunches consisted of peanut butter and jelly sandwiches, and the dinner staple was spaghetti with Ragu sauce—and we were thankful that we had enough to eat!

Today we serve well-balanced meals with variety, so when a House of Hope teen begins skipping breakfast, picking at her lunch, doing strange things at dinnertime (like pouring ketchup over her salad), acting fearful around fatty foods, reading salad dressing bottle labels, wishing everything we served were low fat or nonfat, we take notes. When they make a big deal about drinking a Diet Coke or always having something in their mouths like sugar-free gum or sugar-free candy—something to keep their mouths moving—then we know they have a fixation with food.

Controlling Food

Sheila was scared of food. She told me that she had binged when her family vacationed at the beach. She ate everything she could for four days—she really pigged out. Then she would throw up for three days by drinking water and tickling the back of her throat. Just to be sure she got everything out, she took laxatives. —Sheila, age fifteen

Sheila was what *Zest* magazine calls a "hedged hedonist"—someone willing to do something unhealthy but who compensates for it afterward. We've heard stories about girls buying a half-gallon of chocolate chip ice cream and trying to eat it in one night. Then they would do a hundred push-ups and a hundred sit-ups and drink a gallon of water, believing everything would cancel out.

This extreme behavior is one reason why eating disorders are a touchy subject. Raising the ED issue with teen girls risks sending them underground. Why? If you ask them point blank if they have an eating disorder, they'll deny it. Those who have been borderline anorexic upon arrival at House of Hope often move into bulimic eat-and-purge activity. They do this despite living in a group home situation, where their peers can hear them vomiting in the bathroom. This still doesn't stop girls from trying because they are determined to *control* food.

Pressure to Be Thin

Eating disorders are common, dangerous and difficult to deal with. Those with eating disorders are enigmas wrapped in loose-fitting clothes.

Although boys are sometimes affected, 95 percent of eating disorders involve girls and young women who think they're fat, weigh too much, are depressed about their looks, fuss over fat grams, and obsess about miniscule weight gains. It's my belief that teen girls are heavily influenced by what they see in fashion magazines. Runway magazines such as *Vogue* and *Elle* drip with glamour, and their models must be rail thin or they are banished from the haute couture of Milan and Paris. (From a study done at UCLA, they discovered that the average model weighs 23 percent less than the average woman.)

Teen-targeted publications such as *Seventeen* contain articles on taking laxatives for weight loss or step-by step directions for following the latest fad diet. Reading these magazines puts ideas in a girl's head.

No wonder a significant survey of female attitudes revealed that many feel the greatest pressure to be thin comes from the media, followed by their peers and their family.

Pressure comes from other sources as well. At the same time elementary-age- girls are enchanted by petite figure skaters and pixie gymnasts, they are playing with Barbie dolls, which, if human sized, would have an eye-popping thirty-nine-inch bust and tiny eighteen-inch waist.

If your teens watch TV in the afternoon, they will hear guests on the *Oprah Winfery Show* gush to the charismatic Oprah about "how good you look"—after she's lost another twenty pounds. Elsewhere on the small screen, a survey found that 70 percent of television characters are thin and only 5 percent were overweight. Example: TV's number-one walking billboard for flesh and bones is Calista Flockhart of Fox's *Ally McBeal*(1997–2002), who shrunk from a size 2 to an unbelievable size 0. Are young women turned off by her pencil-thin frame, which can't weigh more than ninety pounds? No, because young women say that it's better to be too thin than too fat.

A boyfriend can place incredible pressure on a young woman. If she gains ten pounds, he'll say, "Well, don't get bigger than that." What's she supposed to think a week later when the scales announce more pounds? What's she supposed to think when she overhears what guys say about other girls—"She's porky," or "Look at those thunder thighs"? This is what she's thinking: "If he says that about her, he'll say it about me."

If you were to walk into a room of girls, I'd guarantee you could read these thoughts in many of their minds: "Look at her. Her legs are so much longer and thinner than mine." "Look at her figure. She looks like Courtney Cox." "She has no pimples. How come I am always breaking out?" "Her hips are perfect. Mine are so huge." "I wish I were thin."

Thinness has not only come to represent attractiveness, but success, self-control, and higher economic status as well. The following are the Thin Commandments, as written by Carolyn Costin, the clinical director of a California eating disorder clinic and author of two books. They are a sad commentary on the warped perspective that society is giving women about their bodies.

The Thin Commandments

1. If you aren't thin, you aren't attractive.

2. Being thin is more important than being healthy.

3. You must buy clothes, cut your hair, take laxatives, starve yourself, or do anything to make yourself look thinner.

4. Thou shall not eat without feeling guilty.

5. Thou shall not eat fattening food without punishing yourself afterward.

6. Thou shall count calories and restrict intake accordingly.

7. What the scale says is the most important thing.

8. Losing weight is good. Gaining weight is bad.

9. You can never be too thin.

10. Being thin and not eating are signs of true willpower and success.

Years of Battle Eating Disorders: Diane's Story

My name is Diane, and I am now blessed with a wonderful family. However, when I was a young girl I was sexually abused.

I placed the memory far away and continued on with life as the "perfect child." I was involved in many extra-curricular activities where I shined, but I always stayed away from boys.

My senior year of high school I went to a party where a boy pushed me into a corner and kissed me against my will. I only remember blacking out. This is when my eating disorder began.

That unwanted kiss had triggered something inside of me. I started limiting my diet to water and crackers. However, I had to be very careful that my "perfect" image wasn't shattered by my need to control something in my life.

A couple of months later I headed to Bible college, and that fall I was sitting with a group of girls when one of them was discussing her own battle to overcome sexual abuse. The memories flooded me as if I had been hit with a brick.

I stopped going to classes and I began overeating. I gained a lot of weight. In my sophomore year of college I began to throw up after meals. I spent a couple of very tumultuous years of partying during breaks, sexually acting out and being miserable in my own skin.

In October of my junior year, I had a very bad seizure and was sent home unable to work or drive. I was finished—emotionally, mentally and physically.

When I came home I started limiting my food intake, taking diet pills, laxatives and exercising up to five hours a day. I lost weight very quickly to the concern of my family. Strangely enough, I liked their attention, and I liked being able to focus on this new obsession. It kept my mind off everything I wished I could erase. I was busy counting calories, worrying about what new diet pill to buy and wondering whether my body looked any thinner then thirty minutes before. I was safe behind my new mask—"a full-blown eating disorder."

When a doctor cleared me to go back to work, I knew I couldn't continue in my current eating disorder, so I switched back to bulimia.

Two years later, the eating disorder went out of control. I was throwing up almost everything that went into my mouth. I couldn't stand to be around food or anything associated with food, and I certainly didn't want it in me. If I did eat without throwing up, I would cut myself as punishment for allowing myself to consume food. My gastroenterologist was very concerned as I know had developed IBS, GERD, hemorrhoids, gastritis, and esophigitis. For the first time in my life I started having cavities and teeth problems. I was moody and angry with everyone, especially myself.

Eventually a counselor declared this was enough and said I needed a residential treatment program. I checked into a Christian program that does all spiritual counseling. The inner healing prayers I received and went through are what lead me to my healing.

I also learned the most important lesson of my life, which is understanding who I am in Christ. I am a precious jewel, God's most valuable possession.

Today I work as a counselor to and lead others on this same journey of healing.

Freedom from Gluttony: Cathy's Story

Once Cathy was the college fraternity's sweetheart, the center of attention, popular and loved by everyone. But after Cathy was married for six years, she found herself fat and eating constantly. These were Cathy's words:

I know what it's like to be overpowered by habits...

I thought I would always be fat: I'd never have a nice figure again. I ate and yet was never satisfied. Devouring a whole loaf of bread with peanut butter at one sitting was normal for me.

I had become a miserable victim of a hopeless cycle. The more I ate, the more I disliked myself; the more I disliked myself, the more I ate! I eventually expanded from a size 12 to a size 18 dress. Occasionally I would attempt to break the terrible treadmill of eating that I was on. But my efforts always ended in disaster. I tried every fad diet imaginable, hating myself for not being able to do anything about my weight. I felt like a huge mistake. I was afraid and alone and in rejection because of my obesity...

One day a friend told me about a House of Hope counselor who might be able to help me. Through counseling I found my hassle with food was a sign of a deeper struggle, an inside conflict. The counselor prayed for a spirit of gluttony to leave me. I fell in a heap on the floor. It was at that point she prayed for God to fill that void that had been left with His love and acceptance.

The counselor was not sure what sin allowed the demonic spirit to come in, but it had to leave in Jesus' name. It was only after those prayers that I began to set goals that could deal with my problem. She helped me find ways to change old habit patterns not only in my food selection but also in physical and spiritual discipline.

After we found the root cause, self-control became easier. My normal weight became a reality. I began a steady, daily weight loss, and today I am wearing a size 12 dress once again. I feel like a new creature because of God.

God cares about you just the way you are. Maybe you have a void in your life. He'll make all things new for you, too, no matter what habit seems impossible for you to break. Nothing is too big for God to change!

What Counselors Suggest Can Be Done by Parents

Since you could go hungry waiting for the mainstream media to present a balanced view of what girls *really* look like, I call on moms and dads to step up and offer encouragement and a counterpoint. Here are some things parents can do:

Watch for overnight changes when their daughter hits her "growth spurt."
Puberty can do amazing things to the body. A five–foot-tall, flat-chested girl weighing 110 pounds in the seventh grade can become a five-foot-four girl weighing 150 pounds who needs a 34C bra as she enters the eight grade! Of course, she's wondering what hit her. She will worry about her new weight or whether someone notices the zit on her face. Parents can help her through this difficult time by telling her stories of how they felt during their growth spurts. They should compliment her growing body. If she develops a large bust in middle school or high school, she will hear friends tell her that if she loses weight, her chest size will shrink. She may start starving herself. *This is when she needs her parents the most.* They can discuss the issue with love and draw her out. If she actually needs to lose weight, parents can counsel her on losing weight the *right way.*

If a teenage daughter is watching what she eats, watch what you say.
Dinnertime comments such as "Getting chubby, aren't we?" or "Do you really think your body can afford that chocolate cake?" will not win anyone the Parent of the Year award. Repeat after me: *If you can't say something nice about a child's weight, don't say anything at all.*

Let me AMEN that to include comments about other people as well. Laughing at portly men or pear-shaped women sends the wrong message and reinforces the vilification of overweight people and the glorification of slenderness. Listen to how a teenager described her friends with eating disorders:

> *Most of my friends with eating disorders weren't fat at all. They were disgustingly skinny and had been disgustingly skinny their entire lives. They had eating disorders because they wanted to please their parents, maintain their weight and look good for the family. One of my friends felt like she had to lose weight because her parents made fun of her pudgy sister, saying things like, "Why don't you lose weight?" She wasn't overweight; she was just pudgy. My friend became bulimic because she didn't want that to happen to her.*
> *—Adrianne, age 15*

Don't even joke about it.

Even saying, "So, eating again?" could be enough to start a girl obsessing about food.

Don't constantly talk about dieting and losing weight in front of your children.

If you're in the midst of a personal struggle with your weight, resist the temptation to give the family a play-by-play description of lost ounces and gained pounds. If the children see you obsessed with counting fat grams and measuring portions, they will become just like you. Gulping diet pills, laxatives or diuretics shows a persistent concern with body image. If you are dieting, don't make a big deal about it. Quietly go about your business.

Even if you're dieting, continue serving three well-balanced meals a day.

Children need nutritious food to grow and to fuel puberty. It does no good when parents skip meals—coupled with making the children feel guilty for being hungry. Parents should continue to cook complete meals and eat with the family, just giving themselves smaller serving sizes.

Give girls the facts about weight.

- ⅄ Fact: The average American woman stands five feet, four inches tall and weighs 130 pounds.
- ⅄ Fact: Supermodels stand close to six feet tall and weigh between 100 and 110 pounds.
- ⅄ Fact: 65 percent of American women wear a size 12 or larger.
- ⅄ Fact: your body shape is much determined by family genes.
- ⅄ On the other hand, the facts also show that eating disorders are dangerous and carry long-term health effects.

Up to 10 percent of the girls with *anorexia nervosa* die from the disease. Those who survive are left with shrunken organs, bone mineral loss (which leads to osteoporosis later in life), low blood pressure, damaged reproductive organs, and an irregular heartbeat, which can lead to cardiac arrest.

Binge eaters develop gall bladder disease, heart disease and certain types of cancer. The stomach acids being regurgitated do not help the digestive tract nor does throwing up make girls skinny. If a teenager eats a salad with lettuce, cheese, bacon and croutons, the first thing to come up is the food that contains the vitamins.

Know the signs of bulimia.

To see if a teenager is bulimic, keep an eye out for telltale signs. Watch for frequent visits to the bathroom, watery eyes and scraped knuckles from gagging, and playing music in the bathroom to muffle purging sounds.

Tell children that they look beautiful—early in life and as often as possible.

Alone in her bedroom, a girl can be looking into a mirror and saying to herself, "You are fat; you are fat. If you could lose just a little more weight, you would be a much better person." If she is talking to herself and saying, "You are fat," who's going to offer a counterpoint? It has to be Mom and Dad. Boost her self-image by reminding her how beautiful God made her. Love her even when she's acting unlovable. You can improve a child's self-esteem by continually complimenting her gifts, talents, inner beauty and character qualities *rather than her appearance*. Let her know that it is not her "outside" that you love or are proud of, but rather her "inside." Love her unconditionally.

Remember that eating disorders are very much about control.

Parents constantly harping on their daughter to "do something" about her weight or vowing to "take control" of the situation are backing their daughter into a corner. Often anorexic girls feel that they have lost all control of their lives, but the one thing they can still reign over is the amount of food they put into their mouths. When anorexia or bulimia becomes a control issue, it's best to seek professional help.

If she's losing weight, it's hard for her to stop.

A girl with an eating disorder thinks: "If I were skinny and beautiful, I'd be popular." This thinking creates a never-ending downward spiral that often leads to a crash. That's why 105-pound twigs think they are fat and have to lose more. Saying, "We've got to fatten you up" is something you should never state to an anorexic teen. This will alienate her more than pull her out of her tailspin.

Invite her to talk to you.

The last people an anorexic teen will approach for conversation about this issue are her parents because of the shame. That is why parents need to take the first step. She wants to hear them express their love for her and tell her that she's the most important person in the world. She needs to hear them say they are willing to help her with anything.

Conclusion

In this section, we've looked at the steps of praying for spiritual freedom and wholeness as well as specific areas where prayer ministry is often needed. After experiencing freedom it's time for Step 5—Setting Up Counseling. In other words, once the hurts are being healed and they are free from the bondage that has held them captive, clients are ready for the ongoing counseling that will keep them healthy.

STEP V

SET UP
COUNSELING

CHAPTER 17

Healthy Boundaries and Relationships

WE HAVE REACHED THE FINAL STEP IN OUR TRIAGE APPROACH TO counseling—physical therapy. This is the point at which an EMT would give a patient a white tag, meaning only minor injuries remains and the patient can be prepared for home care. The EMT would set up a plan for physical therapy.

At House of Hope, when a client leaves our house, we go to Step 5 of our Triage Approach to Counseling, which is physical therapy, or continued counseling. The purpose is to maintain the progress that has been made and to continue the healing process. Counselors are always available to give our teens and parents guidance, healing and direction.

Weekly counseling may or may not be arranged. Either way, House of Hope counselors are always available to give our teens and parents should they have questions or needs. When these future issues arise, counselors may go back to one of the previous steps to address it, particularly praying for inner healing or spiritual freedom.

There are several things that we, at House of Hope believe are necessary for long-term success after counseling. The next three chapters will deal with these three key issues:

1. Boundaries, which create healthy relationships

2. Good self-esteem and knowing their identity in Christ

3. Positive peer pressure from family, friends, community and church

4. Building a Strong Faith

The rest of this chapter will focus on the first key—boundaries. You will learn what areas in your lives need boundaries, how to identify a lack of boundaries, the benefits of boundaries, and how to establish boundaries. Both teens and parents reap rewards from learning about boundaries.

Boundaries—What Are They?

People in general work well when expectations are clear. The real issue is not only clear expectations, but also consistent consequences. As counselors and caregivers we need to be very mindful to work to balance love and boundaries, grace and consequences. We also need to be aware of the traps set by the "charming" clients and/or parents and not succumb to their manipulation.

We all know that a boundary is a border or limit that acts as a dividing line between one person's space and another. But I also believe that boundaries have two sides. They keep others from invading one's space but they also keep you from going past the standard you have set. When there are no boundaries, life is blurry and everything is acceptable. That kind of living and thinking is one of the main reasons we have clients!

There are some areas in life that have natural boundaries over which we have no control. For example, skin is a good and protective boundary. It holds in good things (i.e. blood, organs, bones, etc.,) but keeps out harmful germs and bacteria.

The word "no" is the first word that most toddlers learn to say. Why is it their first word? Because that is the one word they have probably heard the most. *No* protects them from being burned, from unnecessary falls and tumbles, from the stairwell, from putting dangerous things in their little mouths. This word creates a boundary.

As we age, the word *no* also protects teens (and adults) from doing wrong things others want them to do. It also keeps others from doing things to teens that are unkind, unhealthy and ungodly.

We tend to forget that God uses this word, too. When He says no or, "Thou shalt not," He is saying it for our best interest. God does not say "NO" to ruin a good day; He sets boundaries that prevent His children from making unwise decisions that will have life-long consequences.

What Boundaries Do for Teens

Boundaries allow teens to learn and practice self-control.

As they participate in life, they have new experiences. Imagine what it would feel like to be sent to another planet — where *nothing* is familiar, where nothing is OK, where you don't know the rules or the law. How would you live? How would you survive? Teens without limitations are lost and uncomfortable, although they want you to believe differently.

Teens may complain about having boundaries, but they do like to know the limits. Limits provide a safety net that brings a sense of security. Without that limit, anything goes! Believe it or not, those ambiguous boundaries (or no boundaries) are what cause chaos and confusion.

Boundaries clarify unhealthy thinking in regard to self and others.

How far are you willing to go? What are you willing to allow others to do to you? Where is your line in the sand? Better yet, how did you determine where to put that line in the sand? Without boundaries, anything goes, and that is not what God had in mind as He created you and the teens with whom you are working.

Boundaries promote love.

That statement is true, but first it will create a scene! Ask a troubled teenager about the validity to this statement, and you might not like what you hear. How many times have you heard a teen say these kinds of things:

"These rules are stupid."

"Why can't they let me do what other kids to?"

"My parents are old and overly protective."

"I am going to do what I want to do regardless of their rules."

"I hate it when my parents tell me no."

"I may outwardly live by their rules, but inside I am not doing it willingly."

At House of Hope, setting boundaries is one of the toughest jobs for our house staff! Most of these teens come from families where limits have resembled amoebas (constantly changing shape) or have never been established. Consistency (at home) was not an issue because in most cases, it did not exist.

Parents Do Try

I need to stop here and give credit where credit is due. We have had many parents (especially single parents) who have tried to set boundaries with their children but have been unsuccessful in getting the teen to adhere. When we look back at family history, in a majority of cases we find that consistency has not been enforced. Because of overwhelming stress and strain, emotional upheaval and daily demands, it is difficult to stay strong. Exhaustion and frustration can overwhelm parents to the point of just caving in!

You see, there is a battle going on in every family where teens reside. The teen wants to be free, and the parents want the control. Unfortunately that can mean war, but it does not have to be that way. Teens must learn that freedom is earned by becoming responsible.

Parents have a lesson to learn in this process as well. Parents must learn when to set boundaries and when to let go—allowing the teen to make decisions and deal with consequences of those decisions. With love, respect and support, parents need to keep the limitations in place no matter how crazy the scene may become. Inconsistency will destroy the relationship.

It is not only the teens who come to House of Hope with heavy hearts and bowed shoulders! Often there are many tears of shame that fall from the eyes of the parents— tears of frustration, tears of failure and humiliation for having their children in treatment. You can taste the frustration of the mom who wrote these words:

> *I don't know how it happened. Little by little, I lost control. When my marriage fell apart, I gave her everything. I went back to school so I could earn better money. I bought a house, and it was just the two of us for a long time. When I started dating again, everything went south. She did everything in her power to destroy our relationship. She got out of control and started just acting out, even when I was not with my fiancé.*
>
> *She was screaming, punching holes in the walls, lying about everything, stealing, shop lifting, sneaking out, sneaking strangers in, and skipping school. I felt like I lived in a war zone every day. I wanted to give her all the things I did not have. I wanted her life to be easier than mine. Is that so wrong?"*

I like what Dr. John Townsend says in *Boundaries with Teens*

> God made parents to be the guard rails on the twisting road of life. You [parents] need to be strong enough for kids to crash into over and over and over again. You must stay strong so that your teens will learn to stay on track. Guard rails get dinged up. But if they work well, they preserve the young lives that run up against them. (Zondervan, 2006, page 32),

Signs That a Teen Lack Boundaries

What kinds of behaviors indicate that a teen is suffering from "wobbly" boundaries or a complete lack of limitations? Here is a partial list to consider:

- Disrespect! They possess an attitude of disrespect toward authority figures and parents
- They are often mean (physically and verbally) to siblings and friends.
- The teen is constantly challenging rules and requests by authority figures.
- They are quite lazy and unwilling to take care of their responsibilities.
- Moodiness is over-exaggerated with no warning signs.
- Integrity issues are prevalent.
- He or she may not do homework, skip school and run away.
- The teen selects friends that are unsuitable.
- Angry explosions seem to arise without warning.
- Substance abuse or addictive behaviors are prominent. (Drugs, alcohol, smoking, pornography, etc.)
- Violence and physical aggression toward anyone or anything are observed.
- Nothing appears to make the teen happy and the general attitude is negative.
- Sexual activity is considered a casual form of recreation.
- Motivation is lacking on all fronts.
- Chores and household responsibilities are ignored.

Areas That Need Boundaries

God has declared the boundaries of His love so that we can know how to maintain a healthy relationship with Him. In the same way, we need to have boundaries for ourselves and respect the boundaries of others in order to maintain healthy and loving relationships.

It is essential to have boundaries in the following areas to become healthy, happy adults:

- ⊼ Feelings
- ⊼ Attitudes
- ⊼ Values
- ⊼ Desires
- ⊼ Behavior
- ⊼ Time
- ⊼ Abilities and talents
- ⊼ Personal belongings
- ⊼ Space

Warning: If you don't teach teens how to maintain good boundaries with others, their healthy relationships will be stolen from them. As they enter adulthood, they will be angry, bitter, and rebellious.

Healthy Boundaries for Parents

Too often parents take responsibility for the teen's feelings or they feel constrained by a false sense of responsibility that denies them a choice about doing what the teen demands. These are the result of the parent's unhealthy or non-existent boundaries. To help their teen establish healthy boundaries, the parents must take back control of their own lives where they have yielded to others, especially to their children. This is not going to be easy.

One of the reasons that we require parents to enter counseling, attend parenting classes, and visit their teens regularly is to help them build and maintain boundaries. It does the teen very little good to work on his or her issues without tackling the big issues of boundaries. You can make the following suggestions to help families establish much-needed personal boundaries:

⅄ Explore the roots of the conflicts and identify the areas where boundaries (or lack of boundaries) have caused the most problems.

⅄ Get into an accountability group with people who will tell you truth, say no, and help set limits.

⅄ Learn how to give and receive forgiveness.

⅄ When you pray, tell Him the truth.

⅄ Speak the truth to all people.

⅄ Understand the difference between submitting to authority and allowing others to control you.

⅄ Set your limitations and establish consequences for those who ignore your boundaries.

⅄ Give—with no strings attached—to those who legitimately need help.

⅄ Learn to respect others' boundaries.

As I said earlier, learning to set boundaries or re-establishing boundaries is going to rock the boat. You cannot avoid that! I can only encourage you to keep moving forward and not to give up. Keep your eye on the prize.

Overcoming Parents' Stumbling Blocks

There will be times when the teen—and the parents—feel like throwing in the towel out of disappointment and frustration; both may want to run away far and fast. Here are a few stumbling blocks that may try to hinder the process of setting healthy boundaries.

⅄ Not wanting to hurt another person's feelings

⅄ Not wanting to make someone else angry

⅄ Fear of feeling rejected, ignored or abandoned

⅄ Feeling you are being selfish to set limits

⅄ Thinking that God does not approve of your boundaries

⅄ Fear that you will lose your job, friends or position if you set boundaries

⅄ Thinking you will be disloyal to all those family members and friends who have helped you in the past

This is what Drs. Henry Cloud and John Townsend say about setting limits in their book, *Boundaries:*

> God the good Parent, wants to help us, His children, grow up. He wants to see us "become mature, attaining to the whole measure of the fullness of Christ" (Ephesians 4:13). Part of this maturing process is helping us know how to take responsibility for our lives.[1]

As counselors, we must make it abundantly clear with the parents that by not setting boundaries, they are robbing their teens of the opportunity to mature and become healthy and happy adults.

God's Has Authority to Set Boundaries

Who ultimately decides every boundary? The answer to that question is easy. God must be acknowledged as the supreme authority. Teens want freedom, so it is understandable that they will rebel against God, too.

When God's Word talks about submitting to authority, it is the same as honoring and respecting boundaries. The Bible is clear that God expects obedience:

> Obey My voice, and I will be your God, and you shall be My people. and walk in all the ways that I have commanded you, that it may be well with you. —Jeremiah 7:23

> Let us hear the conclusion of the whole matter: Fear God and keep His commandments, for this is man's all. —Ecclesiastes 12:13

His Word has much to say about rebellious attitudes and actions.

> But they rebelled and grieved His Holy Spirit; so He turned Himself against them as an enemy, *and* He fought against them. —Isaiah 63:10

Children are to obey their parents and that means to function within the boundaries that the parents set!

> Children, obey your parents in all things, for this is well pleasing to the Lord. —Colossians 3:20

> My son, keep your father's command, And do not forsake the law of your mother. —Proverbs 6:20

> Listen to your father who begot you, And do not despise your mother when she is old. Buy the truth, and do not sell it, Also wisdom and instruction and understanding. The father of the righteous will greatly rejoice, And he who begets a wise child will delight in him. Let your father and your mother be glad, And let her who bore you rejoice. —Proverbs 23:22-25

Teens must be taught what Scripture says about giving respect to adults, including teachers.

> Likewise you younger people, submit yourselves to your elders. Yes, all of you be submissive to one another, and be clothed with humility, for 'God resists the proud, but gives grace to the humble.' —1 Peter 5:5

> Remind them to be subject to rulers and authorities, to obey, to be ready for every good work, to speak evil of no one, to be peaceable, gentle, showing all humility to all men. —Titus 3:1-2

Discovering Boundaries, Derek, age 17

I am Derek, and I am seventeen years old. My parents divorced when my dad sold drugs to everyone on the block. He was physically and verbally abusive to my mom and me. He continually cheated on my mom, and even bought prostitutes home with him. He called me names and yelled at me. "You are a loser!" "You are worthless and a hopeless mess!"

When I was thirteen, I never went to school. I smoked, drank, took pills, had sex, and did all kinds of bad stuff. I missed so much school because I was always high. I stole money to buy drugs. I even took my dad's gun to rob people, and I hung out with gangs.

Mom finally had enough. I was not listening to her or respecting her in any way. Why should I? My dad didn't! She brought me to House of Hope. I was mad...

I hated it there at first. I would not obey any rule. Miss Sara suspended me. That made me start thinking about my life and the chaos and trouble I was experiencing daily.

I made a decision to try it another way but was not sure I could come back to House of Hope. Finally Miss Sara called and told me I could come back if I was willing to be obedient.

Since then, I have accepted Jesus into my heart. I caught up three grades in school in less than one year. I am also learning how to respect other people's boundaries and submit to their authority. I may not always like it, but because God says I need to do that, I will.

My favorite Bible verse is Psalm 63:1 (NKJV): "O God, You are my God; Early will I seek You; My soul thirsts for You; My flesh longs for You in a dry and thirsty land where there is no water."

The truth is that no one can live without boundaries. The earlier one learns to live within them and respect other peoples' boundaries, the happier and healthier they will be. Life without limits produces chaos. It is my hope that all of us counselors have strong boundaries that we can use in dealing with these hurting teens and their families.

Now It's Your Turn...

Let's check ourselves as counselors:

- ↖ How strong are your boundaries? Do you struggle to set limits with the teens you are counseling? Do you allow them to curse in your office?
- ↖ Are you consistent with your teens? When you give assignments, do you follow up to see if they have completed the tasks? How do you handle their lack of cooperation?
- ↖ Have you ever had a time in your life when you struggled with personal boundaries? What did you do to reinforce them?

What Happens When Parents Let Go

There was structure during the fifties, and parents were definitely stricter. They enforced spoken and unspoken rules that were not to be broken. In the 1950s teens knew what was right and wrong. Everything was black and white, and shades of grey were not discussed. Few climbed out of the cultural box or went on adventures that moved them from their family or birth area. Many married high school sweethearts or college sweethearts and settled down after high school or college to raise two or three children. If you were a teen during the 1950s, you knew the meaning of responsibility! Today, things are different!

Parents can no longer have the "ostrich syndrome," in which parents turn blind eyes and deaf ears to their teenagers. They put their heads in the sand because they either don't want to be involved or don't know how to be involved in their teen's lives.

Here are some stories that House of Hope teens shared about their daily lives before coming to House of Hope. When their parents found out about their children's lifestyle, some were devastated. Their emotions ranged from sadness to anger to guilt, and total disbelief.

> *A typical day of mine would definitely begin with a wake-n-bake [wake up and get high], and then I would throw on some clothes to go to school. At school, my high would usually start to wear off in second period or lunch, so I would go take more drugs either in the bathroom or skip the rest of the day. By 2, I would be over at friends, getting blazed. I came home by 9 only to smoke more weed before I went to sleep."—Emma*

> *A typical day for me before I came into House of Hope would usually consist of me trying to recover from the night before. Hangovers were pretty much an everyday thing for me. When most kids were at school, I was popping a couple of Tylenol to cure the headache and calling around and figuring out what party I was going to that night. My life revolved around going out every night, getting wasted, having sex and then passing out. To me that is what I thought having a perfect life meant, but since I have come to House of Hope I've learned that there is a different way to live."—Leigh*

> *When I was at home the usual day for me started at 6:30 a.m. I would wake up and get ready for school. I would come home at 2:45 p.m. and would usually get on MySpace.com. Then I would watch TV and do some homework. I would get on the phone and talk for hours. When my mom would get home, my brother would talk to her and I ignored her. Then we would start getting into fights and arguments. I would blame my brother and get into fist fights over it. I never handled my anger very well. I went off for the smallest things."—Tina*

> *Before I came into House of Hope, a day for me was as follows: I would wake up, wait until my mom left for work, and smoke the cigarettes I stole from her. Then I would pop*

*as many pills as I could find so I felt comfortable in myself. I
would get a ride from my mom's friend or skateboard or walk
to school. I would wait in the courtyard until first period bell
rang and then go to class. When second-period bell rang,
I would usually find my friends and hit the drug stores so
that we could buy cigarettes and beer. (We knew which ones
would sell to us.) We would get high and drink the "cool stuff."
Then I would run back to school when the last bell rang and
get a ride home with a friend or walk home. By the time I got
home, my sister and mom were there. I'd run to the bathroom, take a cold shower, go in my room and lock my door
until supper time. Usually I would blare the music, light the
candles and wait until my mom went to bed and then sneak
out to go and be with my girlfriend."—Angie*

Boundaries Are Protection

Most teens will scream and shout about having boundaries, curfews
and being supervised. The revealed truth (usually months down the
road) indicates that they like knowing how far they can go and what they
can and cannot do. Working with teens is a balancing act. They want to
know the limits, and at the same time they want their independence.

We cannot put a wall around them and completely protect them from
the world, but as professional counselors working with teens and their
parents, we can set boundaries. Believe it or not, teens really do like to
know where the boundaries are. They want to know just how far they
can go, and they test those limits!

Boundaries keep teens from wandering too far and crossing the line.
They also keep other people out of their space. Whichever side you are
working on, the boundary is a form of protection!

Boundaries allow teens to learn and practice self-control. Boundaries
also clarify unhealthy thinking with regard to themselves and others.
Finally, boundaries promote love. That is a tough one for teens to recognize and understand, but again, with consistency, over time, the teen will
appreciate this expression of love and will become self-governing.

God's Clear Boundaries

Again, it is important that we invite God to every counseling session because He is our example for setting boundaries. He is 100 percent clear about what should be inside the boundaries, or those things that He loves:

- ⅄ Righteousness (Psalm 33:5)
- ⅄ Children (Mark 10: 13-16)
- ⅄ His people (2 Chronicles 2:11)
- ⅄ The world (John 3:16)

In the same way, He is extremely clear about what should stay outside the boundaries because they are the things that He hates:

> These *six* things the Lord hates, Yes, seven *are* an abomination to Him: a proud look, a lying tongue, hands that shed innocent blood, a heart that devises wicked plans, feet that are swift in running to evil, a false witness *who* speaks lies, and one who sows discord among brethren. —Proverbs 6:16–19

This verse says the Lord hates these seven things:

- ⅄ Pride
- ⅄ Lying
- ⅄ Violence
- ⅄ Wickedness
- ⅄ Evil
- ⅄ Evil thoughts
- ⅄ False oaths

God has declared the boundaries of His love so that we can know how to maintain a healthy relationship with Him. In the same way, we need to have boundaries for ourselves and respect the boundaries of others in order to maintain equally healthy and loving relationship.

Warning: If we don't maintain good boundaries with others, our cherished treasures will be stolen from us. These treasures include some or all of the following:

- ⊥ Balanced feelings
- ⊥ Positive attitudes
- ⊥ Strong morals and values
- ⊥ Deepest desires and goals
- ⊥ Acceptable behaviors
- ⊥ Quiet time
- ⊥ Creative abilities and talents
- ⊥ Personal belongings
- ⊥ Personal space

We must help the teens become aware of areas in their lives that show boundary problems and explore the roots of those conflicts. We must teach teens what boundaries look like, what they feel like, and what purpose they serve.

Conclusion

A lack of personal boundaries will manifest itself in unhealthy relationships. For example, a person with unhealthy or non-existent boundaries will often take responsibility for another person's feelings. He or she will feel constrained by a false sense of responsibility that forces him or her to submit to others' expectations. To establish healthy boundaries, he or she must take back the control that was yielded to others.

CHAPTER 18

Good Self-Esteem and Learning Their Identity

I WOULD LIKE TO MAKE A BOLD STATEMENT ABOUT SELF-ESTEEM. Proverbs 23:7 says, "For as he thinks in his heart, so *is* he." If a teen thinks he is a failure, he will live up to that expectation. If a teen believes that she is "a piece of trash," she will become that. A teen's self-image becomes reality.

Our mission is to give teens the right self-image so that God can repair the damage that has been done, put them back together again, and make them whole.

This chapter will teach you how to restore teens' self-esteem through confessing Scripture and how to educate them about their true identity in Christ.

Self-Esteem

If I gave you a quiz right now about your self-esteem, how would you score? Maybe you would do well; maybe you would chalk up your findings as a bad day, getting up on the wrong side of the bed, or some event that has brought you to your knees. Imagine if you will, what a teenager feels like—one who does not have the years of experience or the education to realize that "these moments" actually happen in life but they don't stay forever. To them, the days drag on forever and because they lack the mentoring, nurturing, and coping skills, they start a downhill, slippery slide.

I am not going to give you a pop-quiz regarding your self-esteem; however, see if you can answer these questions:

- ⋏ How do teens develop self-esteem?
- ⋏ Who teaches them about self-esteem?
- ⋏ Is there really such a thing as self-esteem?
- ⋏ How do you build self-esteem in a teenager?
- ⋏ What part does trust play in self-esteem?
- ⋏ Can you improve a teen's self-esteem permanently without changing the family?
- ⋏ What does inner healing have to do with self-esteem?

The answers to these questions are at the core of any counseling philosophy.

As I see it, when a teen's self-esteem has been destroyed, you can be sure that somewhere during the earlier years of his life, he heard lies about himself and chose to believe them. When we present the truth, it looks so different that many teens cling to the lies, even though they have caused a great deal of pain, because that is their comfort zone.

Steve Russo, author of *Protecting Your Teen from Today's Witchcraft*, describes the teen mindset this way:

> Seven out of ten teens say there is no absolute moral truth, and eight of out ten teens claim that truth is relative to the individual and his or her circumstances...The one word that seems to be in the frontal lobes of most teens' philosophy of life is *whatever*. Combine their world views, values, and mosaic style of thinking, and you will realize that they're incredibly comfortable with a number of contradictions in their lives....But keep in mind, they are most likely unable to explain why they feel the way they do.[1]

What is the difference between the lies they have been living with and the truth that we are going to instill in their hearts and minds? Our truth is foundational. We can show it to them in black and white because it is found in God's Word. We can prove it! When the teen accepts God's image of them, the change in their attitude is amazing. Listen to this poem written by one of our teenage boys about his potential.

A Poem: Nate, age 17

(Nate wrote this poem before graduating from House of Hope.)

I am a branch that grows from the vine.
My mission is to rise as high as I can, as long as I can,
Bearing as much fruit as I can along the way.
No one can stop me because I am connected to the vine.
If you cut me, I'll grow longer, stronger and faster.
If you put something in my way, I'll go over it, around it,
Sometimes even under it,
Or I'll find a crack and go through it.
I'll embrace every obstacle along the way,
Since each one is as a rung on a ladder.
Every triumph gives me the hunger I need to climb.
Every adversity gives me the strength and
courage I need to prepare for the next level.
This is who I am.
This is my destiny
For I was born to rise!

Scriptures to Build Self-Esteem

The following are important Scriptures we use to build self-esteem. As part of the program's requirements, we have clients memorize verses. Our purpose is for them to recite them and meditate o them until they get them in their heart.

For I know the thoughts that I think toward you, says the Lord, thoughts of peace and not of evil, to give you a future and a hope. —Jeremiah 29:11

And the Lord will make you the head and not the tail; you shall be above only, and not be beneath, if you heed the commandments of the Lord your God, which I command you today, and are careful to observe them. —Deuteronomy 28:13

When you pass through the waters, I will be with you; and through the rivers, they shall not overflow you. When you walk through the fire, you shall not be burned, nor shall the flame scorch you. —Isaiah 43:2

Jesus said to him, "If you can believe, all things are possible to him who believes." —Mark 9:23

Now this is the confidence that we have in Him, that if we ask anything according to His will, He hears us. And if we know that He hears us, whatever we ask, we know that we have the petitions that we have asked of Him. —1 John 5:14–15

My soul waits silently for God alone, for my expectation *is* from Him. —Psalm 62:5

For with God nothing will be impossible. —Luke 1:37

From the end of the earth I will cry to You, when my heart is overwhelmed; lead me to the rock that is higher than I. For You have been a shelter for me, a strong tower from the enemy. I will abide in Your tabernacle forever; I will trust in the shelter of Your wings. —Psalm 61:2–4

Be anxious for nothing, but in everything by prayer and supplication, with thanksgiving, let your requests be made known to God; and the peace of God, which surpasses all understanding, will guard your hearts and minds through Christ Jesus. —Philippians 4:6–7

Identify: Understanding Who They Are in Christ

There are basic lies that cause even born-again believers to be ensnared in wrong thinking and thus wrong living. A person who has an ungodly belief about their identity will find freedom in knowing their identity in Christ.

During our counseling sessions, have the counselees list, with our help, words that describe the false identity that has controlled their lives with lies. Beside that list, we write what God says. For example:

False Identity	God Identity
Helpless/victim	Hopeful/victor
Burden	Blessing
Fearful	Full of faith
Guilty	Forgiven/redeemed
Trapped/limited	Delivered/free

Then we have a time of prayer where the counselees renounce and break the agreement with the lie of the false identity and replace it with the truth of the God identity. Then we have them declare all that follows.

> I affirm the truth of who I am in Christ. I am a new creation; old things are passed away. I forgive all those who helped me form these lies about myself, including myself. And I choose to receive the truth of who I am in Christ. I renounce the lies and receive the truth. I now am being ruled by Jesus Christ and who I am in Him. With the revelation of the following Scriptures, I am walking in faith and victory, allowing the making of a warrior in, to and through me—to be and to do whatever He has purposed and destined for me, thus accomplishing His will on earth.
>
> *I am...*
> ⅄ God's child (Romans 8:17)
> ⅄ Forgiven (Ephesians 1:7; Hebrews 9:14; Colossians 1:14; 1 John 1:9; 2:12)

⅄ A new creature (2 Corinthians 5:17)

⅄ The temple of the Holy Spirit (1 Corinthians 6:19)

⅄ Delivered (Colossians 1:13)

⅄ Redeemed (1 Peter 1:18–19; Galatians 3:13)

⅄ Blessed (Deuteronomy 28:1–14; Galatians 3:9)

⅄ A saint (Romans 1:7; 1 Corinthians 1:2; Philippians 1:1)

⅄ The head (Deuteronomy 28:13)

⅄ Above only (Deuteronomy 28:13)

⅄ Holy (1 Peter 1:15-16; Ephesians 1:4)

⅄ Elect (Colossians 3:12; Romans 8:33)

⅄ Established (1 Corinthians 1:8)

⅄ Made nigh (Ephesians 2:13)

⅄ Victorious (Revelation 21:7)

⅄ Set free (John 8:31–33)

⅄ Strong (Ephesians 6:10)

⅄ Dead to sin (Romans 6:2,11; 1 Peter 2:24)

⅄ More than a conqueror (Romans 8:37)

⅄ Joint heirs (Romans 8:17)

⅄ Sealed (Ephesians 1:13)

⅄ In Christ Jesus (1 Corinthians 1:30)

⅄ Accepted (Ephesians 1:6)

⅄ Complete (Colossians 2:10)

⅄ Crucified with Christ (Galatians 2:20)

⅄ Alive (Ephesians 2:5)

⅄ Free (Romans 8:1)

⅄ Reconciled to God (2 Corinthians 5:18)

⅄ Qualified (Colossians 1:12)

⅄ Firmly rooted (Colossians 2:7)

⅄ Circumcised (Colossians 2:11)

⅄ A fellow citizen (Ephesians 2:19)

⅄ Built on Jesus Christ (Ephesians 2:20)

⅄ As He is (1 John 4:17)

⅄ Born of God (1 John 5:18)

⅄ His faithful follower (Revelation 17:14; Ephesians 5:1)

⅄ Overtaken with blessings (Deuteronomy 28:2; Ephesians 1:3)

⅄ His disciple (John 13:34–35)

⅄ The light of the world (Matthew 5:14)

⅄ The salt of the earth (Matthew 5:13)

⅄ The righteousness of God (2 Corinthians 5:21; 1 Peter 2:24)

⅄ A partaker of His nature (2 Peter 1:4)

⅄ Called (2 Timothy 1:9)

⅄ The first fruits of His creation (James 1:18)

⅄ Chosen (Ephesians 1:4; 1 Peter 2:9)

⅄ An ambassador (2 Corinthians 5:20)

⅄ God's workmanship (Ephesians 2:10)

⅄ The apple of my Father's eye (Deuteronomy 32:10; Psalm 17:8)

⅄ Healed (1 Peter 2:24; Isaiah 53:5)

⅄ Being changed into His image (2 Corinthians 3:18; Philippians 1:6)

⅄ Raised up (Colossians 2:12; Ephesians 2:6)

⅄ Beloved of God (Colossians 3:12; Romans 1:7; 1 Thessalonians 1:4)

I have...

⅄ The mind of Christ (Philippians 2:5; 1 Corinthians 2:16)

⅄ Obtained an inheritance (Ephesians 1:11)

⅄ Access to the Father (Hebrews 4:16)

⅄ Overcome the world (1 John 5:4)

⅄ Everlasting life (John 5:24; John 6:47)

⅄ The peace of God (Philippians 4:7)

⅄ Received power (Mark 16:17–18)

I live...

⅄ By and in the law of the Spirit of Life (Romans 8:2)

⅄ By faith (2 Corinthians 5:7)

I walk...

⅄ In Christ Jesus (Colossians 2:6)

I can...
⅄ Do all things through Christ (Philippians 4:13)

My life...
⅄ Is hid with Christ in God (Colossians 3:3)

I shall...
⅄ Do even greater works than Jesus (John 14:12)

I possess...
⅄ The Greater One in me (1 John 4:4)

I press...
⅄ Toward the mark for the prize of the high calling of God
(Philippians 3:14)

I always...
⅄ Triumph in Christ (2 Corinthians 2:14)

I show forth...
⅄ His praises (1 Peter 2:9).

Parents Hold the Key to Self-Worth

Who is helping teens build their identity? Who is teaching teens about self-worth and acceptance? Somehow parents have fallen away from their parenting responsibilities and have gotten caught up in the business world. They work eight to ten hours a day. Many have two jobs just to survive. So the nurturing, mentoring and child-rearing has fallen on the shoulders of the teachers and youth pastors. Yikes!

Teens desperately want acceptance and support from their families. While they may do some outlandish things to get attention, underneath all of those behaviors is a deep-rooted desire to be loved by the immediate family. George Barna writes,

Mom is typically the most revered figure in the life of a teenager. Almost 6 out of 10 teenagers (57 percent) say they are emotionally very close their mothers; 9 out of 10 teens contend that emotionally they are at least fairly close to their mothers."[2]

Even if the family is struggling, even if Mom and Dad are out of control, even if there is evidence of abuse, drugs, alcohol, adultery and other problems with Mom and Dad, the teen still has that need to be loved by the family. The teens' worth, value and self-esteem are bathed in family events. Can you now understand why it is imperative that we work toward the goal of family restoration and not just bringing wholeness to the teen?

God Is Erasing the Damage: Brittnee, age 15

I am Brittnee. I am fifteen years old. I have been at House of Hope for ten months.

Growing up I was rejected by my parents. They favored my brother. He could do no wrong. My brother hit me, and I would get punished. My mother verbally abused me, and I hated myself. She would tell me I was no good. She would call me names and tell me I was a mistake. I was so angry that I lashed out at my mom.

I was looking for someone to love me. I was accepted by a group of people at school who took drugs. My life went downhill fast.

I once was a virgin and pure. I had never even been kissed or hugged.

My life was changed by a dealer and drugs.

I had flashbacks like lightning in my head.

Not remembering, I woke up crying in my own bed.

Cops asking questions—why was I bleeding and bruised?

They said I should be dead.

I was raped by a stranger and sexually abused.

I told Mommy and Daddy, "Please don't worry.

At least I am alive to tell my story."

Now I am being healed and no longer sad.
It is in my past and God is my Dad.
He is erasing all the damage that has been done.
Because of Jesus, my life shines brighter than the sun.
I have prayed and been forgiven.
Since coming to House of Hope, my relationship with my mom is awesome. I like the Scripture in Psalm 147:3: "He heals the brokenhearted and binds up their wounds." Jesus is healing my broken heart and is healing my hurts. I want to serve Jesus and help other people who have been hurt like I was.

The teens keep coming. Their names change. Their faces change. The stories still break your heart. Just for a moment, consider what might have happened to Brittnee if she and her mother had not received counseling. What do you think she would be like today? What would she be teaching *her* children?

So many teens arrive at House of Hope feeling utterly worthless. Here is a poem written by one of our girls that painfully expresses those feelings.

What Was It Like? Tara, age 16

What was it like
To be disowned and neglected,
To never have your wants and needs respected?
I never had a father.
My mom was never around.
I only had a stepdad,
Who criticized and brought me down.
Every time my stepdad hit me,
Where was my alcoholic mother?
Where was she
For every bruise I had to cover?

So I turned to sex, deceit and weed.
I found an artificial comfort.
It always left a bad taste in my mouth,
But it temporarily filled my need.
What was it like?
It was hard.
And the road was so long.
And because of God's grace,
I am slowly moving along.
The Lord only gives us what we can take.
He heals our hearts and makes us stronger.
And He loves us with a kind of love
That is impossible to fake.

CHAPTER 19

Positive Peer Pressure

HEALING RELATIONSHIPS ARE VITAL. GOD DID NOT WANT ADAM TO be alone, so He made for him a helpmate. From the beginning of time, relationships have been important, and they still are. We believe that helping individuals to find community, group, church and friend support is a huge determination of success.

This chapter focuses on the following areas of support:

- community
- church
- group therapy.

Community Support

At House of Hope, we create a community of support for our clients even after they graduate. One of our House of Hope graduates, Jenna, did a great job of describing how she felt about this support.

I loved being in the program and loved everyone there. They showed me what true love felt like, and more important, they showed me how to accept love in my life and how to show other people the love of Christ. I know for a fact that I wouldn't be where I am today if it weren't for House of Hope.

House of Hope taught me how to have the courage to let people love me back, but, more important, I also learned to love God with all my heart and to love myself.

Throughout everything that I went through, House of Hope was a door opener to a greater part of my life. I have learned so much and gained back an entire family. I wouldn't still be doing so great if I didn't have such an amazing support system cheering me on as I continue my walk with Christ.

My counselor and house staff from House of Hope are so much more than that to me now; they're family. It's not what I put into the program itself that matters to me now; it's everything that I left the program with. The important thing that I've learned throughout my journey so far is that no matter how many mistakes I make or regardless of what happens, God, my family, counselors and close friends will always be there for me. We all have friends and loved ones that are only in our lives for a short season, but the family I've gained from House of Hope will be in my life forever.

Jenna's story shows how a Christian community can work together to support a wounded person.

Church

In alarming numbers, Christian teens are walking away from the traditional church. Most teens at House of Hope say that church is boring and sermons don't relate to what's happening in their lives. They go to youth groups for fun and food and to hang out with peers. Most are looking for entertainment with very little spirituality.

At House of Hope we encourage parents to select a church that believes in the Trinity so they can participate and interact with the community and build a basis for their family social life. We involve the teens in music, drama, praise and teachings that are Bible-based. We make it perfectly clear what it means to be a true follower of Jesus Christ. It is important to find a church where teens can respond to the message, and where they hear lively music, and where they are allowed to participate—a place where they can find healthy friends. These churches **DO** exist!

The Power of Friends: Bryan, age 17

I was doing fine until I hit fifth grade and met Kevin. After we became friends, he introduced me to his buddies. We looked out for each other, especially when we started stealing stuff from stores.

One of the guys would say, "Hey, let's do a beer run," so we'd walk over to the Cumberland Farms Mini Mart and case the place. I would walk to the back where they kept the beer behind the refrigerated glass doors. Our beer of choice was Red Dog, so when the clerk was busy ringing up a customer, I would grab two quarts, act like I was looking for the bathroom, and then sprint out of the back door. I did most of the stealing.

I was usually gone before the stupid clerk knew what was happening, but one time a lady chased us in her van. She found my friends, but they told her that they didn't know where I went. When the coast was clear, we shared the beer, which got us drunk.

Growing up in the Miami area, it seemed as though I was always getting in trouble. By the time I reached seventh grade, I was kicked out of school. My parents signed me up for some type of Christian boarding program where I came home on the weekends. I know that Mom and Dad had their hands full trying to raise my two brothers and two sisters and at the same time dealing with my problems.

I got suspended from school twenty times; constantly stole candy, sodas, and other food items; and constantly got arrested. The local cops and shop owners came to know me well because they knew I couldn't go into a store without stealing something.

My parents knew they had to do something, so Mom moved the family to a new city so that I would no longer hang out with my old friends. Dad commuted to his accounting job in Miami and would stay down there during the week, coming home on weekends.

It wasn't long before I started making new friends— friends who became so important that I basically stopped going to school. I didn't like hanging around home because I constantly got into fights with Jenny, my sister who was six years older.

Because Dad was gone all the time, I felt as though I should be man of the house. Jenny would get on the phone and make these long-distance calls to her old friends back in Miami, and I didn't like her running up the phone bill. So I would smack her to get her off the phone, but she didn't appreciate my efforts to save the family money. Several times she called the cops, and I was given a domestic violence charge.

I got back at her. Every once in a while I would steal Jenny's car, and half the time she didn't know about it. I also started stealing from cars—stereos, money, whatever I could find in there. I did it to get some money to buy weed.

Meanwhile, the local cops were learning my name, and my brushes with the law earned me a trip to a court-ordered school, but I kept getting into more trouble. I got arrested so many times that I knew how to put my hands in the correct position—behind my back, hands together, fingers pointing downward—to make it easier for the cop to slap the cuffs on me.

The last time I got arrested, I knew this judge was going to be tough. I expected the worst—to be sent to a lockdown facility for eight to sixteen months. This judge had heard about House of Hope, though, and this is where I landed.

> *House of Hope is where I heard the Gospel for the first time and where I learned how important it is to surround myself with good friends. You see, I always got in trouble because the people I used to hang out with were up to no good. Since they were up to no good, I was up to no good.*
>
> *I can see now why one of the rules at House of Hope is that you can't see old friends from your past. I used to break it, but now I see the importance of having friends who can have a positive influence on me.*
>
> *This I do know: The more good friends I make, the less bad things happen to me.*
>
> *A righteous man is cautious in friendship, but the way of the wicked leads them astray (Proverbs 12:26, NIV).*

Brian had to go through a lot of hurt because of his friends. At House of Hope we teach them how to choose good friends.

Group Counseling

We have found at House of Hope that our group counseling provides an excellent means of hearing from others in similar circumstances, sharing one's own pain, and hearing and receiving encouragement. Parents and teens have the benefit of a trained counselor to navigate the participants through difficult territory. In group counseling, people laugh and cry together, bonds are developed, and growth is inevitable. Parents and teens find freedom because they realize they are not alone. Many receive healing just because they are able to identify and relate to others. Because God designed us to live in families and communities, it is important that we teach our clients how to function together based on shared values, mutual responsibilities, and faith principles.

There is usually a good amount of flexibility within the group at the onset when the core values are established. The counselor and parents/teens develop guidelines for confidentiality, boundaries, appropriate behavior, etc. The parents and teens help define these core values and even give specific examples of potential problems and learn how to resolve them. The desired result is that all members have a "buy in" and recognize that their contributions are not just appreciated but vital.

We keep in mind that every group member is in a different place mentally, emotionally and spiritually. We never push anyone who seems to not want to participate in the discussions, rather, we remind them that they are invited to be a part and their input is meaningful.

Conclusion

Positive change can be undermined by bad influences from the community or simply a lack of positive support. Make sure your clients keep open communication with you, find a strong church, and participate in group counseling as needed.

In the same way, the spiritual growth that is experienced at House of Hope needs to be supported after the client leaves the residential program. We encourage clients to continuously build their faith by focusing on the following three areas:

1. Thinking
2. Speaking
3. Hearing

We call this putting "faith into action," and I will describe how we do it in the next chapter.

CHAPTER 20

Keys to Building Faith

GOD HAS GIVEN US FAITH TOOLS TO HELP TRANSFORM TEENS AND parents from a dead existence to a vital relationship with Him. We find it is essential that parents develop their faith along with their teens. Faith runs in families, and we know without faith they can't please God and fulfill their DNA—Destiny Now Arriving!

Three faith tools are essential in defeating the chaos. They are:

- ⅄ Thinking: having a positive thought life.
- ⅄ Speaking: learning to say the right words.
- ⅄ Hearing: the ability to hear from God and listen to others

Thinking: Having a Positive Thought Life

Someone wise once observed, "Satan uses our mind as a dark room where negatives are developed." These negative thoughts can sabotage any person's life. That's why our first strategy for building faith is to get rid of negative thinking.

We find in Romans 12:2 that our lives can be changed by the "renewing of our minds by the washing of God's Words." Proverbs 23:7 says, "For as he thinks in his heart, so *is* he."

Christian speaker and author Graham Cooke has wisely pointed out, "If teens will change their minds, God will change their hearts."

That's why we spend so much time helping parents and teens to bring their thinking in line with the Bible. Our goal is for these teens to reject their past thought lives and adopt the good, acceptable and perfect will of God that will guide their choices and renew of their minds.

We, as counselors and parents, know that mind changes do not happen overnight; they take time.

We teach them that it is not a sin to have a bad thought, but it is a sin to entertain it and put it into action.

We help parents and teens realize that entertaining doubt and fear is like driving a nail with a hammer. Each thought makes a deeper imprint.

Teenager's minds are a battlefield of chaos, with media, music, porn, etc. battling for attention. We offer some simple suggestions for parents to assist in renewing their minds:

1. Turn off the TV, or watch TV as a family.
2. Spend more time together as a family doing things.
3. Read Scripture and talk about it.
4. Attend church together.
5. Get teens involved in a good youth group.
6. Parents should get involved in a life group or home group.
7. Talk about what you are learning.
8. Journal.
9. Have quiet times and listen to God.
10. Have meals with the family; make them mandatory.

In summary, a positive thought life is our first strategy for building faith.

Speaking: Learning to Say the Right Words

Our second strategy is to teach parents and teens how to speak the right words. The words we say have power to develop their faith and create a positive identity based on Scripture. Spoken words can be negative or positive, creative or destructive.

Proverbs 18:21 says, "Life or death is in the power of the tongue. Those who love it will eat its fruit." Words are so powerful! They can be blessings or curses. Our words can work against us or for us. We can speak God's Word of blessings, life and victory, or we can tear other people down.

We have teens arrive at House of Hope carrying labels the size of anvils on their shoulders. Almost all the boys and girls come with their heads down, poor posture, shoulders slumped and downcast because of negative words that have been spoken to them by parents, teachers or peers. They have been told, among other things, that they are no good and that they will never amount to anything. Too many of them have heard the words: "I wish you had never been born." They have been called stupid, ugly, fat, etc.

Guess what? Teens have a way of fulfilling expectations. If they are tagged as problem kids, they live up to those expectations. They quit trying in the classroom and at home. When they quit trying, they begin acting out because they are seeking attention. They seem to be saying, "Look at me! I can be somebody!" But really they are saying, "Help me."

These are hurtful words! These are curses that are spoken over teens every day and cause deep wounds. Think about the damage caused. This is why inner healing and deliverance are so vital to counseling and restoration of the teen. It is important to challenge teens and parents to watch what they say.

How many times have we found that if teens can't get positive reinforcement, they'll find a way to get it negatively? Positive self-talk and affirmative comments are essential but must be taught. Most of us can find more wrong with us than we can find that is right with us. At House of Hope we have to keep reinforcing the fact that we are made in God's image. We focus on His greatness and what His Word says about us.

According to a survey done on the words we speak, the average American utters between twenty-five thousand and thirty thousand words a day (equivalent to a small paperback novel, or a thesis for a master's degree). It would be interesting to wear a tape recorder on our shoulders and record the words we speak. Then we would better understand what is happening to our lives. We would probably be shocked. But God's Word emphasizes the importance of what we say. James 3:10

says, "Out of the same mouth proceeds blessings and curses." Jesus said, "Out of the abundance of the heart the mouth speaks" (Luke 6:46).

To help teens learn how to speak and receive positive words, I have special meetings at House of Hope called "fireside chats." During these meetings, teens speak into each other's lives. I ask them to say one positive comment and then a constructive comment. The teens listen intently to each other because teens *listen* to their peers. Their peers can help them see areas in five minutes that may take us adults five days to get across.

During all our interactions with the teens, our counselors take every opportunity to speak words of encouragement and life. Positive words establish and affirm who they are in Christ (their identity) and give direction for their futures (their destiny). We tell our teens that they are special, loved and deeply valued.

Many teens have a habit of speaking negatively to those around them. We target and lovingly confront negative language such as name-calling or sarcastic statements.

Words can cause teens to feel either belittled or beloved. At House of Hope, we make sure our words always say, "You are beloved."

Speaking Scripture

For each teen, our counselors select a few Scriptures that communicate the Father's heart for that person. The counselor reads the verses with the teen, helping him or her see what God's Word says about them. Sometimes we personalize the Scriptures and ask the teen to put it on his or her mirror and repeat it several times a day. For example, "You are the apple of His eyes" (Psalm 17:8). "You are created in His image" (Genesis 1:27). "You are fearfully and wonderfully made" (Psalm 139:14).

On the following pages you will find key verses that we use to help teens and families strengthen their faith.

Scriptures to Renew the Mind

The Scriptures teach that "as a man thinks in his heart, so is he" (Proverbs 23:7). We cannot think negatively and believe positively and we cannot believe negatively and live positively. Notice the following verses which emphasize the importance of our thought life.

For though we walk in the flesh, we do not war according to the flesh. For the weapons of our warfare *are* not carnal but mighty in God for pulling down strongholds, casting down arguments and every high thing that exalts itself against the knowledge of God, bringing every thought into captivity to the obedience of Christ, —2 Corinthians 10:3–5

I beseech you therefore, brethren, by the mercies of God, that you present your bodies a living sacrifice, holy, acceptable to God, *which is* your reasonable service. And do not be conformed to this world, but be transformed by the renewing of your mind, that you may prove what *is* that good and acceptable and perfect will of God. —Romans 12:1–2

Trust in the LORD with all your heart, and lean not on your own understanding; —Proverbs 3:5

That you put off, concerning your former conduct, the old man which grows corrupt according to the deceitful lusts, and be renewed in the spirit of your mind, and that you put on the new man which was created according to God, in true righteousness and holiness. —Ephesians 4:22–24

Rejoice in the Lord always. Again I will say, rejoice! Let your gentleness be known to all men. The Lord *is* at hand. Be anxious for nothing, but in everything by prayer and supplication, with thanksgiving, let your requests be made known to God; and the peace of God, which surpasses all understanding, will guard your hearts and minds through Christ Jesus. —Philippians 4:4–7

For God hath not given us the spirit of fear; but of power and of love and of a sound mind. —2 Timothy 1:7

For those who live according to the flesh set their minds on the things of the flesh, but those *who live* according to the Spirit, the things of the Spirit. For to be carnally minded *is* death, but to be spiritually minded *is* life and peace. —Romans 8:5–6

> But let him ask in faith, with no doubting, for he who doubts is like a wave of the sea driven and tossed by the wind. For let not that man suppose that he will receive anything from the Lord; *he is* a double-minded man, unstable in all his ways. —James 1:6–8

Scriptures for Daily Confession

> Our minds will be renewed when we discipline our thinking, reject negative thoughts and fill our minds with the truth of Scripture. Therefore, we must confess God's Word because "faith comes by hearing the Word of God" (Romans 10:17).

We don't confess our weakness, our fear or our doubts. Even though we have them. We confess what God says we have. We confess who God says we are.

The book of Hebrews talks about the importance of our professing our faith. Keep in mind that professing is the same as confessing.

> Therefore, holy brethren, partakers of the heavenly calling, consider the Apostle and High Priest of our confession, Christ Jesus. —Hebrews 3:1

> Seeing then that we have a great High Priest who has passed through the heavens, Jesus the Son of God, let us hold fast *our* confession. —Hebrews 4:14

> Let us hold unswervingly to the hope we profess, for he who promised *is* faithful. —Hebrews 10:23

The following Scriptures are a few that are personalized and confessed aloud each day. In this way their faith becomes strong. If these passages do not apply to a particular need, we select other appropriate verses for our teens.

Old Testament
Psalm 23
Psalm 27:1

Psalm 3:6
Psalm 103:1-5
Isaiah 26:3
Isaiah 40:25
Isaiah 40:31

New Testament
Matthew 11:28
Mark 11:24
Luke 17:21
John 10:10
John 14:27
John 15:7
Romans 8:1
Romans 8:31
Romans 8:32
Romans 8:37
2 Corinthians 4:8
Philippians 4:13
Philippians 4:19
Philippians 4:4-7
2 Timothy 1:12
2 Timothy 1:7
1 John 1:9
1 John 4:4

Hearing: The Ability to Hear from God and Listen to Others

The third area in helping them build their faith is to teach them to hear from God and listen to others.

Our identities are formed by what we hear. Romans 12:1-2 says, "Faith comes by hearing and hearing by the word of God." As I mentioned earlier, almost every boy and girl who comes to House of Hope has a poor self-concept because they've heard people speak negative things about them. After these teens hear these words long enough, they believe the lies and start living up to the expectations. Our job is to deprogram them from the lies and then reprogram them with Scripture.

When I meet a teen for the first time, I always look for something positive to say like, "You have a great smile," "I love the color of your eyes," or "Your hair is beautiful." Of course, they do not believe me because they still believe the lies from other people telling them they are trash and unlovable. But with continued healing and affirmation, they eventually accept the truth.

After they have developed a relationship with God, we encourage them to listen to that still, small voice of God and what Scripture says about them and their potential. Teaching a teen how to quiet their minds and their hearts so they can hear from God is no easy task. Most have never attempted this and don't have a clue where to begin.

We try to create some time during the day when they can focus on hearing God without distraction. We find a good time is after breakfast, when they have finished their chores and are ready to go to school. We tell them to quietly focus on Scripture and listen to His still small voice. During this time, we sometimes play praise music. At first, many of them say, "I can't hear God." But over time they learn that God will speak to them if they can quiet themselves to listen.

Teenagers love it when I tell them that God has a phone number: Jeremiah 33:3. He says, "Call to Me, and I will answer you, and show you great and mighty things, which you do not know."

 Most people in our fast-paced world don't listen because they make their schedules too busy to hear from God. If God doesn't send them an e-mail or a text message, then they don't know how to listen.

Because there is so much going on, I have found that I really need to make time to listen every day. I need God to help me get through all of it! Each of us is given the same 24 hours a day. We all have the power to choose how we spend our time.

At the same time we learn to listen to God, we need to learn to each other as well. In today's society, people are not taking quiet, focused time to hear each other. It is vital for parents to listen to their teens, just as much as the teens need to learn to listen to their parents.

Conclusion

This chapter focused on building up faith in teens and parents. The three keys are:

Thinking: Having a positive thought life.

Speaking: Learning to say the right words.

Hearing: The ability to hear from God and listen to others.

As we seek to better identify and correct the teens and parents' distorted views of Christianity and faith in Jesus, we're seeing a new generation of teens emerge. The battle is raging to destroy this generation, but we are winning them back one-by-one!

CONCLUSION

CHAPTER 21

Testimonies from Parents

SO FAR IN THIS BOOK, MOST OF THE TESTIMONIES HAVE BEEN FROM the teen's point of view. However, we are equally involved in the parents' lives, and I want you to see how House of Hope impacts them as well. Many times the parents and families experience just as much healing as the teens. In this chapter you will read nine stories that could have ended in disaster but resulted in restoration instead. Some stories took place only a few years ago, but some go back almost two decades.

Separated from Her Daughter: Beth's Mom

I was born in Pittsburgh, Pennsylvania, and remember my upbringing as very normal and family focused. Our family was involved with community events, local sports and weekly "family-only" events. Sitting down every night for dinner as a family without interruptions was a priority. I remember my dad always making time for each one of his children yet still working two jobs to make ends meet. My mom was always making sure we felt loved.

Work was always difficult in Pittsburgh, and an opportunity for a teaching position became available in Maryland for my dad. My parents decided that's what would be best for the family, and we moved to Maryland in 1984.

I was devastated. Pittsburgh was where I grew up. This was my home, my roots and my best friends of seventeen years. And now my parents were pulling everything from under me with one big jolt and without much notice. I had just graduated from high school, and going to college was going to be hard enough.

I attended college in St. Augustine, Florida, in the fall of 1984, and before I knew it I was in a relationship that I thought would last for the rest of my life.

I met the man of my dreams. He was tall, thin, handsome and played basketball. Any priorities I had before meeting Dan weren't priorities anymore. He became my priority. Whatever he wanted, whenever he wanted it and however he talked to me—it was OK. Before I could blink, I had lost all my friends, all my values and pushed my family aside, and Dan was making my decisions. I had lost who I was.

The relationship became verbally and mentally abusive within the first six months. I made excuses as to why it was going on and would say "It's OK. Dan promised me it wouldn't happen again."

My family finally stepped in and physically removed me from the relationship July 1985. They brought me home to Maryland and tried to keep us apart. I wouldn't listen. I thought I knew what was best and, after all, I loved Dan. He promised me he wouldn't do it again.

In October 1985 I found out I was pregnant. I was 19 and lost. The pressure was on by Dan, and in his mind the only thing we could do was get married and have the baby. We were married February 8, 1986, in Maryland, and our daughter was born March 27, 1986.

The verbal and mental abuse continued and it became so bad I was scared for our lives. I didn't know what to do because I was scared to stay, and I was even more afraid to leave. I finally got the courage to leave. This was only the beginning to what you will read next.

Dan didn't want custody of Beth, but he did want to hurt me so he used Beth to do this. During a weekend visitation he not only relocated within the state without telling anyone, he also decided to keep Beth. It took thirty days for me to see Beth again, and I vividly remember hiding under a car just to see her from a distance.

Within the next couple of months, Dan vanished again with Beth. This time when I went to pick up Beth for our Wednesday evening visit, the apartment was empty. Dan had packed up his things, packed up Beth and headed to Florida.

The court system was involved for four years, and during those years, Beth became the victim. She was back and forth between Dan's temporary custody and my temporary custody. It came to an end August 1992. Dan was awarded full custody. I was awarded reasonable visitation and mandated to pay child support.

Dan continued to live in Florida after he was awarded full custody, so seeing Beth on a regular basis was very difficult. Not only was I dealing with the decision that was made by the judge, I knew firsthand that Beth would receive the same treatment from Dan that I did.

I did everything I could, to the best of my ability with what I had, but that wasn't enough for Beth or me. After eight years of long distance communication and visits, my husband and I relocated to Florida. If the courts wouldn't change custody and see that it was in the best interest of Beth to be fully involved in our lives, then I would have to rely on nature to work things out.

Beth came to live with us the summer of 2000 [when she was fourteen years old]. She also brought along her wounds of feeling abandoned by me, hurts that her dad had just rejected her, and the learned negative verbal and mental behaviors from the last eight years.

Our relationship with her became a living nightmare. We began with weekly counseling, but that wasn't enough. As time went on, Beth was moving at a pace none of us could keep up with. I thought with each episode, I could help her through it. It was at the point where we were afraid of being in the same house with her because we never knew when she would rage. These rages included verbal and physical destruction.

I came to terms with the fact that Beth and our family needed help. I couldn't be the savior anymore. If I wanted any chance of Beth surviving her life, I had to turn it over to God and allow him to work the miracle I thought I could do. He had been knocking on my front door for a long time, and I ignored his knocks. I couldn't ignore them anymore.

I remember getting ready to leave House of Hope campus in January 2002 after I had just finished the process of admitting Beth into the program. I was emotionally, physically and spiritually exhausted. I stopped and began to pray. As tears flowed down my cheeks, I began, "Heavenly Father, I release Beth to you. She is your child. Please take her, hold her and surround her with Your angels of strength and wisdom. I believe this is the right thing to do and have faith You will lead us to where we need to go. I understand we will not be reunited as a family until You say it's time. I am committed to You and Your guidance."

Through the passion and commitment of the servant leaders at House of Hope and messages from God, miracles began to happen. The "do it yourself" toolbox that we had brought with us to House of Hope had been emptied and a "God-centered" toolbox began to be filled with the power of forgiveness, unconditional love, boundaries, being in control of ourselves instead of controlling, listening and communication tips, learning how to say "I'm sorry," and relearning the basics of parenting and relationships.

After numerous parenting sessions, counseling sessions and focused prayer time, our family graduated from the program in April 2003. We will be forever grateful for the opportunities presented to our family to heal and restore our relationships with each other.

It would be very difficult for me to choose the most spiritual opportunity that was given to our family during our time at House of Hope; however, for me personally, I can remember this like it was yesterday. It was a Tuesday night at parenting class. This night was unusual because we weren't learning about life skills, and Dan was present. This was the only parenting night Dan ever attended. It was going to be a night of prayer by a visiting intercessor. This would be a first for me. (This experience I am about to tell you about was completely voluntary and nothing or no one pressured me into this.)

The intercessor asked for all persons interested in being prayed for to come up in front of the gymnasium. The next thing I knew, I was standing in the front of the gymnasium, waiting for someone to pray over me. This is very unlike me. I usually pray very quietly and privately. As I stood holding Beth's right hand and Dan holding her left hand, I was very uncomfortable, nervous and my palms were sweating. I had a strong feeling we were up there for a reason. I didn't know what to expect but felt calmness about what was getting ready to happen.

The intercessor approached me and began to pray out loud. I thought to myself, "Oh my—everyone can hear what she is saying to me." Then something came over me, and I was completely relaxed and I let go of any hesitation. The presence of God was overwhelming. As the intercessor prayed over me, I began to release the hatred and resentment I had toward Dan.

The House of Hope staff gave me some time to pull myself together and realize what I had just experienced. Then Dan and I were brought together face-to-face. Could I do what the intercessor told me I needed to do? Could I look Dan in the eye and forgive him for everything he had done to Beth and me?

With Sara's assistance, Dan asked me to forgive him for the pain he caused Beth and me. I looked him in the eye and very sincerely and truthfully said, "I forgive you." By being confronted with this and dealing with it, I had just accomplished what I never thought I could do. I freed myself from the hurts and wounds of a previous situation that was killing any possibility of present or future happiness. By doing this, truthfully and sincerely, I would now be able to move forward with restoring my relationship with myself, my husband (who had been so patient with me) and with Beth. That's exactly what I did.

Since April 2003 our family has continued to focus on the importance of strengthening our relationship with God, listening, communicating, understanding each other's needs and wants, and always trying to do a better job today than we did yesterday.

Beth graduated from high school with honors in May 2004 and will attend a private university in the fall to study occupational therapy. My husband and I continue to practice the life skills learned at House of Hope with each other and our three younger children, who are four, two and one.

Loving and Caring—But Too Trusting: Missie's Mother

Dumb, stupid, out of touch, naïve—these were the best words to describe me. But there were also other words that described me—loving, caring, active in Missie's cheering squad, proud and trusting. This last word was the one that got me into trouble. Trust! I trusted Missie to do the right things and make the right decisions the way I had done in my life.

I had brought Missie up in the church. I never drank, never did drugs, and never had sex except with the man I married.

I did not sneak out of my house. I did not lie to my parents about where I was going or where I had been. I obeyed the rules. I thought Missie did, too.

There had been some warning signs along the way—a pack of cigarettes, some beer bottles, some friends I questioned, but Missie always had a good explanation for everything.

Then one day I was in Myrtle Beach in a business meeting when the meeting was interrupted for an emergency phone call for me. It was my housekeeper who stayed with Missie, who as now in the tenth grade, when I was out of town. She reported the following:

"Missie was arrested at school today, handcuffed and led off the school property. They found some "crack" and other drug paraphernalia. They have arrested her. We got her out of jail for the night, but she has to appear before the courts tomorrow. We do not know what to do. How soon can you come home?"

My head started buzzing. I got sick to my stomach. I was crying, yet numb.

Later, when I told my mother the story, she looked at me and said, "How did you not know? I did." She went on to tell me what my oldest daughter, Dawn, told her only two weeks earlier. While I was out of town, Missie had been admitted to the emergency room. She had eaten mushrooms and almost died that night.

I couldn't believe what I was hearing. I was devastated. I flew home, and the next morning Missie and I got up early and went to the school principal's office. We learned that someone had reported Missie's license plate and school parking permit to the police when they saw five kids smoking marijuana in her car and passing a pipe.

We left the school and went to a lawyer. The attorney went to court with us and met the juvenile authorities. (Missie was 16 years old.) The court finally determined that if Missie would go for treatment, they would be more lenient with her.

The lawyer then told us about a great drug counselor. He scheduled an appointment with the counselor for that same afternoon. The counselor conducted a one-on-one evaluation of Missie. We learned that Missie's problem was very serious, had been for quite some time, and she needed to be in program care.

The counselor recommended a rehab program in Minnesota and had the appointment set up for her to be admitted two days later. Everything was such a whirlwind, but within three days of my finding out Missie was on drugs, we were on a plane to Minnesota for the twenty-eight-day program.

Missie stayed in this program for twenty-eight days but was allowed to smoke, cuss and see male patients. During this time, she actually learned more about other drugs and how to use them than she had known before she went in.

After twenty-eight days she was definitely not ready to return home, so she was sent to Lafayette, Louisiana, to an outside program and stayed there for five months. During these five months, she was again allowed to smoke, fraternize with male patients, cuss and use all kinds of foul language.

During this time, Missie's roommate became pregnant after sleeping with one of the male patient's. The staff took her to have an abortion. After the abortion, Missie was left to take care of this girl, who was barely seventeen years old. In short, these programs had no discipline or morals.

I visited Missie several times, and at the end of the five months, they felt she was ready to be released. Missie and I talked, and she begged and said she was not ready to face the world alone.

God works in strange and wonderful ways. My husband, Ed, met an old friend, and we went to dinner with him and his wife. During dinner, we began discussing Missie, and I told his wife I was looking for a safe haven for Missie. Her eyes lit up, and she said, "I know just the place, and it will mean so much to her and also to you. It is Christian-based, and the first thing you need to do is meet Sara Trollinger, the founder."

Before long, Missie was in House of Hope, and her life began to turn around. At House of Hope, she was not only putting drugs out of her life, but she was also allowing God to fill in the empty space.

As Sara told me, it took a strong commitment of my time, and this brought Missie and me closer. Missie was not the only one whose heart was touched by House of Hope.

Missie ended up staying at House of Hope another eight months, rededicating her life to the Lord, and finishing high school at Hope Academy.

After experiencing both a secular program and the Christian program at House of Hope, there is no question about where you would want to have your child go—or which is the best program.

At House of Hope, your teen is taught that he or she is a child of God and that He loves them. They also know that their counselors love and forgive them. They begin to fill the emptiness inside with God's love. It builds their self-esteem and their love for themselves.

They make good Christian friends that will help them when they are outside of House of Hope. The graduates of House of Hope have a beaming glow that will fill your heart with joy for teenagers with so much peace and joy.

Missie still had to fight her demons from time to time, but she always came back because of the strong faith she experienced at House of Hope. She is now twenty-six years old, has just finished her Bible Study class at the seminary after graduating from college, and is preparing her life to be used for God in His work. She is engaged to the son of the leader of Campus Crusade in Africa. She plans to open a House of Hope there.

Living in Fear: Tony's Mom

Have you ever felt helpless—at the end of your rope? That's how I felt ten years ago.

I'd like to share a little background information. I was not married when my son Tony was born. He grew up never knowing his biological father. I was a single mother trying to raise two children when I met and married George. Tony was only three when he acquired a stepfather. As it turned out, George was abusive, and for the next ten years of our lives we lived in fear.

Tony was suffering from a life of abuse and rejection. He never knew his biological father, and he grew up with a stepfather who abused him. As he got older, he continued to internalize the abuse and rejection he felt. He was hurting so bad on the inside that he wanted everyone around him to know it and to feel as bad as he did. He shut himself off emotionally. He felt unworthy of being loved and was incapable of showing love to anyone.

I tried to make the best of the situation, trying to keep peace and not upset George, Tony's stepfather; because you never knew what kind of a mood he would be in. There were plenty of times that I wanted to leave, but George made it clear to me that I wasn't going anywhere. Because of his threats to take my children and because I was afraid that he would kill one of us, I stayed in the marriage, hoping and praying that somehow we would all just get out alive.

And then the blessing came: George met someone and left. Under normal circumstances, that could have been a crushing blow. Instead, for my kids and me, it saved our lives.

Because George was the only father that my kids knew, even though they suffered abuse, they also suffered from rejection issues after he left. Now I was alone with three children, trying to sort out our lives and facing the reality of what really happened to us over the past ten years. It was the first time that I was able to slow down, take a step back, and look at what had happened.

I sought counseling for my kids and thought that because I loved them they would be OK. But they weren't OK. I wasn't OK. How could we be? We suffered abuse at the hands of a horrific man for years, and it would be years before we would recover.

My son was so filled with hurt, anger and rejection that the older he got, the more I saw behaviors of George. Because Tony was hurting, he wanted everyone around him to hurt and to feel as bad as he did. He was becoming more and more violent toward his sisters and me—even himself. He was full of rage. He began self-mutilating, cutting himself with knives and sharp objects.

I didn't know what to do to help him. All I saw was a boy, my son, hurting so badly on the inside that he wanted everyone to know it. He went through anger management classes and saw several different counselors. Nothing was making a difference in his life. I was desperate for him, and I didn't know how to help him.

The path that he was on was continuing to escalate in the wrong direction. I knew that God had a great plan for his life, and that it was not supposed to be what past circumstances had made him become. Here was a teen that was headed for major trouble. I was at the end of my rope, feeling helpless. There is nothing worse than not being able to help your teen and watch him destroy himself and everyone around him.

I kept praying, "Where, how, when, what is going to make a difference for Tony?" I was desperate for him. I understood his pain; I just didn't know how to help him. He was on the road to self destruction. He was emotionally and mentally tormented and angry enough to kill someone.

When Sara Trollinger announced that they were going to open a House of Hope for boys, I knew that if there was going to be any hope for my son, it was going to be there. For the first time in years, I felt there was hope for my son to receive healing, to find out who he really is, and to have a fresh start at a new life.

Bringing Tony to House of Hope was the hardest thing I ever had to do, but I knew I had to let him go to save his life. Being separated from him was hard on all of us. It was hard to let him go and give up my rights to him and turn him over to God to take full control of him however He saw fit.

Tony tried to manipulate me and the people around him. He acted out and wanted out and did things that were quite embarrassing at House of Hope. His goal was to get out any way he could, and he tried to make everyone miserable, hoping that he would be kicked out and sent home.

I know that the staff had their hands full, as I knew what Tony was capable of. He played "parent against parent," or "Mom against House of Hope." But I trusted God to use this program and the people that He placed there to help my son. My heart wanted to keep protecting him and shelter him from the sadness he felt being separated from his family and in a strange place. He would cry, beg, plead and bargain with me to come home, and it took all I had to say, "No. When God is ready, you will come home."

He was not making much progress for the first several months, always trying to buck the system and still hoping that if he were "bad" enough, they would kick him out and send him home.

Tony finally started to open up, and started asking questions about this Jesus they were always talking about. It was still a long road from this point but he was finally willing to do whatever it took to get well, to stop being angry, to allow God to heal him and to become the man that God destined him to be.

I am forever grateful to Sara and to House of Hope for their faithfulness in their calling to help teens like Tony and for being there for him when I couldn't be and for the unconditional love that they showered on Tony.

God is the miracle worker. He has truly healed my son. He has removed all his anger issues. He has shown Tony that He is the Father and he will never abandon him. He has restored in him the ability to love and to receive love. We enjoy each other, to laugh with each other. Tony and I now have a very open relationship and are able to just sit and talk-sometimes to all hours of the night. It has been one of the greatest experiences of my life-to finally have a loving, healthy relationship with my son.

If you met Tony today, you would never believe that he was that same person that we have been talking about. He is a young man after God's own heart. His heart's desire is to please God in all things. He is a man of integrity. He is a changed person through and through. He has a great heart of gold; he is the most generous, honest, trustworthy person that I know. He is very active in his church. He finished college. He later went to Bible School. Today he is happily married and is a very successful business man living in the Northeast USA.

Finding the Right Place: Michael's Mom

Michael was diagnosed with ADHD and started taking Ritalin when he was four years old. Mostly due to the medication, he had several mood swings a day.

Starting at the age of four, we had challenges with his behavior. Until fourth grade, he was in public school, but we decided to home school him starting in the fifth grade.

He was rebellious to his mom for several years, but six months prior to House of Hope he was also rebellious to his dad. The breaking point came when we found marijuana and hash in his room and discovered he had used our ATM card to steal $2,000 from our checking account to buy drugs.

We removed Michael from our home in Orlando and sent him to stay with my brother in Ft. Lauderdale, trying to get him away from the people who sold him drugs. My brother was kind to take Michael in, however, he had two boys of his own and he was pressuring us to make a decision about how to help Michael.

When we visited House of Hope, we felt such a peace throughout the campus. You could feel God's anointing on Sara's ministry. Everyone we spoke with was so friendly and helpful. We also had several acquaintances who spoke highly of the program. However, there was a waiting list and they could not accept Michael.

We then researched several other facilities and visited two of them. We found a military-like facility that my husband was leaning toward. The Holy Spirit told me that this was not the place to send our son. I spent hours on the Internet researching, and I found an article in the newspaper on MSNBC.com that showed children at this facility were beaten with chains and polls as a form of discipline. Several children had been removed from the facility, and the police were investigating.

Two days after finding out the truth about this military facility, and more than thirty days after our son left to live with my brother, we received the call we so desperately prayed for: House of Hope had an opening. Michael entered House of Hope when he was fourteen.

House of Hope allowed us to correct our issues as a family and not just correct our child. Most parents don't realize that they can also be part of the problem. We were able to get counseling as well as our son Michael. This allowed us to work out the differences we had with one another.

We learned valuable information at the parent meetings, and the small group sessions helped us realize that we were not alone with the challenges we were having with our child. Parents who were further along in the program than we were gave us hope, and we made commitments to pray for each other. Not only do the children make friendships and encourage each other, but the parents do as well.

House of Hope also brought in guest speakers to teach, and we learned each other's personality styles, which helped a great deal. We were able to write letters of apology to each other and remove the past and have a fresh start.

In order to give Michael a fresh start, we made a choice to move to a different state after he graduated from the program. Applying what we learned at House of Hope to our lives has allowed us to deal with our issues in a more biblical way and it has helped us to reason with our son instead of screaming at him, which is what we did in the past.

We would be lying if we did not say that we still have some challenges. He is still a teenager! It is how we deal with the challenges now that has made the difference. Michael attends a small Christian school, and he is enjoying it. He has made lots of friends but still calls Florida "home." We keep him very busy with soccer, basketball and baseball.

House of Hope has been a blessing to our family, and we appreciate all the staff that helped us to be successful in this program.

Finding Purpose in Life: Ronnie's Mom

My name is Tina and my son, Ronnie, is a graduate from House of Hope. House of Hope literally saved our lives.

About six years ago, we lived in a nice home and our family looked like the typical, happy family. But that was all on the surface. We were a family of four: Ed, my husband; Paul, my oldest son who had just recently joined the Air Force and moved away from home; Ronnie, who was fifteen; and of course me.

When Ronnie reached the age of fifteen, he began to be difficult and started getting in many fights with Ed. When

Paul, his brother, moved away, Ronnie felt he was losing his best friend and was very lonely. Ed was unable to handle the changes he was seeing in his son. That, along with being unable to find a job, put Ed into a terrible depression. It seemed that the once beautiful family was now a battle zone.

In November, Ed, Ronnie and I took a trip to Holland. During our trip, we received a call from our neighbor telling us we had several kids staying in our home and the police had come. We were shocked and asked Ronnie if he had given anyone the combination to our door. He denied it at the time, but told me later that he had. Fortunately, nothing was stolen, but the incident destroyed our vacation and required numerous trips to court to testify against the students.

Our finances became a total mess, and Ed and I were looking at bankruptcy and losing our home. Things were really falling apart.

I knew Ronnie was so very unhappy, and I was terrified that he would try to take his own life. It was a thought I could not bear. When he was home, Ronnie would lie in his bed crying, and I would lie down beside him and cry along with him.

At the same time, Ronnie's anger was out of control. He told me he wanted to control it, but he just couldn't.

To find help for Ronnie, I contacted at least six different programs all over the country. But every time there was a roadblock of one kind or another that made it impossible.

Up to this point in my life, I had always believed in God, but I had never really known Jesus, and I never had a relationship with Him. I always felt that I controlled my outcomes, and it was up to me to make things happen. But one day at work, I had yet another eye-opening experience. I prayed to God to help me. I knew what a great person Ronnie was and what a great man he could be. But without help, I knew Ronnie would be dead within a year.

It was a miracle. Only a few hours later, an acquaintance told me about House of Hope, a treatment facility that was not across the country but in town. I called House of Hope, and they made an appointment for us right away. Ronnie was willing to go because he knew I wanted it for him. He was going for the wrong reasons, but at least he agreed to go.

The trip through Ronnie's recovery was difficult, and the progress was slow. Ronnie played the game and thought he would fool everyone. After he had been in the program for about eight months, he just about convinced me to take him out. Since I was relocating and wanted him with me, I told him I would take him out.

He seemed to be doing so much better, but Ms. Sara convinced me that taking him out would be the wrong thing to do. She said he was like baking brownies. They could look great and smell wonderful but still be raw inside.

As painful as it was, I backed out on my promise to Ronnie. I believe that was the breaking point. Ronnie finally realized he couldn't play his way through any longer. He received the counseling to be delivered from his oppression and to heal his broken heart. He finally was listening with his heart.

House of Hope counseled me as well, and that is when I found Christ. Going to the Tuesday evening parenting classes and praising the Lord with Ronnie was such a beautiful experience. He and I both found what we never even knew was missing. Finding Jesus through the teachings and counseling at House of Hope changed both of our lives.

Ronnie is now thirty-one years old and doing well. He still has his life difficulties, but they are the normal ones and, because of House of Hope's counseling and teaching, he confides in our Lord to see him through. Ronnie's dream is to become a minister and help others who are on the same path of destruction he once walked. Now, both Ronnie and I have a purpose in life.

Overcoming the Results of Sexual Assault: Nicole's Mom

When your seven-year-old daughter is sexually assaulted, the only way to express how you feel as parents is complete and utter despair. Even though it truly is not your fault, the sense of guilt and failure is overwhelming.

Once the initial shock is over, you try to fix what happened. You wonder, "Where do we start? How do we repair the extensive damage to our little girl?"

We did everything the experts recommended to do. Years went by, and by the time our daughter was thirteen years old, she was exhibiting all the behaviors that victims of sexual abuse exhibit. The anger, low self-esteem and lack of trust, combined with drug abuse and promiscuity, were destroying her.

Even after all the years of secular counseling we had attended, we had no answers. We were helpless and losing our daughter. We tried hospitals and treatment centers. Nothing helped! Nothing was working.

I can still remember calling out to God in despair. "Please, God, please help us save our daughter!" A few days later a counselor told us about a place called House of Hope. They explained that it was a Christian residential treatment program in Orlando. We called House of Hope and told them about our desperate situation. The next day, we all sat in Sara's office, and although there were a lot of tears when we left Nicole that day, we had a sense of hope we never had before.

We completely committed to the program, and our whole family attended weekly counseling. The deep healing that we all experienced was truly a miracle!

I will never forget our daughter's face after she had been in the program about two months. You could see the peace that God was restoring, right on her face. She was singing and smiling again! We knew at that moment that God was healing her, and she was going to be OK.

Our daughter graduated from House of Hope fourteen years ago. She is a married woman now with a beautiful daughter of her own. She is a thoughtful daughter and a very kind and gentle person. She is just a wonderful, generous individual, and we are so very proud of her.

Our whole family met Jesus at House of Hope, and our lives are forever changed. We know that God led us to House of Hope for the healing we needed. We are continually grateful to God, Sara and the staff at House of Hope. We experienced a miracle.

A Mother Trying to Make Things Right: Jenni and Danny's Mom

I was a "mother on a mission" and determined to make my children's lives better even though I was a single mom, and the struggles were many. Little did I know how much I also had to learn.

Before I was divorced, my children, Jenni and Danny, grew up with an alcoholic father who was abusive to the entire family. This paved the way for them to have extreme emotional problems after the divorce. Their father abandoned us, and Jenni and Danny had no contact with him afterward. At the time, it felt like a blessing not to have contact with him.

However, Jenni began rebelling and hanging out with other rebellious teens. Disrespect, drinking and drugs became her way of life. Our lives were reeling out of control.

I knew she needed help, and I couldn't live with myself if I let things go further. I began to take her for random drug tests, and, of course, they were positive. I signed her up for a voluntary outpatient drug program in the county where we live. She had meetings several times a week and random drug tests. We also went to outpatient counseling. I never wanted to be "blamed" later if I didn't do the right thing. She continually came up positive on the drug tests but also learned ways to make the drug tests come out clean, so it was difficult to tell exactly how she was doing.

Nothing improved. Her schoolwork went downhill. She skipped classes and never got up on time for school. She ended up failing school because of missing more than eight classes.

The outpatient drug program counselors told me that Jenni was on a downhill course and was not responding to the program, so she was dismissed. They told me she needed inpatient residential treatment. The words were difficult for me to hear because I had tried so hard to get her on the right path. Why had the situation become so desperate and out of control?

I found House of Hope and made an appointment. The counselor was warm and understanding as well as the rest of the staff. She knew how desperate the situation was becoming and had a place set up for Jenni.

I had no idea how I was going to pay any money, but I was continually told that "no one would be turned away because of money." I turned my financial worries over to the Lord and knew in my heart this was the right thing to do and that the Lord would bless it. The first several months were the most difficult with many tearful goodbyes. Gradually, I could see hope returning.

I attended parenting sessions on Tuesdays and began to learn many things about my wayward teen and also about myself. During this time, Jenni accepted Jesus into her heart and a transformation began that no earthly mother could have accomplished. Only God alone could do this job!

At the same time Jenni was taking baby steps on her path to becoming healed, my son Danny grew more out of control. Danny had been plagued by ADHD his entire life and had emotional problems and scars from his abusive father. By age twelve, he had been "Baker Acted" into a crisis center due to a suicide threat. He had gone to multiple counselors and became so out of control that he was placed on four medications at the same time to keep him under control.

School problems were insurmountable. The vice principal had my phone number on speed dial! Danny, like Jenni, began to seek alcohol and drugs for comfort.

As a single mother, I was so overwhelmed with Danny's problems that it became difficult to help Jenni at the same time. I finally brought Danny to House of Hope, too.

Once again, I had no idea where finances would come from. Now I had two children in residential treatment and a business to run. We lived almost an hour and a half away, and the trips back and forth were taxing.

I have two older daughters who were a great deal of support. They helped with visits and driving. It made a tremendous difference.

All during this time, God blessed my business over and over again. The business doubled, tripled and quadrupled. It became unbelievable!

Danny was saved also, and Jesus became a big part of his life. The seeds that were planted then are so much a part of Jenni and Danny now.

It has been seven years since Jenni entered House of Hope, and it has been almost six years since Danny entered there. There have been struggles and there have been hard times since then. God does not promise a life without struggles, but He helps us through them. Danny is presently in an adult residential treatment center and has achieved success only through his belief in Jesus. Jennie is married, has a baby, and doing well as a mother and wife.

I don't believe either of my children could have survived had they not been at House of Hope. The seeds that were planted changed their lives forever and mine, too.

We are forever grateful for the help and care we received.

"They Give You Back Your Child": Terryl's Dad

It was July 2003. I was tense, hardly breathing, confused and upset. We had problems. Big problems! Terryl, our sixteen-year-old daughter, who not more than one year before appeared to be a normal, church-going fourteen-year-old was now drinking, smoking pot and cutting herself. She would go for hours and hours without telling us where she was. She was angry, defiant and rebellious. It was scary, and we needed help.

After we experienced yet another confrontation with Terryl, we sent an email to Sara Trollinger and House of Hope. "We have a daughter who is out of control," we wrote. "Would anyone talk with us? Did anyone know what to do? Did anyone know what she needed? Did anyone have any answers?"

Within minutes a calming message returned via email. Typing a message of understanding, concern and hope, Sara and her staff invited us to visit House of Hope that morning.

Our children had always been our priorities. They had never been in daycare. I had helped in elementary school by teaching math to Terryl's classmates. Cindy had been in the PTA and participated in all things supportive. We had done our best to raise all four of them with the understanding that Christ was significant in our lives and could be in theirs.

Terryl had made a commitment to Christ at an early age. We hoped and prayed that she might be inoculated from the perils of the world. That was not to happen. As Terryl entered high school, we began to see major changes occur in her life. Her care for dress changed. Over time she became angry and sullen. Soon she became distant, and it was a challenge to keep up with where she was and whom she was with. Her stories were never quite straight. She was no longer telling us the truth. We never could be sure when she walked out the door where she was going to be. As we caught her in lies, it seemed she was constantly on some kind of restriction. Formerly a good student, she was now an F student.

Terryl, had consistently and without fail attended church for years, but now she found reasons not to go to her favorite Bible study or to youth group.

Then the trouble really began. Alcohol and drugs were found. There were more restrictions, arguments and turmoil. We found letters she had written describing her hurt, despair and hopelessness. During this time Cindy and I had begun to have some problems as well. So I was afraid for Terryl and my marriage, and soon I was afraid our lives were unraveling.

The night before we called House of Hope, Terryl had been drinking. Terryl had been staying with her older brother and his wife for almost a month while she "got things straight" and had just returned to our house a week earlier. Soon we were back to the same things. We needed to be around Terryl twenty-four/seven just to keep her under some kind of supervision. We wondered if we had failed as parents. We did not know what to do, what else to try or where to turn. The one thing we knew for certain was that Terryl was in trouble.

Our marriage was suffering, and Garrett, our younger son, was in pain. Cindy was angry: she was angry with Terryl and angry with me, and I felt the same. What I learned later was that I was angry with God as well.

What was wrong with my child? What went wrong? Why was this maturing child acting so self-destructively? What had happened to my family?

For Terryl, all of this was a nightmare. She was regularly drinking and using drugs, sexually active and depressed. What we did not know until later was that she had become what was called a "cutter." Even as she was entering House of Hope, we thought she might be suicidal.

We visited House of Hope, and before we left, Cindy knew this was exactly where Terryl needed to be. For me, the thought of sending my daughter away was traumatic. We could not afford House of Hope. Yet we were assured, "If

Terryl needs to be here, we will make it happen!" Within a week, Terryl was living at House of Hope.

I have been asked what brought the changes. First, you need to know what the changes are. Cindy and I have never been happier in our marriage. In all the twenty-one years we have been married, this is the best time of our lives. House of Hope put us back together. We very well might have been divorced by now. House of Hope helped me see that the direction I was going in all aspects of my life needed to be under God's scrutiny.

Today Terryl works two jobs and is preparing for her senior year in high school. She is trustworthy and a delight to be around. She is communicative and eager to talk about the things that cause her discomfort or joy. We see her invest herself in her friends with authenticity and purpose. She shows her concern and love to her brother and to us on a daily basis. When she says she will be home at 11 p.m., she is! She has a renewed spiritual commitment to Christ, and it is apparent in how she speaks and handles herself around her friends.

It took almost a year of being at House of Hope. The first weeks and months Terryl was surly and self-destructive. Prayer made the difference. House of Hope touches heaven with its prayer warriors, the staff, and Sara. We thank God daily for the prayer warrior ministry. Terryl was never the same. Prayer changes things!

At House of Hope, each child is dealt with individually. On her first Sunday home after being discharged, Terryl found some Vodka and drank almost a half a bottle. She was drunk. It was traumatic! The next day the staff dealt with the distraught and clearly depressed Terryl with love and compassion. She felt it. She knew she was loved. It was a turning point. She had experienced grace.

At House of Hope, Sara, Sandra Carpenter and the staff loved Terryl! Even when it was hard for us to be around her, they loved her in the same way Christ loves his children.

Through the power of Christ in their lives, they loved my child. For that, Cindy and I are forever grateful. The miracle is that they worked so hard with Terryl, and when their work was done, they gave our daughter back to us. That is what they do at House of Hope: they give you back your child.

Mother Finds Healing While Daughter Is in Program

My daughter was fifteen when she entered the program, and this is the story of what happened from my perspective as her mother.

Our story began when our youngest daughter turned twelve. It seemed like overnight she turned into this person that I did not know. She entered middle school, and the trouble began. Her language pattern changed drastically. She was swearing a lot and speaking street slang most of the time. The phrases we heard repeatedly were disturbing, to say the least.

When she was at home the phone was glued to her ear behind a locked bedroom door, which was against house rules, but she didn't care. The defiance grew stronger every day. Family participation was nonexistent. I was beginning to be afraid of what she might do. The violent tendencies she was developing were frightening. I really thought she was doing drugs.

After several months her father and I were so discouraged, we knew we needed help. We had been called to the school several times for unruly behavior, so I contacted one of the school counselors to see if they could help.

We were referred to a counseling group that our health insurance would cover. Our daughter's attitude by this time had become very hostile. We continued the counseling until it became such a chore that we almost had to tie her up to get her there. Our insurance quit paying, so we quit going. Our home situation continued to deteriorate daily. My husband worked nights and I worked out of our home.

I didn't know it then, but I was too broken and insecure in my own "stuff" to be able to stand up to my daughter. I was afraid of her. My husband just vented in anger and took it all out on me; he didn't know why I couldn't "stand up to a kid."

Meanwhile our older daughter sought her own refuge with her peers. She was out of high school and working full time. What a mess!

My father was terminally ill during this time and my mother was caring for him at home out of state. I was also under the pressure of my mother telling me that this situation was going to kill my dad.

I was such a mess already, but I also had to deal with my mother-in-law's constant negativity. I couldn't do anything right in her eyes.

I'd ask my husband for help, and he would tell me to take care of it. He and his mom had a pretty volatile relationship.

We tried another counselor that had been recommended and paid out-of-pocket for her group sessions. The parents had separate sessions with her. I was given a test for depression, and I scored big with suicidal depression. My way of coping was to hold everything in and not express what I was thinking or feeling. I was sent to my doctor with the test results and was put on medication. The situation grew progressively worse, and we were paying a lot for to go to counseling and make no progress. Enough was enough: we quit.

During this time we had several drug tests done on our youngest daughter, and to our surprise, she was clean every time. We also tested our older daughter and were stunned to find her results were positive! Needless to say, by this time we were becoming more and more desperate!

All this progressed to the point where our youngest daughter threatened my life because I wouldn't let her go to a football game. What an ugly night that was. On this particular day, in a fit of rage she screamed at me that she had been thinking of how she could get rid of us. She had come up with this plan: she was going to come into our room while we were sleeping and shoot us and then burn the house down so it looked like we died in the fire.

I'd had enough counseling to know that she had detached herself from the family because she kept referring to us as "you people." While she was yelling this from the back seat, I was driving in pretty heavy traffic. When we got home, the rage continued until she was standing there with a gun in her hand. There was so much arguing and her screaming that it was very hard to keep focused. I managed to back her into our bathroom, and in her rage she yelled that she would shoot me and then herself.

All I knew was to cry out to Jesus, and I did. At that very instant the phone rang. The phone must have rung fifteen times, which was odd because the answering machine always picks up after three rings. There was a struggle, and I managed to get the gun. I answered the phone; it was a neighbor who was coming to be with me.

I called 911, and they kept me on the phone until the police arrived. The officer arrived and realized he needed backup. They tried to reason with my daughter, but had no success. I told them to "Baker Act" her because I knew she was a danger to herself.

The officers carried my daughter—my baby—out of our home, shackled and cuffed. I was too numb to cry or feel anything at this point. They put her in the back of the police car and drove her to a crisis unit. She was like a mad man, screaming and throwing herself around in the back of their car, and the language was unbelievable. I had to go and be with her until she was "processed," and I had to fill out all the paperwork. This ordeal took about six hours.

I got home right before my husband came home from work. I had to tell him what happened. I don't think that he believed me at first, but then I showed him all the paperwork.

She was in there for fourteen days. She was given every type of drug test known, and no traces of drugs were found in her body. We were relieved to hear that. She was "labeled" with Oppositional Defiant Disorder. What were we supposed to do with that? That's when we heard about House of Hope through a business associate.

We really needed help. We knew that we couldn't do it by ourselves. For the good of all concerned, we arranged for the three of us to meet with the staff. We had to trick her to get her to come with us; we even put the child locks on the back doors so she wouldn't jump out of the car. After our meeting, we were put on the waiting list and they scheduled us to start counseling. Our parents thought we were making a huge mistake.

After only two weeks of counseling, we were called and told that there was an opening for us. Praise God! What an extremely difficult day that was. I wrestled with my thoughts and doubts all day. My daughter barely spoke to me and didn't even say goodbye when I left her. Deep down I knew this was the best solution. I do remember sleeping very well that night because I had a peace inside knowing where she was and that she was being cared for.

After orientation, her anger and hatred hadn't disap- peared, but we did notice a softening. She actually hugged us when we saw her for the first time after orientation. After a few months, we started to notice a real change in her. She was talking to us, and we even had some conversations. She was so anxious to share what she had learned about Jesus.

I looked forward to her phone calls every week and was sad when she had to hang up. She was trying so hard to succeed. She caught up in her schooling; she had been almost two years behind. We were so proud of her accomplishments.

Home Phase was wonderful. She was a new person and so grounded in the love of Jesus. Our family life was pretty good. Something I had only dreamed about before.

My counseling was a huge success! It was a long, tough road, and I had to do a tremendous amount of work. But I did it! I didn't realize that I truly did have an anger issue. Since I was a small girl, I had been told that I was to be quiet and behave perfectly. Basically, I was taught that my thoughts and opinions had no merit. I was to be seen and not heard.

As I grew, my art talent began to develop and I was recommended for the art program starting in seventh grade. My family didn't understand what I was doing. Why couldn't I be like my brother? My artwork was my escape.

I sought out the wrong type of friends, but they accepted me as I was. I got married at twenty, had a baby and moved to Florida. We had our second daughter three years later and lived with my mother-in-law. All was OK for a few years; then she turned against my husband and me. "We were no good; we had no business raising children, etc." Since I was at home, I received the backlash.

My way of dealing with it was to stuff it down and keep on stuffing and stuffing—until it finally came out in counseling. The day I admitted I had a problem I floated out of the office. After all these years I was finally being affirmed for who I was, for who God made me to be. God loves me just the way I am.

Psalm 139 took on a new meaning for me. The love I received was what I had craved for so long. Through counseling, I dealt with the problems in my marriage, my insecurities, and my problems, and—yes—I quit taking anti-depressants! I was able to deal with life in such a new and positive way. Jesus was living through me. I felt good about myself for the first time in my life. A spiritual awakening had taken place in me. Joining a church family added much needed support, and daily reading of the Word made life seem easier.

A few months after we started the program my husband and I rededicated our lives to Jesus and that's when everything really started to fall into place. Our family forgave each other and committed to one another.

During our time in the program, we discovered what our daughter's problem was. She told her house staff that her friend's stepfather had molested her. She was twelve and obviously didn't know what to do. The man threatened her if she said anything to us.

Finally, we knew what she needed! The puzzle pieces had all come together. Her counseling took on a new aspect, and she excelled. She had been freed from this heavy burden of guilt.

Through our determination and the unconditional love and guidance we received from the staff at House of Hope—and of course knowing that Jesus loves us even more—we are enjoying life.

We were all in the program for eighteen months. We started going to church regularly. We saw our family coming together more and more. Our family had been restored as per the vision of Malachi 4:6. Glory to God!

We have had our fair share of disappointments and trials. Our daughter strayed from what she had been taught, but the seeds that were planted are growing again. Knowing that God will never leave us or forsake us and that He will never give us more than we can handle (even when we say, "How much more, Lord?") just seems to make it easier and the joy even sweeter.

It has been eighteen years since our daughter was a resident at House of Hope. She is now married and has blessed us with two beautiful grandchildren—our "double portion." Our older daughter served on staff at House of Hope. I have been leading worship and ministering in nursing homes. I have found my calling. I can't imagine my life without it. My husband witnesses to his coworkers regularly. God is so good!

House of Hope launched us to where we are today. We know that we will be serving the Lord for the rest of our days in whatever He has for us to do.

CHAPTER 22

Testimony from a Counselor

JUST AS PARENTS FIND THEMSELVES CHANGED AT HOUSE OF HOPE, many of our counselors do as well. Here is a story of a wonderful young lady who came to us for a summer internship and ended up working with us as a counselor for eight years.

From Naïve to Equipped: Lauren Holmes, LMHC

As a licensed mental health counselor, I focus on helping families in crisis from a Christian perspective. Let me say from the outset that I never thought that God would lead my life in this direction. I can honestly say that the experiences, life lessons and maturity in my profession are a direct result from my association with House of Hope. What a joy it has been to work with Sara and the teens at House of Hope Orlando. It truly has changed my life forever and has given me insights into family challenges that I would have never gotten had I not been working there.

This book will provide you with real lasting answers to counseling difficult family issues. The approach House of Hope takes toward counseling works, and as a therapist, I wish that this book was around when I first got into the arena of counseling teens and families.

When I graduated from Palm Beach Atlantic University with a degree in psychology, I thought it would be a wonderful experience and a natural extension of my education to work for a summer as a house mom at House of Hope. When I applied for the position, Sara told me that working with these teens would change my life and my perspective on life forever. I thought at the time that she may have been over-stating the opportunity. How could a summer job change my life forever?

As I sit in my office today, nearly thirteen years later and reflect back on my eight plus years at House of Hope, it is obvious to me that my counseling practice, knowledge of the dynamics of families with troubled teens, and my outlook on life in general are all a direct result of the time spent at House of Hope working with Sara Trollinger and her staff. A few of my reflections and things I have learned are included in the following pages, but let me first share a glimpse of my journey.

My childhood was wonderful, with an extremely normal family. I grew up in the country, on a lake, in the outskirts of Orlando. My mom and dad have been married for almost forty years. My brother, cousins and I spent most of our time living in either Florida or North Carolina. Both of my parents have a deep-seated faith in Jesus Christ, so my brother and I grew up going to First Baptist Church Orlando.

My father is my hero. He has an adventurous spirit, always looking for fun and excitement. Dad has worked for major companies, and has owned and operated his own successful businesses.

My mother, equally loved, is the complete opposite of my Dad; she is a quiet, calm, elementary school teacher. She keeps our family on course when my father's adventuresome personality gets out of hand.

I share this with you so that you can understand how foreign it was for me when during my internship one of my young female clients came to me with her arms cut up by razor blades. Nothing in college, my family life or my personal life prepared me for a situation like that.

As a part of the house staff, I lived in the house with my group of girls. I ate with them and slept in the same house and knew them on a level that was bone deep. Some of these girls came from the street as a result of a family crisis that caused them to run away. Family crises exist in all types of families, from the wealthy to the impoverished. Regardless of family background, financial position, religion or anything else, if a girl has been on the street for more than a day she after has become involved in drugs and illicit sex. Violence, either mental or physical, is also a big part of the mix. The virtues of purity, trust, self worth and faith are stripped away quickly. The teen goes into survival mode, doing what is necessary to survive, and yet projects a façade that says to the world, "I can make it on my own."

You might guess how the association with these junior and high school girls affected me. I was a fresh college graduate, from a fine Christian home, with lots of love and affection, so every young person that I met gave me a new and different insight into the effects of a failed family life. The problems and issues that we dealt with were many times the result of a lack of godly influence. Family incest, sexual experimentation, stealing, occult involvement, drug use, self-abuse, familial jealousy, rape, deaths—all were part of the patterns that I learned how to deal with as a house staff.

Early on, Sara learned that helping the teen was not enough. She insisted that each teen's parent become involved in the process. First we started with the child, presenting godly principles, Bible immersion and what family normalcy looks like. The girls were expected to keep their rooms clean, dishes washed, clothes modest, and language controlled. Significant, clear boundaries were established so that each child began to learn how to live in a society that respected the rights of others. For some this came quickly; for others, it took some time.

Rarely did we ever find a "bad" teen. What we found was a family that was dysfunctional, either because of violence, drugs, alcohol, sexual incest or parents' lack of knowledge about parenting. We used a holistic approach to working with the parents, teaching parenting skills such as setting boundaries, appropriate discipline and the healing impact of including God in their daily lives.

My summer job turned into more than eight years working with Sara and her staff. My life and my family's lives were changed forever. The insights that I learned from House of Hope have enabled me to understand and provide help to hurting families and teens. I believe that the material and life lessons contained within the pages of this book will provide solutions for you. Chances are you will never get the opportunity to serve with Sara Trollinger and the staff at House of Hope, but I encourage you to investigate House of Hope's powerful approach to counseling. It will prove to be a life-changing method for you in caring for teens God's way.

Epilogue

HAVING WORKED INTENSIVELY WITH TEENAGERS FOR FORTY YEARS, I have learned that I must make a conscious effort to find time to replenish my strength—mentally, physically and spiritually.

First and foremost, I must take time daily for prayer and Bible study. My most uplifting times are when I listen to the Lord and write down what He says to me. I've missed a few sessions, but He's always there. As I tell the teens, God has an easy phone number—Jeremiah 33:3. When I call on Him, He answers and tells me great and mighty things.

Fellowship with other like-minded Christians is something else I need and find time to do, which may include playing cards, Scrabble or board games, and shopping.

For a mental vacation, I love playing Suduko, going to the beach, completing crossword puzzles, reading and traveling.

I make time for physical exercise, which includes walking, time on my treadmill and working in the yard.

I also find that spending time with the teenagers can actually be refreshing and encouraging. One of my favorite weekly treats is called "fireside chat," where I spend an hour with the boys and girls separately at House of Hope every Wednesday afternoon. That's when we encourage each other, share testimonies and usually have "treats" to eat.

For spiritual support, on Monday nights I attend an intercessory prayer group.

I am not a believer in "burn out." I often share with the staff that we don't burn out if we make the right personal choices to spend quality time building ourselves up in God's Word and prayer, being mindful of the fact that only through Jesus with the power of the Holy Spirit can healing be found. I also encourage each staff to receive ongoing triage counseling. Being on the front lines, we need it.

When teens and parents initially come to House of Hope, they are without hope—shoulders slumped, heads down, rebellious, angry. I try to look beyond their despair and depression and find something positive about each one and encourage them. They usually have such a poor self-concept they don't believe me.

What a joy it is to see how they change when they find Jesus and begin their healing process. It is obvious when growth and healing are taking place. These are the moments I live for. In awe, I get on my knees and thank God for them. I am blessed to be a small part of what God is doing with this generation of parents and teens.

The two sayings that guide me are: "God will be as big in my life as I allow Him to be," and "Don't ever give up!"

At the end of each (usually 12-hour) day, I am blessed and fulfilled with a grateful sense of awe and significance that God counted me worthy to be a small hand extended to help change a life—one at a time. For me there is no greater call then seeing a young life set on course to follow God and be reconciled and restored to his or her family.

I've talked a lot about spiritual triage, using the medical emergency metaphor to share important counseling concepts. Every emergency room physician is well acquainted with the "golden hour" concept. The golden hour concept refers to that period of time when critical care is needed. For teenagers it's that critical time when they are in the midst of addictions, rebellion and many other issues when they must receive emergency care. When they arrive at our doors, this is their golden hour of response time—and our golden hour as counselors.

Our society is ready to turn over the reigns to teenagers. They are hearing the siren call of the world's lust. This is our golden hour; we must make a difference; we cannot give up. Whether it's in your home, your youth group or your counseling practice, be willing to fight for whom God fights—our hurting teens and families.

Counseling Tools

Counseling Conversation Starters

At the beginning when a teenager first arrives at House of Hope, we will ask them questions such as these to help them open up.

1. The five most important things I want out of life are:
2. The main motivation in my life is:
3. If I could be without fear of failure and had a strong sense of confidence that whatever I tried would succeed, I would do the following:
4. Women are:
5. I feel most important when:
6. To me being successful means:
7. The three nicest compliments I have ever received are:
8. Men are:
9. The most desirable compliment that I would like to be given would be:
10. To me sex is:
11. The three people I most admire in the world and want to be like are:
12. The quality or qualities that really attract me to these individuals are:
13. My biggest dreads, fears, worries and negative thoughts are:

14. I worry about:
15. The most prominent (normal) emotions in my childhood home were:
16. My childhood dream about what I would be "when I grew up" was:
17. The five things that de-motivate (discourage) me most in life are:
18. I de-motivate myself most by:
19. My favorite color, food and movie are:
20. Jesus Christ is:

Client Evaluation Questionnaire

Counselors fill out this form at the beginning of treatment and keep it in the client's file.

Client Name:_____

Date of Birth:_____   Age:_____   Sex:_____   Race:_____

Home Situation

Lives with:

__biological mother/father   __stepmother/father

__relative placement   __foster/group home

__other: _____

Condition of living situation

__clean	__odor-free	__tidy	__spacious
__own room	__low crime	__dirty	__smelly
__messy	__crowded	__shares rm	__high crime

Caregiver commitment:

__seeking placement   __enthusiastic

__not seeking placement   __not enthusiastic

Child is SSI Recipient: __yes   __no

Psychosocial Stressors
(if more than one year ago, indicate date of event)

__high crime neighborhood   __single parent home

__parental neglect or abandonment __overcrowded living situations

__divorce/remarriage of parents   __physical or sexual abuse (years:___)

Mental Health Status
(check all that are problematic)

__no problems   __insight

__hallucinations   __clouded consciousness

__orientation to person   __judgment

__delusions   __strange thought processes

__orientation to place   __ability to reason

__suicidal ideation   __strange mannerisms

__orientation to time   __attention span

__homicidal ideation   __perseveration

__recent memory   __remote memory

__affect (anxious/depressed/fearful/angry/other: _____)

__motor activity (lethargic/restless/other: _____)

Emotional/Behavioral Symptoms

__Physical aggression   __tantrums/disruptive

__toileting problems   __depressed mood

__threatens/intimidates   __argumentative

__sleeping problems   __anxious mood

__property destruction   __noncompliant/defiant

__eating problems   __low self-esteem

__lies/manipulates   __provokes others

__substance abuse   __suicide gestures/attempts

__steals/shoplifts   __blames others

__sexual acting out   __somatic complaints

__breaks curfew   __irritable/easily annoyed

__swears/verbal abuse   __obsessive/compulsive behavior

__runs away   __angry/resentful

Emotional/Behavioral Symptoms
(continued)

__hyperactive/impulsive   __tics/stereotypy/odd movements

__truancy   __spiteful/vindictive

__self-injury

__Other: _____

Mental Health/Behavioral Treatment History

Previous treatment

__in-clinic therapy   __in-home services

__medication therapy   __crisis unit

__impatient/residential   __none

__other: _____

Treating Agency   Dates of Treatment

_____   _____

_____   _____

_____   _____

_____   _____

Prior Diagnoses: _____

DD: Autism MR (Level: _____) PDD None

Familial Diagnoses: _____

Previous meds: _____

Current meds: _____

Legal Involvement

__none   __charges pending

__on probation   __previous placement in detention

__previous arrests   __doing community service

__charges dropped   __other:_____

Counseling Checklist

This is for the counselor to keep in their client file to make sure they have covered all of these important topics.

House of Hope Counseling Checklist

Name: _____ Intake Date: _____

TOPICS	ISSUES TO BE ADDRESSED	DATE	STAFF
I. Prayer Ministry	Sins of the father and generational curses		
	Soul ties/soul hurts		
	Deliverance/occult		
	Restoration ministry		
	False beliefs /self-esteem		
	Documentation of special prayer ministries		
II. Issues	Anger management		
	Forgiveness		
	Rebellion/submission to authority		
	Abandonment/rejection		
	Codependency		
	Fear		
	Abuse (emotional, physical, spiritual, sexual)		
	Personality testing		
	Identity		
III. Life Skills	Therapeutic letter exchange		
	Communication		
	Boundaries		
	Accepting responsibility		
	Integrity (character, honesty, respect to others)		
	Making decisions and wise choices		
	Relationships		
	Developing intimacy		
	Hygiene		
	Conflict resolution		

TOPICS	ISSUES TO BE ADDRESSED	DATE	STAFF
IV. Spiritual Life	Born-again/baptism		
	Prayer life development		
	Making the Word relate to your life		
	Developing your praise and worship		
	Having a grateful heart		
	Learning to listen to God		
VI. Parenting Issues	Loving your child		
	Discipline and parenting styles		
	Developing character in your child		
	Conflict resolution in the family		
	Creating a positive family environment		
	Boundaries with your child		

Behavior Checklist

Counselors keep copies of this checklist in the clients' files and fill out a new one periodically to assess progress.

Client: _____ **Age:** _____ **Sex:** ____

Counselor: _____ **Date:** _____

No at All	Just Little	Pretty Much	Very Much	
0	1	2	3	1. Picks at things (nails, fingers, hair, clothing)
0	1	2	3	2. Distractibility, or attention span problems
0	1	2	3	3. Doesn't like or doesn't follow rules or restrictions
0	1	2	3	4. Excitable, impulsive
0	1	2	3	5. Fights constantly
0	1	2	3	6. Sucks or chews (thumb, clothing, blankets)
0	1	2	3	7. Headaches
0	1	2	3	8. Carries a chip on his/her shoulder
0	1	2	3	9. Mood changes quickly and drastically
0	1	2	3	10. Difficulty in learning
0	1	2	3	11. Restless in the "squirmy" sense
0	1	2	3	12. Basically unhappy
0	1	2	3	13. Restless, always up and on the go
0	1	2	3	14. Destructive
0	1	2	3	15. Tells lies or stories that aren't true
0	1	2	3	16. Shy
0	1	2	3	17. Gets into more trouble than others the same age
0	1	2	3	18. Stomach aches
0	1	2	3	19. Denies mistakes or blames others
0	1	2	3	20. Quarrelsome
0	1	2	3	21. Pouts or sulks
0	1	2	3	22. Steals
0	1	2	3	23. Disobedient, or obeys but resentfully

No at All	Just Little	Pretty Much	Very Much	
0	1	2	3	24. Other aches and pains
0	1	2	3	25. Fails to finish things
0	1	2	3	26. Feelings easily hurt
0	1	2	3	27. Problems with eating
0	1	2	3	28. Unable to stop a repetitive activity
0	1	2	3	29. Cruel
0	1	2	3	30. Childish or immature (wants help he/she shouldn't need, clings, needs constant reassurance)
0	1	2	3	31. Daydreams
0	1	2	3	32. Disturbs peers
0	1	2	3	33. Speaks differently from others the same age (baby talk, stuttering, hard to understand)
0	1	2	3	34. Vomiting or nausea
0	1	2	3	35. Sassy to grown ups
0	1	2	3	36. Feels cheated in the family circle
0	1	2	3	37. Worries more than others
0	1	2	3	38. Lets him/herself be pushed around
0	1	2	3	39. Fearful (of new situations, new people or places, going to school)
0	1	2	3	40. Easily frustrated in efforts
0	1	2	3	41. Cries easily or often
0	1	2	3	42. Boasts and brags
0	1	2	3	43. Wants to run things
0	1	2	3	44. Bowel problems (frequently loose, irregular habits, constipation)
0	1	2	3	45. Bullies others
0	1	2	3	46. Doesn't get along well with peers in the home
0	1	2	3	47. Problems with sleep (can't fall asleep, up too early, up in the night)
0	1	2	3	48. Problems with making or keeping friends

Glossary of Terms Related to Spiritual Warfare, Oppression, Cults, False Beliefs, and the Occult

alchemy—a medieval chemical science and speculative philosophy aiming to achieve the transmutation of the base metals into gold (with the aid of a mysterious psychic substance), the discovery of a universal cure for disease, and the discovery of a means of indefinitely prolonging life. (It is emerging in modern times in connection with many present-day occult doctrines and groups.)

All Hallows' Eve—October 31 witch festival

amulet—an ornament with a magic spell or inscribed with a sign. It is often worn around the neck or on the wrist in hopes of warding off evil or to help its wearer.

ankh—looks like a cross with a ring shape at its top. This is used in satanic rites and is dangerous to keep.

apparition—a ghostly figure; appearance of a "ghost" or specter.

apport—an object is dematerialized at one point, then carried by the energy of the medium's control spirit to its destination, and materialized there in its original state.

asherah—images of the Canaanite goddess, Asherah, whose worship was lewd

astral projection—the practice of traveling by spirit apart from the body

astrologer—one who forecasts the supposed effect of the positioning of heavenly bodies upon human affairs and earthly events

augury—the practice of divination

automatic writing—writing under a trance induced by spirit or demon powers; the spirit writes.

Baal worship—the worship of the foreign god Baal, which was prohibited by God

Baha'i—eastern religion originating in Iran (Persia) which believes that peace, unity of all religions and brotherhood are the final and essential revelation of God. They reject the Trinity and the blood atonement. They believe Jesus was only a prophet, and the writings of their prophet are the final authority and revelation. They believe Christianity has passed and that Baha'u'llah came to announce a new age

baphomet—Goat of Mendes; Satanic symbol; the goat's head

bewitch—spiritually influence by witchcraft through the casting of a spell

black magic—witchcraft. This is sometimes called Black Art and is used for selfish and evil purposes against a person.

black mass—a religious ritual of Satan worship

blood subscription—(or blood pact). A written expression of occult intention or Satanic devotion which is signed in human or animal blood; any contract with Satan signed in blood.

Buddhism—eastern religion with many forms—two hundred sects and sub-sects in Japan alone; most sects are polytheistic, pantheistic or atheistic.

cartomancy—fortune telling with cards (card laying)

charm—an act or spell having magic power, or something worn by a person to bring good luck or to ward off evil

charming—procedure in magic using the chanting or reciting of a magic spell or incantation; to affect, compel, endow with supernatural powers, control or protect by spells, charms or supernatural influences

chiromancy—divination by examination of the hand; palmistry

charmer—an enchanter or magician

Children of God—founded by David Berg (who calls himself "Moses"); an organization emphasizing "forsaking all" for Jesus; includes all material possessions and their allegiance to families and teaches sexual freedom which includes fornication, group sex and wife swapping. "Moses" listens to a guiding demon called, "Abrahim."

Chiun—called also Remphan; a god of the Phoenicians, whose worship was abominable to God

Christian Science—practitioners attempt to convince the sick that their illnesses are a delusion of the mind, and by denial of the reality, they will be healed. Other beliefs are: a pantheistic god (god is everything); hell and eternal punishment do not exist; a denial of the blood atonement and bodily resurrection of Jesus, and the denial of the Trinity. The writings of Mary Baker Eddy are used coequally with the Bible.

clairvoyance—the ability to spiritually discern things through spirits that are not yet discerned by the human senses

color therapy—method used in New Zealand for psychic diagnosis (divination) and healing of disease based on psychic theories of light and color

conjure—to summon a spirit, often by incantation

consulting a medium—seeking aid or information from one who contacts evil spirits

control spirit—a medium's personal familiar spirit which encourages, enlightens and speaks through him about the things of the psychic world of evil spirits

coven—an assembly of thirteen witches

crystal gazer—a spiritualist who uses a crystal ball to look into the future

curse—to call death, injury or calamity upon a person in response to spirit invocation

cutting in flesh—a heathen practice, including tattoos, gashes, castrations, etc., usually done in mourning for the dead and to propitiate deities, but forbidden to the Israelites

death magic—the practice of passing on the illnesses of the living to the dead by placing an article belonging to the sick living person (or a charm or spell) in the grave or coffin a dead person

demon—a disembodied evil spirit under the leadership of Satan

denial—of the Trinity or the deity of Jesus Christ or His bodily resurrection or His second coming

direct voice—while in a trance, the medium's vocal apparatus is taken over by his control spirit or another spirit, and the words and inflections that come forth are in a totally different voice than the medium's, sometimes in a foreign language or in a heavily accented language

divination—the practice of foreseeing of foretelling future events or discovering hidden knowledge by means of reading omens, dreams, the use of lots, astrology, necromancy, etc.

dreamers of dreams—expression used to describe some false prophets who pretended to receive revelations from God through dreams, or who received information in dreams from a demonic source and said it was from God

eclectic—acceptance of good in all religions; still searching for "truth" and not acknowledging Christianity is founded in the *person* of Jesus, not just the teachings of Jesus

ectoplasm—a substance held to produce spirit materialization

elemental spirits—heathen deities and beliefs; more specifically sinister angelic powers and demonic spirits

eidetic imagery—of or relating to voluntarily producible visual images (by psychic means) having almost photographic accuracy

enchantments—the use of any form of magic, including divination

ESP—extra-sensory perception. Telepathy, clairvoyance, mind reading, diagnosis of disease and prescription of cures by clairvoyance; water witching (or dowsing) pendulum or divining by rod usage

EST—(Erhard Seminars Training) pseudo-western religion founded by Werner Erhard, followed by such notables as John Denver. Their philosophy is that there are no absolutes except the absolute of "Whatever is, is right;" God is man and man is God; life is perfect, with no difference between right and wrong.

etheric body—an apparition in visible form; a specter of recognizable shape and form

excursion of the soul—astral projection; the soul leaves the body and travels on a different plane of consciousness

false apostle—any person claiming to be a genuine minister of God but not possessing a divine commission nor displaying genuine fruit

false christs—antichrists, imitators and pretenders who claim to be the Messiah. Jesus warned His followers not to be deceived by them

false prophet—any person claiming to possess a message from God but not possessing a divine commission, nor displaying genuine fruit. More specifically *the* false prophet mentioned in the Book of Revelation, who will come prior to Christ's return and deceive many

false teacher—any person claiming to be a genuine teacher of God but not possessing a divine commission nor displaying genuine fruit

false visions—or dreams and divinations. The revelations of false prophets and ministers which they claim to have received from God; used as methods of deceiving God's people

familiar spirit—a demon, usually impersonating a deceased person, who provides information and guidance to and through a medium

fetish—an object believed to have magical power to protect or aid its owner; broadly, any material object regarded with superstitious or extravagant trust or reverence

fire walking—the practice of walking through fire or on white-hot stones, usually by the fire walker placing himself or being placed in a hypnotic or spiritualistic trance

foreknowledge—precognition, premonition or clairvoyance concerning an event or circumstance that will occur in the future

fortune-telling—the practice of foretelling future events by supernatural means

Free Masons—a secret lodge whose religion is not sectarian. It accepts all creeds and religions but declares on page 619 in *Encyclopedia of Free Masonary* that it is not Christianity. Jesus Christ is left out. Masonary does not teach His divinity or the blood atonement. They regard the Bible as only one of many sacred books, along with the Koran, et. al. They bind themselves with an oath of secrecy with a penalty of having their throat cut and tongue torn out. Their plan of salvation is growth in character and by good works

graphology—the study of handwriting for the purpose of character analysis. This is a borderline case. Perhaps not all instances of graphology are occult-based, but the study is frequently used much as a horoscope would be, to determine future events by analyzing one's handwriting

graven image—a carved image or statue of wood, stone or metal, generally used as an idol

ghost—disembodied soul; the "spirit or soul of a dead person" believed to be an inhabitant of the unseen world and appearing to the living in bodily likeness; actually, an impersonating evil spirit or demon

Hare Krishna—an eastern religion, ISKCON (International Society for Krishna Consciousness) worships and has a personal relationship with a god that emphasizes love and service. It is a works system of salvation. The mantra must be chanted. Believes in reincarnation by atoning for sins and reducing Karmic debt.

hex—to affect by an evil spell; to jinx; also, a person who practices witch-craft: a witch

Hinduism—eastern religion that believes in reincarnation, polytheistic (e.g. Brahma, the creator; Vishnu, the Preserver; Shiva, the Destroyer), idolatrous, a works system, denies claims of Christ that He is the only way to God

horoscope—a chart showing position of planets and stars with their signs of the zodiac; used by astrologers to foretell events of a person's life and give guidance

incantation—written or verbal spells spoken or sung as part of a ritual of magic; a formula of words changed or recited in a magic ritual

incense—material used to produce a fragrance when burned. The burning of incense is not necessarily an occult practice. The reason for its inclusion in this list is that it is frequently used in séances, meditation, chanting incantations, and so forth and is closely connected with occult rituals and experiences

incubus—evil spirits supposed to lie upon persons in their sleep and more particularly, to have sexual intercourse with women by night

Islam—An eastern religion that teaches: 1) Allah is the one true God, and the Trinity is false because it is polytheistic; 2) Allah sent many prophets, including Jesus, who was sinless, but Muhammad is the last and greatest. 3) The Koran is the final message of Allah to man. 4) There will be a Day of Judgment when Allah will decide who will go to Paradise, a place of sensuous delight and gratification, and who will go to hell. Islam rejects the crucifixion and resurrection of Jesus as a way of salvation.

Jehovah's Witnesses—pseudo-western religion whose beliefs are 1) Christ returned invisibly in 1874; 2) denial of deity of Christ; 3) denial of the personality of the Holy Spirit; 4) denial of the bodily resurrection of Jesus; 5) rejection of hell and the eternal punishment of the wicked.

karma—the net spiritual sum of all good and bad acts and works from each persons' prior lives. Reincarnationists try to explain this as the reason for the quality or status awarded each person in this present life.

They believe the Karma varies continually with the good and bad things one does in this present life

legerdemain—sleight of hand; performance of minor magical tricks

letters of protection—magic letter or lucky letter by which the writer or holder solicits psychic protection from accident or calamity

levitation—a person or object rises or floats in the air in seeming defiance of gravitation; a common occurrence at séance

looking in the liver—a form of augury; prediction of the future by position or condition of the liver of a sacrificed animal

lyceums—a system of spiritualist training schools founded in Britain by Andrew Jackson Davis

macumba—powerful and prevalent type of spiritism in Brazil

magic—supernatural power over natural forces by use of charms, spells and so forth (not to be confused with sleight of hand tricks)

magical healing—healing of diseases, not by medical but by occult means; e.g., spells, charms, amulets, incantations, etc.

magician—a person who claims to understand and explain mysteries by magic, which is the art or science of influencing or controlling the course of nature, events, and supernatural powers through occult science or mysterious arts. One who perform wonders by deception or by actual occult power

Manifest Sons of God—a pseudo-western religion whose doctrine teaches that God is forming a special overcoming company within the body called, "The Manchild Company." This "company" is perfected through "revelation" teachings; believers are equal with Jesus and claim to have the only key to the Kingdom of Heaven; adds to the Scripture in the book *Christ Unlimited* by H.D. Voss

mark of the beast—imprinted tattoo or sign upon those who subjugate themselves to the antichrist

materializations—something that has been materialized, especially an apparition; the appearance in bodily form of the "spirits of the dead," actually impersonating demons

medium—an individual held to be a channel of communication between the earthly world and the world of spirits

mesmerism—hypnotic induction held to involve "animal magnetism;" broadly, hypnotism

metaphysics—confusing soul and spirit, trying to contact God with the mind instead of the spirit

mind expansion—techniques by drugs, hypnosis, transcendental meditation, self-hypnotism and metaphysical healing of the body

mind science—the false teaching that the mind is the only reality; matter, sickness, and sin are not real, just errors

Molech—called also Moloch or Milcom; an idol that was worshiped and to which living children were often sacrificed by burning

Mormonism—pseudo-western religion with the following beliefs: 1) God, our Father, was once a man, Adam, who was later exalted; 2) pre-existence of the soul as "spirit children," whom the gods produced through their celestial wives; 3)polygamy (at one time); 4) denial of virgin birth; 5) rejection of hell and the eternal punishment of the wicked

mystic—a follower or expounder of mysticism and occult experiences

necromancy—conjuring spirits of the dead for the purpose of revealing the future or influencing present events

New Age Movement—a worldwide, loose organism of cults whose design is to usher in the "Lord Maitreya" (the antichrist), world rulership and world government, the new world of peace and prosperity through a transformation of higher states of consciousness (realizing one's own "god-hood"). It believes that "all is one" and that we only need to make positive affirmations to change the world. In her book *Aquarian Conspiracy*, Marilyn Ferguson says that this "one-world" concept is being engineered by mysterious invisible intelligences who are guiding from behind the scenes. Many of the New Age writings were received through automatic writings. Their symbol is the rainbow.

nirvana—the sea of nothingness, which is the ultimate goal of the reincarnation *ista*

numerology—the study of the occult significance of numbers; numerical symbolism

observer of times—person who has a superstitious regard for days regarded as lucky or unlucky, as decided by astrology or superstition

occult—secret or mysterious, relating to supernatural agencies or forces

occult textbooks—books which contain rituals, spells, magic potions, occult instructions and information, and detailed explanations of psychic and magic practices. There are countless books of this nature, but some of the best known and most often used are the following: *Satanic Bible, Secrets of the Psalms, Sixth and Seventh Book of Moses, The Book of Venus, I-Ching* and *Tetrabiblos.*

omens—occurrences or phenomena believed to portend a future event; augury

oneiromancy—divination by means of dreams

Ouija board—a flat wooden surface with the alphabet and other signs, used to obtain spiritualistic messages about the future or other hidden knowledge; the pointer is moved by evil spirits

palmistry—reading a person's character or future by studying the lines in the palm of a hand

parapsychology—the study that investigates the psychological aspect of supernatural phenomena such as telepathy, clairvoyance, apparitions, etc.

passing through fire—idolatrous practice of child sacrifice by burning; particularly abominable to God

pentacle—(pentagram) a five-pointed – or sometimes six-pointed – star used as a magical symbol

phrenology—reading a person's character or future by the conformation of his skull

physiognomy—the art of discovering temperament and character from outward appearance

planchette—a small board supported on casters at two points and a vertical pencil at a third, and believed to produce automatic writing when lightly touched by the fingers. Also, the movable indicator on an Ouija board

potions—in an occult sense, a liquid mixture or dose which supposedly endows the drinker with supernatural abilities or knowledge

poltergeist—a mischievous ghost who is said to be responsible for strange noises such as rappings, knockings, or the movement of objects

pornography—pictures, novels, TV shows, films, etc.; sexual deviations

precognition—knowledge about an event not yet experienced by means beyond the physical senses

premonition—uneasy anticipation of an event without any conscious means of knowing why

presentiment—a feeling that some specific evil is going to happen in the future

principalities—order of powerful Satanic angels and demons

prognosticators—astrologers who predicted the future

PSI—symbol for the transcendent aspect of human personality. From letters of the Greek word *psyche* (soul)

psychic—a person who is sensitive to non-physical forces and their significance in the material world

psychic phenomena—events that cannot be explained by natural references; hence are attributed to non-physical or spiritual forces

psychokinesis—movement of physical objects by the mind, without use of physical means

psychometry—extrasensory divination of facts concerning an object or its owner through contact or proximity to the object

physical phenomena—such as telekinesis (attempts to control movement of matter by thought), levitation, table tipping (attempts to neutralize gravity by psychic means), astral projection (attempts to project the so-called astral diagnosis by wooden rod and treatment by color). These things can happen, but the power behind them is demonic.

radiesthesia—the "science" of determining psychic information by use of the ord and pendulum

rhabdomancy—divination by rods or wands

reincarnation—Karma

Rosicrucianism—a secret cultural cult brotherhood dedicated to helping men understand their cosmic relationship and use their inner powers to achieve their highest potentials. Their teachings include reincarnation, pantheism (nature is the visible symbol of God), occultism, divinity of man, etc. They invite all religions into their membership.

sabbat—a midnight assembly of diabolists (witches and sorcerers) held to renew allegiance to the devil through mystic and licentious rites

Satanism—devil worship, frequently involving a travesty of Christian rites; prayer to the devil, black masses and so forth

Satan worship—secret societies, blood pacts

Scientology—basically a psychological method of attempting to remove from the subconscious mind all traces of neuroses and emotional hang-ups (called engrams) which come to man from previous incarnations. This process, dianetic therapy, consists of a program conducted by an auditor to reduce their effect upon the subconscious. An e-meter is used to register emotional reactions when the person replies to probing questions. One is free from engrams when the e-meter registers no emotional reaction. This is accomplished by facing up to the problem and ridding oneself from the neuroses.

séance—a group gathered to communicate with spirits; a medium presides at a séance

séance of passivity—the process of blotting out all conscious thought so a spirit can take control of a medium and speak through him

séance of vocal reality—many sounds are produced through the medium's vocal chords— not just voice but music, sound effects, instruments and so forth. The sound vibrations are distinctly produced through the vocal apparatus of the medium

séance of lights—preceded by a half-hour meditation during which each person prepares himself for the coming of the spirit; in this séance, a darkened room fills with drifting lights until it becomes a mass of colors, each light indicating the spirit of someone who has passed on

séance of trumpet revelation—a metal trumpet, made of aluminum or sheet metal, is used. When the medium enters his trance, the trumpet rises (by demon control) slowly from the table and moves around the room, stopping at intervals in midair. The spirit's voice speaks through the trumpet.

séance of transfiguration—in this séance, the transfigured form of a loved one who has died appears

séance of levitation—soul travel; the phenomena of spirit development whereby a medium or an advanced convert to spiritualism can leave his body by completely yielding to a control spirit; he is not completely disunited from his body but is able to take conscious flight from it to distant places (also known as astral projection)

seer—one that practices divination; a crystal gazer

seducing spirits—demons whose intents are to deceive a believer and ultimately pull him into apostasy

specter—a visible disembodied spirit; something that haunts or perturbs the mind (phantasm)

spell—a spoken pattern of words with magic power

spirit guide—control spirit; familiar spirit that attaches itself to a medium's personality and sets as the medium's personal contact and channel with the spirit world

Spiritism—worshiping spirits

Spiritual Frontiers—a pseudo-western religion founded by Arthur Ford in 1956; an association of ministers and laymen who contend that "communion with the saints" means personal communication with the "beloved dead." They believe ESP, psychic gifts, hypnosis, séances, etc. all have a vital place in the church

Spiritualism—the belief that departed spirits commune with living people, usually through a medium but sometimes through other psychic phenomena

Spiritualist—one who believes that the spirits of the dead can and do communicate with the living by means of a medium, or by other supernatural means, e.g., meditation, automatic writing, rappings, etc.

soothsayer—one claiming power to foretell future events, interpret dreams and reveal secrets; a fortune teller

sorcery—divination by alleged assistance of evil spirits; strictly forbidden by God

sorcerer, sorceress—one who practices sorcery; a sorcerer is a wizard or warlock (male), and a sorceress is a witch (female)

soul transmigration—the supposed process of passing at death from one body or being to another

stargazers—those who worship the stars, the sun, the moon and other heavenly bodies; practice forbidden by God

succubus—(plural succubi or succubae) demons assuming female form to have sexual intercourse with men in their sleep

table lifting—psychic lifting of a table either by levitation, psychokinesis or telekinesis

talisman—an object bearing a sign or character engraved under astrological influences and thought to act as a charm to avert evil and bring good fortune; something producing apparently magical or miraculous effects

Taoism—eastern religion (pronounced "Dowism") – nature is full of conflict between yang and yin, but they perfectly balance each other; Yang—male, Yin—female; good— evil; light— dark, etc. There is no personal Creator-God. It has degenerated into a system of magical practices and incantations. Polytheistic.

Tarot cards—a set of twenty-two fortune telling cards with unusual and often repulsive symbolic figures printed on them

tea leaf reading—fortune telling by reading omens in tea leaves

telekinesis—the apparent production of motion in objects (as by a spiritualistic medium) without contact or other physical means

telepathy—(or mental telepathy) communication from one mind to another, without use of the ordinary physical channels of hearing, seeing, touching, etc.

thaipusam—primarily Far East religionists who torture and abuse their bodies

The Way International—pseudo-western religion that believes 1) there is no Trinity and Christ has no deity; 2) the founder, Victor Wierville, has the correct and reliable interpretation of Scripture. It claims to be the restoration of first-century Christianity, and many of its teachings are Scriptural.

Theosophy—founded by Helena Blavatsky, a medium, in 1875. Annie Besant, leader after the death of Blavatsky, announced in 1925 her son, Krishnamurti, an Indian mystic, was the new Messiah. Major errors include: 1) pantheism (the belief that God and the universe are identical). God does not exist as a personality but is rather the expression of the physical forces of nature. "Everything is God and God is everything;" 2) divinity of man and rejection of the blood atonement; 3) reincarnation; 4) denial of deity of Christ.

trance—an unconscious or semi-conscious state of partially suspended animation, usually caused by spirit activity

transcendental meditation—concentration on the spiritual realm in order to transcend or go beyond material or empirical experience to the higher reality of the spirit world; usually entails repeated prayers or chants similar to magical incantations or spells

transfiguration—an occurrence, usually in séances, where the form of a "departed loved one" takes the place of the medium's body and speaks and gestures to those attending the séance; a form of materialization

umbanda—similar to Macumba, it is also a prevalent cult in Brazil and is totally based upon spiritualistic principles

Unification Church—(Moonies); a pseudo-western religion with the following beliefs: 1) Sun Myung Moon believes that he is the Messiah for this age; 2) the writings of Moon, "Divine Principle," take precedence over the Bible; 3) all existence is dual: Father God and Mother God, yin and yang, etc. Each part of existence has its dual aspect; 4) Jesus failed to redeem man physically and spiritually; 5) Moon believes he is to finish the task uncompleted by Jesus

Unitarian—pseudo-western religion that denies the inspiration and infallibility of the Scriptures, the virgin birth, and the deity of Jesus, is anti-Trinitarian, anti-supernatural or miraculous, and believes in the ultimate salvation of all men. Salvation is by works through the reformation of man's character.

Unity School of Christianity—similar to Christian Science with additional error of reincarnation. Its major beliefs are: 1) pantheistic view of God; 2) no difference between the deity of Christ and the divinity of all men; 3) rejection of blood atonement; 4) the denial of Satan, hell, and eternal punishment. It publishes the magazine *Unity*.

Universalism—belief in the ultimate salvation of all men

voodoo—a religion derived from African ancestor worship involving spells, necromancy and communication with animistic gods

warlock—a male witch—one who works black magic

wart removal—non-medical removal of warts by spells, incantations, magic potions or an occult pact

white magic—witchcraft used supposedly for good and unselfish purposes

witch—a woman who practices the black arts; one who has supernatural powers through evil spirits

witch doctor—a professional worker of magic in a primitive society (and presently in all societies because of the influx of numerous occult practices); similar to a shaman or a medicine man

witches' Sabbath—a midnight assembly of a coven of thirteen witches for performing rites

witchcraft—the use of sorcery or magic; intentional interaction with the devil or a familiar spirit

wizard—a sorcerer

Worldwide Church of God—a pseudo-western religion that claims that no other religion's work is proclaiming the true Gospel of Christ. They deny hell and eternal punishment of the wicked. Salvation is by doing the works of Christ; they don't believe in blood atonement; they reject the Trinity; the soul is said to be asleep between death and resurrection

worship of demons—heathen practice forbidden by God

zodiac—an imaginary belt of planets and constellations in imaginary twelve "houses" which astrologists believe affect human experience; represented by the astrological signs

zombie—the voodoo snake deity; the supernatural power that according to voodoo belief may enter into and reanimate a dead body

APPENDIX C

Potential Strongholds and Oppresion Related Groupings

The bold headers are types of potential strongholds in a person's life, and the items listed under those headers are associated symptoms that may require prayer, ministry, and counseling.

Abandonment
Emotional abandonment
Loneliness
Not acceptable
Not belonging
Not wanted
Rejection
Self-pity
Victim

Accusation
Criticism
Fault-finding
Judging

Addictions
Alcohol
Caffeine

Cocaine
Computers
Escape
Food
Gambling
Marijuana
Nicotine
Pornography
Prescription drugs
Reading
Sex
Sports
Street drugs
Tranquilizers
TV
Video games

Affectation
- Mutilation
- Playacting
- Pretension
- Sophistication
- Theatrics

Anxiety
- Apprehension
- Burden
- Dread
- False responsibility
- Fatigue/heaviness
- Fear
- Nervousness
- Weariness
- Worry

Bitterness
- Anger
- Blame
- Complaining
- Hatred
- Judging
- Murder
- Resentment
- Retaliation
- Root of bitterness
- Temper
- Unforgiveness
- Violence

Bound Emotions
- Hindered emotions
- Repressed emotions

Competition
- Driving
- Jealousy/envy
- Possessiveness
- Striving

Control/Appeasement
- Denial
- Dominance
- Double-binding
- False responsibility
- Female control
- Male control
- Manipulation
- Possessiveness
- Pride (I know best)
- Selfishness
- Witchcraft

Covetousness
- Abandonment
- Anger
- Discontent
- Greed
- Hatred
- Kleptomania
- Material lust
- Murder
- Passive aggression
- Rage
- Resentment
- Spoiled little boy/girl
- Stealing
- Temper tantrums

Deception
  Confusion
  False burden
  Lying
  Pride
  Self-deception

Depression
  Death wish
  Defeatism
  Dejection
  Despair
  Despondency
  Discouragement
  Hopelessness
  Insomnia/oversleeping
  Morbidity
  Self-pity
  Suicide attempt

Failure
  Performance
  Pressure to succeed
  Striving

Fears
  Anxiety
  Bewilderment
  Burden
  Dread
  Fear of authorities
  Fear of being a victim
  Fear of being attacked
  Fear of cancer
  Fear of death
  Fear of demons

Fear of failure
Fear of future
Fear of infirmities
Fear of intimacy
Fear of man
Fear of performance
Fear of poverty
Fear of punishment
Fear of rejection
Fear of sexual inadequacy
Fear of sexual perversion
Fear of singing
Fear of violence
Harassment
Heaviness
Horror movies
Intimidation
Mental torment
Over-sensitivity
Paranoia
Phobia
Superstition
Worry

Financial Bondage
  Greed
  Irresponsible spending
  Job failures
  Job losses
  Poverty
  Stinginess

Grief
  Crying/weeping
  Heartbreak
  Loss

Sadness
Sorrow
Trauma

Identity Confusion
Deception
Homosexuality
Lesbianism
Pornography
Trauma
Unprotected

Idolatry
Appearance/beauty
Clothes
Food
Ministry
Money
Position
Possessions

Indecision
Compromise
Confusion
Forgetfulness
Indifference
Procrastination

Infirmities/Diseases
(These can have physical or spiritual sources. Pray for discernment to know the difference.)
Accidents (falls, cars)
Anorexia/bulimia
Asthma
Barrenness/miscarriage

Cancer
Congestion in lungs
Diabetes
Fatigue
Heart circulatory problems
Multiple sclerosis
Mental illness
Migraines/mind-binding
Physical abnormalities
Premature death

Insecurity
Inadequacy
Ineptness
Inferiority
Loneliness
Self-pity
Shyness
Timidity

Jealousy
Distrust
Envy
Selfishness
Suspicion

Mental Illness
Compulsions
Confusion
Hallucinations
Insanity
Madness
Mania
Multiple personalities
Paranoia
Retardation

Schizophrenia
Senility

Mind-Binding
Anger
Bound emotions
Confusion
Double-minded
Migraines
Occult

Mind Idolatry
Arrogance
Ego
Intellectualism
Pride
Rationalism
Self-importance
Self-righteousness
Vanity

Occult
Accident proneness
Antichrist
Astral projection
Astrology
Automatic writing
Black magic
Clairvoyance
Crystal ball
Death, suicide
Dispatching demons
Divination
Eight ball
ESP
False gifts

Fortune telling
Gypsy
Handwriting analysis
Heavy metal music
Horoscopes
Horror movies
Hypnosis
I Ching
Idolatry of _____
Indian burial ground
Indians
KKK
Levitation
Mental telepathy
Necromancy
Non-Christian exorcism
Occult jewelry
Occult/witchcraft books
Ouija board
Pagan temples
Palm reading
Past life reading
Pendulum
Psychic healing
Science fantasy
Séances
Sorcery
Spell or hex casting
Spirit guides
Spiritism
Tarot cards
Tea leaves
TM
Victim
Voodoo
Water witching

White magic
Witchcraft
Yoga meditation

Rebellion
Anti-submissiveness
Disobedience
Independence
Lying
Self-will
Stubbornness
Undermining

Rejection
Fear of rejection
Mistrust of others
Not wanted by others
Perceived rejection
Self-rejection

Religious Spirits
Antichrist
Catholicism/other
Legalism/rules
Masonic
New Age
Traditionalism

Retaliation
Cruelty
Destruction
Hatred
Hurt
Sadism
Spite

Satanic music
Heavy metal
Rock and roll

Self-Accusation
Anger
Condemnation
Guilt
Inferiority
Self-hate
Self-punishment

Sexual sins
Adultery
Bestiality
Defilement/unclean
Demonic sex
Exposure
Fantasy lust
Fornication
Frigidity
Homosexuality
Incest
Incubus
Lesbianism
Lust
Masturbation
Pornography
Premarital sex
Prostitution/harlotry
Rape
Sexual abuse
Succubus

Shame
Anger

Bad boy/girl
Condemnation
Embarrassment
Guilt
Hatred
Inferiority
Overweight/underweight
Self-hate

Strife
Arguing
Bickering
Contention
Fighting
Mocking
Quarreling

Trauma
Accident
Emotional abuse
Little girl/boy
Loss
Physical abuse
Sexual abuse
Shock
Victim
Violence

Unbelief
Doubt
Rationalism
Skepticism

Unforgiveness
Bitterness
Pride

Religious (no need to)

Unworthiness
Inadequacy
Inferiority
Insecurity
Self-accusation
Self-condemnation
Self-hate

Victim
Appeasement
Helplessness
Hopelessness
Mistrust
Self-pity
Suspicion
Trauma

Violence
Cruelty
Destruction
Feuding
Hate
Murder
Retaliation
Torture/mutilation
Victim

Withdrawal
Alcohol/drugs
Blocked intimacy
Escape
Fantasy
Forgetfulness
Indifference

Isolation
Loneliness
Passivity
Procrastination
Sleepiness
Stoicism
Withdrawal

Notes

Preface

1. "Evangelicals Fear the Loss of Their Teenagers," *New York Times*, http://battlecry.com/pages/nytimesarticle1.php (accessed October 6, 2006)

Chapter 1: Overview of Triage Counseling

1. "The Jukes-Edwards Story: Truth and Myth about Max Jukes," www.rfrick.info/jukes.htm

2. George Barna, *Real Teens* (Ventura, CA: Regal Books, 2001).

Chapter 6: Testimonies of Inner Healing

1. "Suicide Fact Sheet," Center for Disease Control and Prevention, http://www.cdc.gov/ncipc/wisqars (accessed April 19, 2006).

2. Florida Suicide Prevention Coalition, http://www.floridasuicideprevention.org/the_facts.htm (accessed June 14, 2007).

3. "Youth Suicide Fact Sheet," American Association of Suicidology, http://www.suicidology.org/associations/1045/files/Youth2004.pdf4 (accessed December 28, 2006).

4. "Suicide Fact Sheet," Center for Disease Control and Prevention, www.cdc.gov/ncipc/factsheets/suifacts.htm (accessed April, 19, 2006).

5. "Facts for Teens," National Youth Violence Prevention Resource Center, http://www.safeyouth.org/scripts/teens/docs/suicide.pdf (accessed 2002).

Chapter 7: Disaster Lurking on the Internet

1. Daniel Okrent, "Raising Kids Online," *Time* magazine, May 10, 1999, http://www.time.com/time/magazine/article/0,9171,990919,00.html

2. "Fatal Addiction" Ted Bundy's Final Interview, Focus on the Family / Pure Intimacy, http://www.pureintimacy.org/gr/intimacy/understanding/a0000082.cfm (accessed 2004)

3. Lakshmi Chaudry, "Date-Rape Site Taken Down" http://www.wired.com/politics/law/news/2000/03/34941, (accessed March 14, 2000)

4. "Internet Pornography," http://www.enough.org/inside.php?tag=stat%20archives#6 (2006)

5. "Cyber Tipline Fact Sheet," http://www.missingkids.com/en_US/documents/CyberTiplineFactSheet.pdf (updated weekly).

6. Hughes, Donna Rice (March 28, 2000). Senate Hearing, Keeping Children Safe from Internet Predators, citing *Washington Times*, Jan. 26, 2000, http://www.protectkids.com/donnaricehughes/powerpoints/SenateHearing2000.ppt#1

7. Hughes, Donna Rice (March 28, 2000). Senate Hearing, Keeping Children Safe from Internet Predators, citing MSNBC/Stanford/Duquesne Study, Associated Press Online, Feb. 29, 2000 http://www.protectkids.com/donnaricehughes/powerpoints/SenateHearing2000.ppt#1

Chapter 8: Mass Media Culture

1. Victor Strasburger, "Children, Adolescents and Advertising," December 2006, http://goliath.ecnext.com/coms2/summary_0199-6084083_ITM (accessed May 2007)

2. Ibid

3. Pellegrini, *Billboard Magazine*, Jan. 23, 1999, http://www.goodfight.org/e_eminem.html (accessed May 2007).

Chapter 9: Teen Sexuality

1. Peter Kramer/Getty, "NBC News, *PEOPLE* Magazine commission landmark national poll," Jan. 31, 2005, www.msnbc.msn.com/id/6839072 (accessed May 2007).

2. Gary Langer, "ABC News Poll: Sex Lives of American Teens: Gauging U.S. Teens' Sexual Behavior" May 19, 2006, http://abcnews.go.com/Primetime/PollVault/story?id=1981945 (accessed June 2007).

3. Ibid

4. "Abortion Surveillance, United States, 2003," released Nov. 24, 2006, accessed at www.cdc.gov/mmwr/preview/mmwrhtml/ss5511a1.htm (accessed May 2007)

5. National Right to Life, "Abortion in the United States Statistics and Trends", http://www.nrlc.org/abortion/facts/abortionstats.html (accessed June 2007)

6. Ibid.

7. Nancy Gibbs, "Grassroots Abortion War," *Time* Magazine, February 15, 2007, http://www.time.com/time/magazine/article/0,9171,1590444,00.html (accessed June 2007).

8. Sharon Jayson, "Teens Define Sex in New Ways," *USA TODAY*, October 19, 2005, http://www.usatoday.com/news/health/2005-10-18-teens-sex_x.htm (accessed June 2007).

Chapter 15: Freedom From Sexual Perversion

1. Oral Sex Among Adloescencts: Is It Sex or Is it Abstinence? Volume 32, Number 6, November 2000, http://www.guttmacher.org/pubs/journals/3229800.html (accessed June 2007)

2. Price, "A Developmental Perspective of Treatment for Sexual Vulnerable Youth" [electronic version]. Sexual Addiction and Compulsivity, Volume 14, Issue 2, 2007 pp. 225-245

3. Ibid.

Chapter 17: Healthy Boundaries and Relationships

1. Henry Cloud and John Townsend, *Boundaries*, (Grand Rapids, MI: Zondervan, 1992, p. 169).

Chapter 18: Good Self-Esteem and Learning Their Identity

1. Steve Russo, *Protecting Your Teen from Today's Witchcraft* (Minneapolis, MN; Bethany House, 2005), p. 24.

2. George Barna, *Real Teens* (Ventura, CA: Regal, 2001), p. 69.

Author Biography

SARA E. TROLLINGER IS FOUNDER AND PRESIDENT OF HOUSE OF HOPE, a Christian non-denominational residential program for troubled teenagers, headquartered in Orlando, Florida. Founded in 1985, House of Hope Orlando has helped to restore the lives of thousands of teenagers and to reconcile families. It serves as the national model for seventy-four faith operated Houses of Hope across the nation.

A native of Asheboro, North Carolina, Sara received a bachelor's degree in education from the University of North Carolina and a master's degree from the University of Florida and a doctor of divinity degree from International Seminary. During Sara's twenty-five-year teaching career in Orange County, Florida, she taught elementary and junior high students and worked with emotionally handicapped youth. She also taught behind bars in the Orange County Juvenile Detention Center.

Sara witnessed firsthand at the detention center how the social service system was nothing more than a revolving door for those teenagers. They would come and go, repeating their negative behaviors time and again. She saw the need for troubled teens to understand life-changing principles based on God's Word. The teens needed Jesus in order to find a lasting solution.

This was her inspiration for starting House of Hope, a rnon-denominational esidential home where troubled teens could learn to accept responsibility, submit to authority, and get along with peers and adults. Starting this faith ministry with only $200 and five prayer warriors, House of Hope has changed the lives of thousands of young people, their families and countless friends. The beautiful ten-acre campus of House of Hope Orlando is debt free and consists of six residential houses, a chapel, Hope Academy School, a gymnasium, a counseling center, a cafeteria, administrative offices, three staff houses and a ministry house.

Sara received Jesus Christ as her personal Savior at a Billy Graham Crusade in 1951. Several years ago she was featured in Billy Graham's *Decision Magazine* in an article entitled *"Where Are They Now?"*

Sara has been a guest on numerous local and national television broadcasts, including *The 700 Club, Trinity Broadcasting Network, 100 Huntley Street* and scores of radio programs.

She has received numerous awards for her work, including:

2006—Award for Outstanding Achievement from the Women's Executive Council

2005—Front-page article in the *Wall Street Journal* about House of Hope

2003—Outstanding Republican Woman in Central Florida

1999—Federated Republican Women Award (1999)

- ⅄ National Humanitarian Award from the Religious Alliance Against Pornography,
- ⅄ Paul Harris Fellow Award from Rotary International,
- ⅄ Florida Champion Award from Florida Family First
- ⅄ Orlando Habitat for Humanity Award (1998, as its first recipient)
- ⅄ Governor's Point of Light Award (2000) from Florida Governor Jeb Bush
- ⅄ 2002 Women of Distinction Award from the Citrus Council of Girl Scouts
- ⅄ 2003 WMFE Speaking of Women's Health Award
- ⅄ Women Who Make Magic Award

Sara has served on the national boards of Enough is Enough and Coalition Against Pornography.

Other Books by Sara Trollinger

Other books by Sara Trollinger are available. To order any of these books, please contact House of Hope by calling, emailing or visit the House of Hope website.

407-843-8686
E-mail: sara.trollinger@nationalhouseofhope.org
Visit our Web site: www.nationalhouseofhope.org

Coming September 2007
Exciting **NEW** Curriculum for Counseling Teens

Caring for Teens God's Way

"I am so pleased to be co-sponsoring this project with the curriculum titled, "Caring for Teens God's Way published by the American Association of Christian Counselors" with this book and two videos.

—Sara Trollinger, Founder of House of Hope

Breakthrough
Becoming Intimate with God

by Sara Trollinger

Breakthrough is a handbook on listening to the Lord based on Sara Trollinger's personal experiences. In it, she offers background information and guidance on how you, too, can hear the voice of God.

If you doubt that God speaks today, here is living proof...documented evidence...that he is right there just waiting for you to listen...

- ⋏ What does God sound like?
- ⋏ Does He have a big booming voice?
- ⋏ Or is it a thought that comes to us?
- ⋏ How do we hear Him?
- ⋏ How do we get in touch?
- ⋏ What does He say?

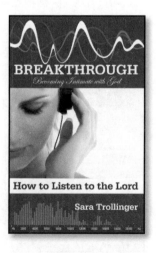

Unglued, Tattooed & Renewed
Compelling stories from teens whose lives have been drastically changed

By Sara Trollinger

Teens talking to teens...about their lives, about their turnarounds, and about their hope for the future makes this book so appealing to other teens and parents.

In their own voices, you will hear from more than two dozen teens who share their raw but real stories. What they have to say will amaze you and leave you with the impression that no problem is too big for God to overcome.

"Any teen reading this book—or parent of a teenager—will come away inspired."

—Sheila Walsh, Women of Faith
conference speaker and acclaimed singer

Unglued and Tattooed

by Sara Trollinger

Unglued and Tattooed: How to Save Your Teen from Raves, Ritalin, Goth, Body Carving, GHB, Sex, and 12 Other Emerging Threats. Unglued and Tattooed, written by Sara Trollinger, Founder and President of House of Hope, Orlando, is a guidebook for parents that will create countless opportunities to educate, provide awareness, and spread the message about the kind of world our teens are faced with today. This book addresses the top twenty issues teens face today.

In *Unglued and Tattooed* you'll learn:

Unglued and Tattooed gives parents of all styles and backgrounds the practical advice on how to influence their kids' behavior without losing them, and how to inspire and motivate them without alienating them. *Unglued and Tattooed* will give your teen — and you — a brighter future.

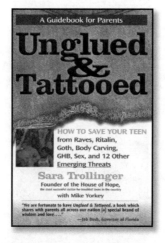

Let's Weigh Our Words

by Sara Trollinger

Let's Weigh Our Words is an invitation to the life of real, authentic and unfeigned faith. Sara Trollinger helps you weigh your words in light of the powerful promises in the Word of God. She then provides the tools, confession, and affirmations to transform your language patterns and speech so that you are aligned with that Word.

Let's Weigh Our Words includes...

- ⋏ The Importance of the Words We Speak
- ⋏ Let's Weigh Our Words
- ⋏ Power of the Tongue
- ⋏ Balance
- ⋏ A Challenge for Confessing God's Word
- ⋏ The Power of the Spoken Word
- ⋏ Blessing Your Children

Prayers, Promises, and Advice for Moms

by Sara Trollinger

Prayers, Promises, and Advice for Moms is designed to encourage your faith to grow. This book is filled with the Word of God, and there are promises for every need and every weakness including...

- ⊥ Promises
- ⊥ God's Word works
- ⊥ What God's Word says to you
- ⊥ Prayers for your children
- ⊥ Ways to show love and affirm your child
- ⊥ Discipline and guidance suggestions
- ⊥ How to be a good role model for your child

House of Hope Information

National House of Hope is a non-denominational, not-for-profit organization established to develop a network of Christian residential programs for troubled teenagers ages twelve to eighteen across the United States and internationally. Sara Trollinger's vision is to establish a House of Hope within driving distance of every major city in America and other countries.

Because House of Hope is a ministry that is run on faith alone, all of the local facilities rely on donations from caring people in the community to help support teenagers during their stays. National House of Hope receives no government funding.

If you would like to contact National House of Hope to make a donation, learn more about the organization or attend one of our training seminars on starting a similar program in your hometown, please contact:

Sara Trollinger
National House of Hope
P.O. Box 560503
Orlando, FL 32856

(407) 843-8686
houseofhopesara@aol.com
www.nationalhouseofhope.org